# WHO SAID IT
# WOULD BE EASY?

# WHO SAID IT WOULD BE EASY?

## ONE WOMAN'S LIFE IN THE POLITICAL ARENA

# Elizabeth Holtzman

## with Cynthia L. Cooper

ARCADE PUBLISHING · NEW YORK

To my parents and my brother

Copyright © 1996 by Elizabeth Holtzman and Cynthia L. Cooper

FIRST EDITION

Selection from *Circles on the Water* by Marge Piercy copyright © 1982 by
Marge Piercy. Reprinted by permission of Alfred A. Knopf, Inc.

*Library of Congress Cataloging-in-Publication Data*

Holtzman, Elizabeth.
    Who said it would be easy? : one woman's life in the political arena
/ by Elizabeth Holtzman with Cynthia L. Cooper. — 1st ed.
        p.        cm.
    Includes index.
    ISBN 1-55970-302-4
    1. Holtzman, Elizabeth.   2. Legislators — United States — Biography.
3. United States. Congress. House — Biography.   4. Women's rights —
United States.      5. United States — Politics and government —
1945–1989.   6. New York (N.Y.) — Politics and government — 1951–
I. Cooper, Cynthia L., 1950–    .  II. Title
E840.8.H66A3     1996
328.73'092 — dc20                                              96-1622

Published in the United States by Arcade Publishing, Inc., New York

Distributed by Little, Brown and Company

10  9  8  7  6  5  4  3  2  1

BP

Designed by API

PRINTED IN THE UNITED STATES OF AMERICA

# Contents

# Introduction

$N$EW YORK 1 NEWS SET UP ITS TELEVISION CAMERAS in my office in New York City's Municipal Building, and Dominick Carter, one of the city hall reporters, flipped through the notes on his pad as he prepared to interview me. I worried that the vital concerns of the city would be tossed aside once again. Misinformation dominated the political race under way that fall of 1993, trampling the real issues to fragments. As the only woman elected to a citywide position, I stood at a crossroads, my reelection by no means guaranteed. Worse, no thoughtful analysis seemed likely to emerge. I expected little from this interview.

As always, I yearned to discuss the issues. During the twenty years I had spent in public office challenging Watergate, crimes, discrimination, and police brutality, concern for issues had always fired my enthusiasm. As the camera and microphone were flicked on, Dominick proceeded to conduct his interview. He asked intelligent questions. He didn't play games or take unfair jabs. I relaxed, relieved. Then Dominick lobbed a puffball question. How did I feel about my two decades of public service? Without warning, my emotions rose; a tear formed in the corner of my eye. This was rather uncharacteristic of me and, of course, became the headline in the next day's city tabloids.

At the moment Dominick asked that question, a flurry of images sped through my mind. I had jumped into the gritty world of politics as a young woman, only thirty years old, filled with idealism and confident about my ability to make a difference as an elected official. I encountered some of the worst in politics, including Richard Nixon, Nazi war criminals, crooks, and machine politicians. But I also met heroes and heroines, such as Peter Rodino, Betty Friedan, and Simon Weisenthal. I had the opportunity to work for civil rights, push to end the war in Vietnam, fight for the environment, and strategize laws to improve women's rights.

I remember reading *Portrait of a Lady* in college and strongly identifying with the young woman protagonist. Henry James sends Isabel Archer out into the world soaring like an arrow, buoyed by an expansive optimism. At the end of the novel, James brings Isabel down to the reality of an evil, complex earth. The destruction of her optimism is the novel's theme. Of course, mine is not an imagined life. Without the steady hand of a novelist's pen, my life has naturally followed its own trajectory and been marked, like all lives, by strengths, frailties, insights, and blind spots. But had my optimism, too, been destroyed?

If so, I certainly had a lot of company: in the mid-1990s most of the public was sinking in the quicksand of cynicism, despairing about politics, government, and the ability to secure justice. Liberals, crushed in a lurch of sentiment to the right, watched their ideals bulldozed. Politicians with a liberal philosophy became scarce. And twenty years in politics had tested my convictions, too. I had learned the hard way about the obstacles that stand before any social reformer. I had served in three distinctly different elected positions — member of Congress in the years from Watergate to Reagan; district attorney in one of the nation's largest DA's offices; comptroller of New York City during a time of fiscal distress and heightened social need. Whatever the position, new and often shocking barriers had appeared. In some instances, however, I was able to surmount them. There were successes; change did take place; and therein lay hope and possibility. In that sense I parted ways with Isabel Archer — I still believed in the ideals that had originally propelled me.

In trying to secure change, I used many tactics: building coalitions, finding common ground, getting the facts to outsmart the opposition, alerting the public, mobilizing the grass roots. Those that worked may suggest ways of vanquishing present-day obstacles. Where the strategies didn't work, the failure may have been due to my own personal limitations in not identifying the right approach or following through properly. And in some cases the problems I tried to fight, such as mindless militarism or wholesale political greed, cannot be overcome without prolonged, intensive efforts by many, many people.

From my earliest years I had learned that some predicaments could be surmounted by focusing on solutions and taking action. My family didn't dwell on why a problem had entered our lives or the psychology that may have motivated the people who caused it, but on what to do about it, and those positive values followed me into public life. Whenever political discussions strayed into chatter about personalities or the private lives of public officials — myself or others — I felt we were being distracted from the serious considerations at hand and, as if by instinct, moved back to the issues.

Can we elicit the strength and determination to overcome the obstacles of these harsh times? The best of liberalism is defined by a generosity of spirit, compassion for others, respect for diversity. Liberal struggles are characterized by an irrepressible, some may say irrational, hope — one that refuses to be intimidated or discouraged.

In the struggle for the woman's right to vote in the nineteenth century, Susan B. Anthony faced pervasive ridicule and constant defeat. She responded by saying, "Failure is impossible." Anthony didn't live to see the changes she fostered, but the changes happened because of her.

Too much has succeeded for us to give up. In my own lifetime I have seen legal segregation in America shattered, tyranny in the Soviet bloc and Eastern Europe crumble, and apartheid fall. Evil can be vanquished. Nelson Mandela can become president of South Africa. But, of course, other evils often rush to take its place. That is why our work is never finished. As the Talmud says, our responsibility is not to finish the job, but we may not shrink from beginning it.

I never fully answered Dominick Carter. There was simply too much to say for a short interview (and I did have to dab my eyes). I wouldn't have given up the opportunity to be in public office for anything. For me, the challenge of trying to get the government to budge provided constant adventure and, when I was successful, genuine satisfaction. Venturing inside the maze of politics and government for two decades taught me volumes about who wields power and the methods that can be used to impel them to do justice. The fact is that for those of us who care about educating children, sheltering the homeless, feeding the hungry, giving opportunity to women, minorities, and other victims of bigotry, saving the environment, reforming our electoral process, and creating jobs, there are still ways to make positive change.

The forces striving for greater human dignity cannot be stopped. All over the world, people carry on the struggle for human rights. A river can be dammed or diverted, but ultimately it will break through the barriers or go around them. Perhaps my experiences will help open a new channel.

# WHO SAID IT WOULD BE EASY?

# 1

## Getting Involved

*P*OLITICAL TALK CHARGED THE ATMOSPHERE in our home when I was growing up during the 1940s and 1950s in Brooklyn. My aunts and uncles and grandparents, all Jewish immigrants from Russia, gathered around our kitchen table, bantering and exchanging views about events in Europe, activities in Washington, current issues of the day in New York. They were various shades of liberal; politics was as natural to them as eating and reading. Since the newspapers presented clashing ideological perspectives, each relative had a favorite and waved it as support. I remember watching their opinions skip back and forth between bites of food and family updates.

My parents, Sidney and Filia, met as teenagers on the Lower East Side of New York City in the middle of the 1920s. My father's family had emigrated from Pinsk in Russia when he was four years old, and my mother and her family came from Bielaya Tserkov in the Ukraine when she was twelve. My mother's love of learning drew her to the public library, where my father shelved books in one of his many part-time jobs. He began to introduce the works of literature to her that he admired. Ten years later, after he had finished law school and she was well on her way to a Ph.D. in Russian, they married.

My brother Robert and I arrived, together, in August 1941. We were twins, and Robbie actually was born first, preceding me by a full thirty minutes, a point that he never let me forget. Despite being twins, Robbie and I were very different. He was gregarious and outgoing; I was so shy as a young girl that I hid under the bed whenever guests came. My mother tried to coax me out, but from my vantage point under the bed, I discovered a wire grating holding up the mattress. I grabbed onto it and resisted her entreaties. Eventually I stopped hiding, probably because I became too big to fit under the bed anymore. In adult life I still felt twangs of shyness and found myself uncomfortable in new social situations, unsure whether I could find the right things to say. Oddly, campaigning didn't bother me, and sometimes I think I unconsciously entered politics as a way to overcome my shyness.

Growing up as a twin was like having a shadow. Robbie and I were very close, but we weren't always talking to each other. We could be very competitive. After my father taught us chess in elementary school, winning was a do-or-die proposition for both of us. I was spurred to victory because if I lost, Robbie teased me for hours, having mastered a range of techniques to get to me.

Yet there were times when my brother was my closest friend. In grade school we loved to play stickball in the empty lot a block from our Ocean Parkway home. With my thick reddish hair braided into long pigtails, I was good at athletics, a tomboy. Still, when the neighborhood boys set up full-fledged team games at the lot, they sometimes refused to let me play because I was a girl. Then I'd go back home and play handball in our garage. Or I would slip away to read a book, letting my imagination and feelings wander freely through Louisa May Alcott and Charles Dickens, the Brontë sisters and Arthur Conan Doyle's stories of Sherlock Holmes.

In 1952, when Robbie and I had just turned eleven, my parents took us on vacation to the oceanside in New Jersey. We swam daily in the Atlantic. When we came home, Robbie developed a high temperature and became lethargic. There were endless visits to different doctors and diagnostic tests with long, difficult names. The results were devastating — Robbie had contracted polio and had to be hospitalized. I was terrified by his illness. What would happen to him? Why was he stricken and not me? Medical books and analyses and trips to specialists became our family routine. My mother visited my brother every day in the hospital and reported on his condition. Sometimes she allowed me to accompany her. Slowly he began to improve, and finally, after a grueling six months, he was released. Eventually Robbie's health improved to the point that he ran track in high school. He later became a doctor.

Although we lived modestly, my brother and I never lacked for anything. When I announced that I wanted to be an astronomer, my father immediately bought a telescope. At another point I was determined to be an artist. My mother signed me up for lessons at the Museum of Modern Art. Each week I traveled to Manhattan by subway and immersed myself in profound artistic activity with clay and fingerpaints. The fact that I had absolutely no talent did not prevent my mother from continuing to indulge my fantasies.

Because my mother was fluent in Russian, she was recruited during World War II to work in a classified job in the Office of Censorship. When she completed her Ph.D. in Russian, she began teaching evening classes at Brooklyn College, and later she taught at Hunter College, becoming the head of the department. Her decision to pursue a career was completely natural, never in question. Our house brimmed with academic hubbub. College students were constantly in and out of our living room for serious teas with meaningful discussions, and professor colleagues of my mother's often joined us for dinner. Everyone greeted my mother with tremendous respect.

Deeply concerned about social justice, my mother joined picket lines when she could to support workers fighting against labor inequities. She let us know that violence was to be rebuffed and told me how disturbing she found racism in America. And I can remember in grade school coming home from school and sitting with my mother as she watched the McCarthy hearings on television in dismay. From an early age, I fully understood that serious injustices were occurring.

My father was a lawyer with his own practice, representing individuals with ordinary problems — some civil and some criminal. In his frequent courtroom appearances he carved out a personal niche, with his rich baritone voice and ability to quote at will from Milton, Shakespeare, and the Bible. The demands of his practice kept him in the office late, and he rarely ate dinner with us on weeknights, but on weekends he slipped away with Robbie and me on various adventures, often ending at the merry-go-round at Coney Island.

In his own way, my father was as unusual as my mother. He always had a kind or complimentary word for everyone he met. Every man was handsome, every woman beautiful. He liked people and enjoyed making them feel good. I fully realized the extent of my father's popularity when I traveled around New York City after being elected to office. People often came up to me at public events to tell me they could never forget my father, usually describing a specific instance in which he had gone out of his way to be thoughtful.

My father's parents were extremely poor, and economic adversity had marked his life. His mother had died when he was in his teens, and he worked as a stevedore at the Bush Terminals and hauler at the Fulton Fish Market to support his own father and two sisters. Marked by these hard times, my parents always insisted that both Robbie and I have a profession or skill so that we could provide for ourselves.

My mother's parents lived in the upper unit of our two-family home, extending our little family unit. Mornings, when we were little, my brother and I crept upstairs to their apartment because Grandpa arose early to attend synagogue. Before he left he made breakfast for us, boiling eggs and breaking up little bits of toasted bread in them.

A dignified man with a thick mustache, Grandpa was sometimes serious to the point of severity. He rarely said anything about his past, and only from my mother's stories did I come to appreciate how complicated a man he was. She told me how Grandpa had owned a successful dry goods store in Bielaya Tserkov, a small town outside Kiev. After World War I, pogroms swept through the town. Jews were subjected to violent assaults by citizens and soldiers of many uniforms — White Russians, various Ukrainian forces. Attackers stopped Jews on the street and stripped them of any belongings, even eyeglasses. Soldiers burst into the homes of Jews, murdered them, and carted away their property.

Because their street was considered to be inhabited solely by Christian families, my grandparents' house was spared from attack, and Grandpa often gave sanctuary to Jews who were fleeing for safety. To me, Grandpa was a hero. On one occasion, my mother recounted, more than fifty strangers, including women and babies, were crammed into the family parlor, seeking refuge from a pogrom. My mother was terrified. Grandpa told the group he would do whatever he could to help them, even if it meant using up all of his own money in an effort to bribe attackers. "But," he said, "I am not God and I cannot guarantee life for any of us." His actions taught me the meaning of courage: that whatever the risk, I had a personal responsibility for others, even strangers.

Grandpa's house was skipped by soldiers on that occasion, but later they did come to search for Jews. Once soldiers went through my grandparents' entire house looking for a Jew who they thought was hiding there. After searching and finding nothing, the soldiers noticed the family dog sniffing at the basement window. Ripping open the basement entry, the searchers discovered the man. Enraged, the soldiers seized him, and my grandfather as well. They had stood Grandpa up against a wall, my mother said, and aimed their guns at him when, miraculously, an officer who knew my grandfather happened along and ordered the soldiers to let my grandfather go.

When the Communists took control, they confiscated Grandpa's business, but he still continued to make his way in Bielaya Tserkov until a final indignity changed his mind. He became determined to get out of Russia when my mother was forced to leave the gymnasium. To earn one of the prized seats in the school, she had studied for years, passed all the difficult exams, and surmounted a rigorous quota system that strictly limited the number of Jews. When she turned twelve, the Bolsheviks took over and simply told her to go home and not return. According to the new authorities, she was part of the bourgeoisie and had received enough education. My mother was crushed, and my grandfather decided they had no future in Russia.

My brother and I made my mother repeat the story of their escape from Russia many times. Grandpa had insisted on bringing dozens of others along, orchestrating the escape of fifty people — his whole family, relatives, business partners, children of friends, even infants and blind and frail elderly. With Grandpa in the lead, they rode on open horse-drawn wagons through blizzard weather, skirting soldiers and hazards, as they made their way across Russia. En route robbers accosted them, seizing, among other things, my grandfather's breadbasket. Grandpa had hidden gold coins under the bread, and the thieves, probably without even knowing it at the time, ran off with most of his money. Still Grandpa kept the group moving. Finally they reached the Romanian border, where, evading guards, the group waded across the Dniester River to safety.

By the time Grandpa reached the United States, he had no money whatsoever. Everything was gone, and like so many immigrants, he and my grandmother had to begin again. Grandpa started with a pushcart, built his business up, and opened a store, only to endure and overcome more hardship during the Great Depression. Having lived through the pogroms, the Russian Revolution, and the depression, he had an intimate knowledge of the impact that government could have on people's lives.

Implicit in my grandparents' actions was always a fierce sense of optimism. If as a Jew you were restricted from education by a quota, you would find a way to study anyway. If the Bolsheviks took away your business, you would start up again. If life wasn't possible in Russia, it would be possible elsewhere. Adversity was an unavoidable fact of life. You took it in stride. I learned from Grandpa that no matter how hard life knocked you down, you picked yourself up and went on. Even though pain and difficulty might be involved, there was no barrier that couldn't be overcome.

Being a Jew was a natural fact of my life. While neither of my parents was religious, they wanted Robbie and me to be exposed to traditional Judaism. Indoctrination fell to my grandparents. On the high holy days Robbie and I dressed up in new holiday clothes and walked with them to the synagogue a few blocks away. The synagogue was orthodox, with the women sitting separately, although there was no curtain or partition between the men and women. Despite the division, sometimes I sat with my grandfather anyway. I watched with a sense of awe when he pulled the prayer shawl over his head in what seemed to me a mysterious and private prayer.

At the synagogue I usually sat with my grandmother, who dressed up elegantly for the Jewish holidays. She was as dignified as my grandfather but not as serious. Her great disappointment in life was that her gender had stopped her from becoming a doctor, and she had wanted my mother to become one. A Zionist, she impressed upon me the importance of the state of Israel. Listening to the radio at home on the day that Israel was established, she called me over. "You must never forget this day," she told me. I never did.

Our formal religious education, however, ran into a few difficulties. Robbie and I went to Hebrew school every day after regular school. On the way, a local bully named Paddy regularly waited for us and tried to beat us up. We did learn some Hebrew. Unfortunately, there were some older boys at the school, and from them we learned to smoke at a rather tender age. Upon hearing that, my mother instantly ended the trips to the Hebrew school. From that point on a rabbi came to our house to give us lessons.

Robbie and I took lessons separately. I had a theological tangle with the rabbi when he described the world as being five thousand years old. Having just visited the Museum of Natural History, I asked how it was possible that the world was only five thousand years old, if dinosaurs lived millions of years ago? The rabbi had no answer, but would in no way alter his opinion. Neither would I. After another unresolvable disagreement, my mother ended the Hebrew lessons for me altogether.

My Hebrew was solid enough for recitation on Passover, the holiday I most enjoyed. Before the big night, my grandmother and my great-aunt Susie would make gefilte fish by hand, sometimes letting me grind the raw fish. For the seder, great-aunts and uncles and cousins came to our house by the dozens, laughing and teasing and joking. When the seder started, Grandpa led the prayers with great seriousness. Then the children, including my brother and me, chanted the all-important four questions in Hebrew. One special prank was played on our great-uncle Nathan. Children were supposed to "steal" a special matzo called the *afikomen*. Since the seder couldn't end until every person ate a piece of the *afikomen*, customarily the children were paid some small amount of money to give it back. We conspired to slip a piece of matzo in Uncle Nathan's pocket, tell him it was the *afikomen*, and scold him for stealing it instead of letting the kids do it. We did this every year. Every year he would protest that he hadn't done it. Every year he was overruled. We all laughed giddily at this staged comedy. These family celebrations left in me a deep sense of rootedness, the feeling that I belonged.

I also understood at an early age that Jews were not always welcome. When I was a child our family spent the summer at a small cottage on the South Fork of Long Island. Along the road, I often saw signs: "Restricted. No Jews Allowed." Our neighbors on the South Fork made no effort to conceal their anti-Semitic feelings, but we tried to rise above it. One summer an emergency shattered any further illusions. My brother smashed his thumb badly in a boating accident, and my mother ran to the neighbors' house, pleading with them to let us use their phone (we had none because installations were restricted during the war) to call a doctor. The neighbors refused. Frantic, my mother sent me racing down the road to call for help. While my brother got the medical aid he needed, we could no longer ignore the intensity of the hatred at our doorstep. My parents sold the property shortly thereafter. I learned the harsh realities of anti-Semitism, and by extension the need to oppose bigotry of every kind.

Religion also brought about the only lapse in my parents' dedication to the equality of upbringing for Robbie and me. My parents demanded the same standards from each of us, but society did not always have the identical models for girls and boys. As a result, my brother was given a bar mitzvah; as for me, I never had my bas mitzvah. In those days the ceremonies were rarely conducted for Jewish girls, and I remember feeling left out as I watched the bar mitzvah activities swirling around my twin.

In our education, Robbie and I were both encouraged to excel. We attended all of the same classes, and whenever something happened to one of us, it affected us both. In the first grade a teacher in the local public school slapped me. My mother abhorred physical violence and instantly removed both Robbie and me from the school. We were promptly enrolled in another school.

Grandpa drilled both Robbie and me each day in our arithmetic tables. We had to know them perfectly. Books were everywhere around us. My parents kept a large library, and my father, who loved to read about ancient Greece, always brought us books with beautiful engraved pictures and leather bindings. I read voraciously, and to this day I still discuss the books I am reading with my parents.

After the third grade, my parents decided to send my brother and me to the Ethical Culture School in Brooklyn. A progressive private school, Ethical Culture was unique — a system of study in which we learned tremendous amounts without realizing it. We listened to weekly lectures on ethics from the school's founder. Respect for our classmates was a paramount value. If we raised our hand once, we couldn't raise it again. We had to give someone else a chance to say something. We were taught that listening and valuing the contributions of others ranked as high as showing you knew the answer.

Robbie and I advanced quickly enough in our studies to skip fifth grade, and in sixth grade at Ethical Culture I met Becca Folkman. Like me, Becca had long braids and played a mean game of softball. She was also one of the smartest people I had met, and an excellent actress, snaring the part of Rosalind in *As You Like It* while I was relegated to the lesser role of Phoebe. Becca became a lifelong friend, and we remained close even though we entered different high schools and colleges. Later she and I became roommates, sharing a large rent-controlled apartment on Manhattan's Upper West Side until she left for Paris and marriage, and I went off to Brooklyn and politics.

When high school began, my brother and I enrolled at Abraham Lincoln, a public school in Brooklyn. For the first time we were separated in our classes. This came as something of a relief for us both. I filled my life with friends and a host of extracurricular activities, ranging from the school choir to the newspaper to the new great books club. Robbie and I joined forces again in our junior year to mount a political campaign for president and vice president of the school. Robbie was the presidential candidate and I ran for vice president. I especially enjoyed organizing the effort. We came up with the slogan "Win with the Twins," and it actually worked: we were both elected. We immediately went about bridging a racial divide among the students. The black students comprised a tiny minority and often sat separately in the cafeteria, unfortunately isolated from the rest of the students. Robbie and I planned a giant victory party at our house and made sure that all the black kids were invited and welcomed. Hundreds of kids, black and white, made their way to our backyard, and the party was joyful and carefree.

Throughout my formative years, I followed the guiding philosophy of my grandparents and parents: life always presented problems, but the key was not to let the problems drown you. You had to look for solutions and keep moving forward. There was, however, one of Grandpa's admonitions I never understood. When my brother and I were about ten, Grandpa sat us down and told us, "Don't trust anyone," he said. My life was full of many loving people — parents, aunts, uncles, friends, Grandpa — whom I trusted implicitly. Grandpa's words made no sense to me. To this day, I wonder what he meant.

Robbie and I were barely seventeen when we headed off to college in 1958 — he to Harvard and I to Radcliffe. I found college intimidating at first and felt inadequate, but after a while I recovered my self-confidence and thrived in its environment, making many lasting friendships. Linda Davidoff, a classmate whom I met in a politics and literature course, had me join her in handing out flyers in Boston for a professor who was running for the U.S. Senate as a peace candidate. When, much later, I decided to run for the Senate, Linda became my campaign manager.

Politics on campus were largely nonexistent at the time. The big issue at the Radcliffe-Harvard commencement was whether the diploma would still be in Latin, and protesters wore togas to mark their dismay when it was not.

I did develop a passion for one issue in my senior year at Radcliffe that, in retrospect, probably told more about the shape of my career than I understood at the time. The senior women in the dormitory had a 1:00 A.M. curfew. Each of us had a key to the dormitory, and when we came in, we signed in under an honor system. Many women commonly stayed out after the curfew but put down a sign-in time before 1:00 A.M. Though a lie, it was regularly overlooked. I thought the curfew for seniors was silly and began a campaign to abolish it. Why should we have to lie? My parents had taught me that you were never to lie, that your word was your bond, and that if you made a pledge, you kept it. To my astonishment, there was opposition to my proposal. Some classmates wished to keep the curfew, even if it meant falsifying the sign-in sheet. They believed that the curfew, though ignored, protected the image of Radcliffe women. To them, their image was the critical consideration. Try as I might, I couldn't begin to understand their point of view. Much later I learned that in so many cases appearances are everything. At any rate, my effort to abolish the curfew finally succeeded, and seniors were relieved of the burden of double lives.

This campaign also brought my first bad press experience. A student reporter, Mike Churchill, interviewed me for the *Harvard Crimson*, but the article he wrote completely missed the point. I let Mike know my reaction. After some tense discussion, Mike and I became friends. Years later, I actually tapped him to manage the final campaign effort in my first race for the House of Representatives.

After getting my degree in American history and literature, I was determined to go to Europe for a year. My parents wouldn't assent to my simply taking off and traveling. While still hoping to convince them, I dashed off a single law school application, to Harvard. To me, law school was a distant and far inferior second choice. When law school accepted me, the decision about what I would do after college was made.

Harvard Law School was hardly a bastion of liberalism in the early 1960s. Nearly the entire year-long course in constitutional law was spent on the interstate commerce clause. We raced through the Bill of Rights in about a week, although the professor had enough time to let us know that he thought *Baker v. Carr*, which created the concept of one person, one vote, was wildly wrong.

Our class of 500 students had only one African-American student, and 20 or so women. Unknown to us, quotas were in place for both. A property professor, Barton Leach, went out of his way to humiliate the women, announcing at the outset of the term that women in his class of 120 would be treated differently. He used the Socratic method to call on students in the class — except the five women. For women, he held "Ladies' Day." The women law students had to stand at the podium and respond to a barrage of questions, many condescending, from the professor. None of us protested this double standard, although I despised the class and never studied for it.

Only by accident did my involvement in politics — with a small p — take off at Harvard. In the spring of 1963 I saw a notice about a lecture on civil rights. I normally didn't attend extracurricular events at the law school, since most of them seemed to me to be pointless. But this talk was being given by William Higgs, a white civil rights attorney from Mississippi who was actually involved in bringing about social change. Only a handful of students showed up. We were at once riveted by Higgs's vivid depiction of how he had helped James Meredith desegregate the University of Mississippi. His descriptions told us, for the first time, how law could be used as a tool for social justice. As he concluded, the amiable Higgs invited us to come to the South to help civil rights lawyers work on their cases. I signed up then and there.

After exams that year, four male classmates and I set out by car for the South with the promise of $40 a month. We pulled the car up at the office of the Student Non-violent Coordinating Committee — SNCC — in Atlanta, where we were to get our assignments. When we announced ourselves, the SNCC workers stared blankly. They had never heard of us. They suggested that we might drive to Montgomery, Alabama. The U.S. Court of Appeals for the Fifth Circuit was hearing cases, and all of the civil rights lawyers in the South would be there. We got back into the car and headed out again. On the way to Montgomery our car, conspicuous with its northern license plates, was pulled over by a trooper. He was not friendly; he simply wanted to harass us. Pegged as outsiders, we were learning quickly that law enforcement did not necessarily welcome civil rights workers.

Civil rights workers were harassed, assaulted, killed. In June a segregationist assassinated black civil rights leader Medgar Evers in Mississippi. And more horrors were to come. A Birmingham church bombing killed four African-American girls in September 1963, and the next summer the Ku Klux Klan murdered three student civil rights workers — James Chaney, Andrew Goodman, and Michael Schwerner — drawing nationwide attention.

At the federal courthouse in Montgomery, I met C. B. King

from Albany, Georgia. The Albany movement was one of the most vibrant segments of the civil rights campaign in the South. C. B., as he was called, was in his mid-thirties. A medium-sized man, he wore black-framed glasses and had a deep baritone voice. He was a man who never diminished the English language by saying something in ten words when twenty could do, and he loved to roll his tongue around big words and toss them out with oratorical flourishes. He would say things like "night is when the mellifluous odor of honeysuckle wafts on the evening zephyr." The only black civil rights lawyer in the southwestern part of the state, C. B. King was much more than an attorney who helped get SNCC workers out of jail. He played an integral part in the movement, joining peaceful demonstrators on the streets and sidewalks as they marched or kneeled to protest segregation. I asked C. B. if I could work for him, and he politely agreed.

One of my friends who had found a position in Savannah drove through Albany and dropped me off at King's law office in a part of town called "Harlem." The second-floor office was nestled above a café, or more accurately a juke joint. The office consisted of a few rooms with a reception area, where the secretary, Ann Butler, was constantly busy. Law books took up most of the wall space, and thankfully so since C. B. had been denied access to the law library used by white lawyers. Between the books crawled roaches so big that the word was pronounced with two syllables — ro-ach. The jukebox in the café downstairs could blast out a rocking rhythm that set the floorboards pulsating.

When I arrived, C. B. had already been joined for the summer by Dennis Roberts, a white law student from Boalt Law School in Berkeley, California. They greeted me warmly. And then for the next two hours they proceeded to relate every story of violence and brutality to civil rights workers that had taken place in Albany, in the surrounding area, and in the whole South. The words "bloody," "beatings," "arrest," and "jail" hammered at me. They seemed to leave out not a single one of the gruesome details.

I was scared. All I wanted to do was to leave town and get back to New York as fast as I could. When they saw that the stories had taken effect, C. B. took me to the home of an elderly black woman with whom I was to stay the night. She lived in an old, tiny house in the black section of town. My host could see my agitation and asked what was wrong. I responded unconvincingly, saying I was fine. The woman gave me a cup of tea and sat me in a rocking chair. We talked about law school, my parents, her family — everything except what was on my mind.

Slowly I grew calmer and began to look around. The house had wooden floors, turned gray with years of mopping and sweeping; they were spotless. A sense of dignity and pride shone in the cleanliness. I wondered about the woman sitting in front of me, trying to help me. My mind walked through the daily indignities she encountered simply because of the color of her skin. There were no sidewalks in her part of town, as there were in the white section. White people would never address her as "Mrs." but called her by her first name, as if she had no complete identity. Whites forced blacks to use segregated public facilities, movies, restaurants, and hotels, and inferior schools. Blacks even had to stand aside at grocery stores so that the white people could pass through the lines first. In a dozen other ways I couldn't even imagine, she was treated as a second-class citizen here in her hometown. But the well-scrubbed floors told the story of a person whose spirit had not been broken by a society that demeaned her. Extraordinary courage had to be summoned to keep a sense of personal dignity in an atmosphere of violence and humiliation.

Leaving tomorrow would be easy, I thought. Get on a plane. In a few hours, LaGuardia and home. I could leave behind the things C. B. and Dennis described — heads bashed, vicious sheriffs, ugly insults. I would be safe. I stole another look at the woman's face, worn and kindly. She can't leave, I said to myself. For me to run away would be cowardly, abandoning people in need, abandoning values I had been taught to cherish. How would things change if people like me fled when danger presented itself? She was the real face of civil rights. If she could survive the brutality of a lifetime, I could survive the brutality of a summer. I wasn't going to let myself be intimidated.

Had I spent the night in a hotel, I probably would have picked up and left Georgia the next day. When I appeared in the morning at C. B. King's office, pen and legal pad in hand, he registered surprise. And then he put me to work. Now that I had weathered his test, we were going to be good friends.

My job was to help C. B. in his legal work, and he had plenty of it. Blacks were peacefully protesting against the totally segregated society, and protests inevitably resulted in arrests and criminal charges. C. B. King defended the protesters. They came to him from miles away. One set of clients, demonstrators from a nearby town, had been arrested trying to desegregate a library.

Everywhere, the whole apparatus of police chiefs, police officers, sheriffs, state troopers, and judges enforced segregation and ensured that no blacks got out of line. Most local whites believed that local blacks would feel perfectly content with the segregated status quo, if it were not for "outside agitators." That meant people like me, and we were not safe in the white community.

At first the SNCC workers viewed me a little suspiciously. I dressed much more conservatively — linen skirt and matching top. Most of the young men wore overalls. And I probably held more conservative political views than many of them, too. Some of them even thought I was a secret FBI informer. Winning their confidence took time.

The Albany movement was especially known for its singing. Whether at church meetings or SNCC gatherings, the freedom songs were on everyone's lips, sung with great gusto and verve. Singing was a way of joining hands, stiffening resolve, stoking courage. I loved the singing, the words: it all still rings in my ears.

Since I was staying for the summer, C. B. arranged for me to be housed in more comfortable quarters with the Nobles, a very warm, middle-class black family. The Nobles were teachers with an attractive home and an extra room, which they turned over to me. They offered me meals, comfort, advice, made me feel secure and cared for. And soon I was accepted similarly in the black community everywhere in Albany.

The evening after I settled with the Nobles, I called my mother to let her know where I was. I had already learned a lot. I whispered into the phone that the lines were tapped. I also mentioned that I was being followed by the police. Don't worry, I told her with great assurance. My mother was immediately worried. She thought

I had gone crazy, she told me later. This was America, she thought, not Russia. The police didn't follow ordinary people around and listen in on their telephone conversations. Her mind was not at ease until Joni Rabinowitz, another activist from New York, made a trip back North a short while later. Joni kindly called my mother to report that I was fine and had not lost my mind. While my mother was reassured that I was okay, she realized that the system wasn't, and of course that created a different cause for concern.

Right after July 4, the Albany police shut down the black swimming pool. In this unbearably hot weather black kids had nowhere to swim. The city had another pool, but for whites only. Some blacks decided to buy tickets to the white pool and integrate it. I stationed myself outside the pool area to observe how the city would respond.

A big wire fence circled the "white" pool. Close to twenty police officers stood by. There were many white kids swimming in the pool, having a great time. Outside the fence stood the black kids, their fingers holding onto the wire, looking longingly at the white kids splashing about. What were they feeling? I kept wondering. Was it anger? Hurt? How would the rejection affect them?

And what about the white adults who had gathered to help police keep blacks out of the pool? What kind of sheer meanness would make them send armed cops to keep kids out of the only swimming pool in town on such a hot day? (A decade later I thought of this scene as I watched first graders in my congressional district being bused to schools in Canarsie, where white parents were waiting to greet them with hisses, catcalls, and spitting. Racial hatred has no geographical boundaries, I learned.)

The first black people to try to buy tickets were arrested and dragged away by the officers. I stood near the black people supporting the civil rights action. Whites across the way started shouting, calling for police violence. A police officer pushed his way up to me and asked me for some identification. When I didn't respond at once, the officer declared that I looked suspicious. In fact, the officer said, now leaning forward as if threatening me, I might even be an escaped convict. He let me know this was a power struggle, and I was going to lose. I knew he would arrest me if I didn't give in, so I took out my Harvard student card, which the officer snatched up, looked at intently, and then handed back and walked away.

The pool remained segregated that summer, and I could never get out of my mind the picture of the little black kids slumping against the fence, the slant of their backs showing their resignation.

A lot of C. B.'s work was concentrated in Baker County, which had a spectacular record of antiblack violence. In 1943 a white sheriff named Claude Screws, angry at a black army veteran, had arrested him late at night for the supposed theft of a tire. The sheriff and two other law enforcement officers handcuffed the man and drove him to the courthouse square. The officers let the man, still handcuffed, out of the car and knocked him to the ground, beat him for thirty minutes with their fists and a two-pound blackjack, and then dragged him, unconscious, through the courthouse yard into the jail, where they left him to die on the floor. Charged with federal civil rights violations, the sheriff was exonerated in a shameful case decided by the U.S. Supreme Court, *Screws v. United States.*

It wasn't long before an incident in Baker County demanded C. B.'s attention. He represented a man facing the death penalty on a charge of attempted murder. The case was serious enough that Donald Hollowell, an older, more experienced black attorney from Atlanta, came down to help out.

The case involved a white sheriff in Baker County, L. Warren Johnson. Sheriff Johnson was an enormous, hulking man — well over six feet tall and close to 300 pounds — and he had been an assistant to Sheriff Screws. Charlie Ware, whom C. B. represented, was black, short and thin, probably not weighing over 125 pounds. Sheriff Johnson showed up at Charlie Ware's home one night. The reason was not entirely clear, but it seems that the sheriff had a personal interest in Ware's wife. The sheriff called Ware out to the porch, handcuffed him, and put him in his official car. The sheriff then spoke into the radio mike in his car and said Ware was coming at him with a knife. He shot Ware in the neck — not once but over and over and over again. Amazingly, unlike the man in the Screws incident, Ware survived. Surviving meant that Charlie Ware got charged with attempted murder of the sheriff. C. B. and Hollowell were defending him.

Merely going to Baker County on Ware's behalf presented dangers, especially for black lawyers. The U.S. Justice Department and FBI refused to provide any protection, despite the requests of C. B. and Hollowell. Faced with this rebuff, the two lawyers devised another plan. They asked me to accompany them on the drive to Baker County, even though it was also dangerous for black men to be seen with a white woman. They thought that if I looked like a U.S. Justice Department lawyer, they might have a possible cloak of protection. I was to ride in the backseat of their car until we got to the outskirts of the town where the trial was to take place. From there, I would walk into the courthouse, carrying a briefcase and dressed in my most "lawyerlike" clothes, stay all day, walk back out to the edge of town, and then ride back with them.

C. B. and Hollowell were convinced that we would be ambushed en route. The drive from Albany to Baker County was hauntingly beautiful — and terrifying. The road passed through lush green fields where cows grazed. Magnificent trees spread from either side of the road. Every time the sun glinted on the leaves of the trees, I heard a sharp intake of breath from the two lawyers in the front seat. They thought the sun was catching the barrel of a rifle. I could hardly breathe at all.

The Baker County courthouse was in Newton, a tiny town. The only thing remarkable about it was the massive and imposing courthouse. I walked into the courthouse, trying to look very much like a Justice Department lawyer, even though I had never seen one. The interior of the courthouse seemed like the set for *To Kill a Mockingbird*. The main chamber where the trial took place had a high ceiling with a fan spinning slowly and a small balcony for black observers, who had to sit separately. The judge sat on a raised platform with a spittoon on the floor to his right — he would read the newspaper, spit into the spittoon, and swivel in his chair from side to side. Looking through the open windows, curious farmers in straw hats stood outside, chewing on long stalks of grass. There were a lot of spectators: I don't think they had ever seen black lawyers try a case.

After about a week, the all-white jury convicted Ware. This was not a surprise, given the location and circumstances. The conviction was overturned later because of the exclusion of blacks from the jury, in violation of the constitutional right to a fair trial. The plan by C. B. and Hollowell to assert Ware's right to legal representation — and to survive it — had at least succeeded. We had expected the worst, considering that most days we were driving at speeds of at least a hundred miles an hour to and from Baker County. We left unharmed.

Nothing, however, prepared me for Americus, Georgia. SNCC had scheduled a demonstration for voting rights in this small town not far from Albany. On August 8, black and white protesters, led by SNCC activists, including Zev Aelony, began a peaceful march. Like all civil rights workers, they adhered to policies of nonviolence. Three SNCC field workers were beaten horribly and then arrested. Zev, the field workers, and several others were charged with an offense that carried the death penalty — inciting insurrection against the state of Georgia.

The next evening, a large group marched to protest these arrests. Most of the protesters were young — between thirteen and twenty years old. They were met by the city police, state police, the sheriff, and deputized white citizens, all armed heavily with guns, clubs, and cattle prods. The whites savagely attacked the civil rights demonstrators in a violent, bloody episode. Protesters were clubbed, smashed, burned with the prods. One youth's leg was broken; another required two dozen stitches in his head. Several, including a man of sixty-seven, had their heads split open.

C. B. was called upon to defend the civil rights workers. It was an especially worrisome case because of the capital charges involved. Could these young people face execution? More troubling, we learned that the protesters had been charged under a law declared unconstitutional over twenty-five years earlier. This bothered no one in Americus. The trials were sure to proceed and to result in guilty convictions, no matter how good a job C. B. did. At the same time, the police and the deputized civilians eluded charges of brutality. We could not ignore the gravity of the situation.

Volunteer lawyers, such as Mike Finkelstein, came down from the North to help us out. We appealed to the federal government to take action. The federal government did nothing. "There is no evidence of police brutality in Americus," declared one Justice Department spokesman.

By this time SNCC had accepted me as one of its own. SNCC knew the civil rights atrocities in Americus needed public attention, and the leadership decided that I should go to Washington along with some other SNCC workers to hold a press conference. Our mission was to expose the bloodbath in Americus and the failure of the Justice Department to respond to the violent illegal behavior of law enforcement. Julian Bond, who handled press relations for SNCC, decided that we should show the bloody shirts from the Americus demonstrators. En route to Washington, I stopped in Atlanta and met with Julian. He gave me responsibility for the shirts.

I had packed the shirts carefully in my suitcase. They were light summer shirts, stiff and heavy with blood. In Washington, on a bright and sunny day, I lifted them out of the bag in front of the Justice Department. Criticizing the Kennedy Justice Department for not protecting the marchers in Americus, we demanded that it act without delay.

Big, imposing government buildings surrounded us. I knew the government had committed serious injustices in the past, but I kept looking at the buildings. Why didn't anyone inside them care? Why weren't they enforcing the law? At its essence, the civil rights movement thrived on the sheer faith that America would take notice and act. We were caught up in a crazy optimism, believing that if we held up the evidence and told the world the truth, someone would have to respond.

That summer Washington didn't listen. No one charged the police or others who assaulted the protesters with wrongdoing, while the capital charges lodged against the SNCC workers were pressed by the state of Georgia. Civil rights lawyers countered the charges against the SNCC workers with a case in federal court, heard by a special three-judge panel that included court of appeals chief judge Elbert Tuttle. Tuttle, a Republican, knew the law was unconstitutional; in fact, he had been the lawyer who originally challenged its legality. In contrast to the Justice Department, whose failure to act betrayed a profoundly cynical attitude toward civil rights workers, the federal court ordered the state of Georgia to stop the prosecution.

On my return South, I attended a hearing in Atlanta before

Chief Judge Tuttle. So many civil rights cases had to be appealed because federal district judges in the South (with the sole exception of Judge Frank Johnson in Alabama) consistently upheld segregation. The Fifth Circuit sidestepped the federal district judges and enforced the U.S. Supreme Court's mandate to end segregation. Significantly, many Fifth Circuit judges, including Judge Tuttle, were Republicans, appointed by President Dwight D. Eisenhower. They were people of character and courage. From the back of an ornate, wood-paneled courtroom, I watched Constance Baker Motley, one of the chief lawyers for the NAACP Legal Defense Fund in New York, present a case to the court. Judge Tuttle listened closely to the argument of Mrs. Motley, an African-American woman who is today a federal judge. He treated Mrs. Motley with deep respect. At last I felt a renewed sense of hope. Some people in positions of power understood what justice meant.

After a few hot months in the South, I was beginning to learn. About the depths of bigotry. About how our federal government, including the FBI and the Justice Department, sided with the forces of segregation and the status quo. I learned that segregation was propped up forcibly by the police and sheriffs, who could with impunity act against black people who simply wanted to use a public library, register to vote, or swim in the town pool.

When I left the South that summer, I took the train up to Washington, D.C. There was going to be a big rally for civil rights, and I wanted to hear Dr. Martin Luther King Jr.'s speech. The train started in Waycross, Georgia and stopped at dozens of small towns and cities, a freedom local making its way to the nation's capital. At every stop the doors opened to more and more people, almost all black, bounding onto the train and filling it with anticipation. Change was in the air.

That fall, eight or so of us from different law schools who had worked in the South gathered together. We began to brainstorm. How could we encourage other law students to make the same journey? What could we do to expose the situation in the South further? How could we draw attention to the struggle and at the same time give civil rights attorneys the assistance they needed?

We decided to set up our own organization, called the Law

Students Civil Rights Research Council, or LSCRRC. But good intentions did not automatically translate into positive results: an administrative structure was needed. We got tax-exempt status, raised money, and set up an office in New York, which I helped direct during the summer of 1964. We recruited law students from across the country to work in civil rights. Eventually we were able to send hundreds more law students south.

While assisting LSCRRC, I got a full-time summer job working for the NAACP Legal Defense and Education Fund, Inc. The "Inc. Fund," as it was called, assigned me to work on a U.S. Supreme Court brief challenging the miscegenation statute in Florida, which made it illegal for blacks and whites to marry. The case, *McLaughlin v. Florida*, led to a Supreme Court ruling that states could not prevent people of different races from marrying.

But my work in the South had a serious downside, too. The *Harvard Law Record* published an interview with me in which I criticized the FBI for failing to protect civil rights attorneys and workers. The *Record* went to a large number of law school alumni. Almost as soon as they got it in the mail, the Georgia Alumni Association of Harvard Law School asked the faculty to expel me. The faculty refused to do so. Then J. Edgar Hoover wrote a letter to the *Record*, defending the FBI and attacking me. I was startled that Hoover would pay attention to me, a mere law student. No one took Hoover lightly. The dean of the law school, Erwin Griswold, called me in, recommending that, for my own good, I respond to Hoover. The whole period of the McCarthy era flashed before me. Was Hoover going to prevent me from graduating? Would I be blackballed as a lawyer? Luckily, Hoover had certain facts wrong, so I could easily refute him. I did become a lawyer, but one who had understood early on that challenging power was rarely welcomed.

After law school, many of my classmates applied for jobs in the big Wall Street law firms, but most of these firms in those days weren't very interested in the women graduates. I was nervous about my future. Thanks to Helen Buttenweiser, an older woman lawyer who was a member of the respected Lehman family in New York, I was able to make headway. I had met her during my work in the civil rights movement, and she helped me get a job. At the time a small, barely known firm, Wachtell, Lipton has since grown into one of the country's most successful. Wachtell provided excellent legal training, teaching me rigorously high standards.

I had been at Wachtell for about two years when I got a call from a former Harvard classmate who was a top aide to New York City mayor John Lindsay. Would I consider a position as an aide to the mayor? After suffering from a bout of mononucleosis that year, I was ready for a change of pace. I longed for a chance to get involved in public activity. I accepted the position.

Named as the first woman assistant to the mayor, I worked as the mayor's liaison to the Parks, Recreation and Cultural Affairs Department. The head of the Parks Department was August Heckscher, an elderly, patrician gentleman who upon learning of my hiring, was not amused to learn that a twenty-six-year-old woman would be making policy for his agency. I worked hard and succeeded in making some changes. With the help of a wonderful Parks Department engineer, Dan Garvey, we got safety matting installed under all the playground equipment in the city and built two dozen prefabricated minipools at neighborhood sites. I loved my work — it was challenging, and being inside government gave me a chance to help people.

I have no doubt that spending one civil rights summer in the South had in a roundabout way brought me to city hall and set my sights on public service. My southern experience had given a new dimension to the pogroms and injustice from which my family had escaped. The civil rights movement had inspired me. I saw ordinary people, without weapons but armed with the rightness of their cause, confront sheriffs, police dogs, arrests, beatings, imprisonment, and harassment. Blacks and whites had built a unifying bond. African-American families had opened their homes to me, fed me, and given me friendship and emotional support. Having witnessed how black people and white people had joined in the effort to end segregation, sharing danger and joy, I was saddened later to see polarization arise. In my summer in the South I saw the faces of courage — people involved in a monumentally heroic struggle. And what is more, they succeeded. In towns so antebellum that black people were forced to step off the sidewalk to let white people pass, transformation *had* occurred.

Throughout the years, whenever an issue seemed too difficult or a political battle too perilous, I would think back to those experiences. Even as the country moved to the right in the 1990s, I pictured the determination of those in the civil rights movement. If Jim Crow could come tumbling down, then what injustice was so entrenched and intractable that it, too, couldn't be dismantled? I learned optimism and hope.

# 2

# Power and Corruption

## POLITICS

$T$HE WATERGATE STORY SEIZED PUBLIC ATTENTION not long after I was first elected to Congress. Jimmy Breslin later wrote in his book about Tip O'Neill, the former Democratic majority leader of the House, that my defeat of Congressman Emanuel Celler in Brooklyn in 1972 was a key to the impeachment of Richard Nixon.

At the time it occurred, June 17, 1972, the Watergate break-in barely rippled across my consciousness. That very day, I suffered a break-in at my own campaign office in Brooklyn. Three days before the primary election on June 20, thugs burst into our headquarters in the early-evening hours and roughed up my campaign workers. We rushed Mike Churchill, my campaign manager, to the emergency room. Fortunately, he wasn't seriously hurt. We never found out the intruders' identities, but there was no escaping the possibility of dirty politics.

I ran against the odds — all of them. At the age of thirty, I challenged the most senior member of the House of Representatives. Emanuel Celler was eighty-four years old, a fifty-year incumbent, and almost an institution.

My idea to run for Congress was actually inspired two years earlier by a remark Pearl Marcus, my parents' next-door neighbor, made in November 1970, when she returned from voting. My parents had moved from Ocean Parkway to a home in the Flatbush section of Brooklyn. Seeing me, Mrs. Marcus came by to chat. "I can't believe that man is still on the ballot," she said. "He's been there far too long, and he's way too old." When I asked what she meant, she responded almost wearily. "Celler," she said, "Emanuel Celler."

At the time I felt like a seasoned political veteran. In the mid-1960s my political activities had focused on ending the war in Vietnam. Like so many others I had marched and written letters, trying to stop the killing.

In 1969 I campaigned for Mayor John Lindsay's reelection bid, picking up basic campaign techniques by slogging through Bay Ridge with petition carriers to get Lindsay on the ballot. I helped organize Lindsay poll watchers for election day. After leaving city hall, I began thinking more seriously about elective office and ran for Democratic state committeewoman. My race pitted me against the Democratic political machine for the first time, and I won.

When I became a state committeewoman in 1970, I continued my antiwar activities with the Take Brooklyn Out of the War Coalition. Despite our organizing activities and the nationwide strength of the peace movement, I became aware that much more had to be done to bring the war to an end and tackle domestic needs.

I longed for a more active role, especially after I left my job in Lindsay's office in 1970 and became an associate in a large Manhattan law firm. The fulfillment and satisfaction weren't the same: making playgrounds safe for kids provided many more exhilarating moments for me than representing large corporate interests at a law firm. My city job had involved creative thinking, planning, and analysis — things I enjoyed doing and did well. In an elected position I might be able to do more, to fight for civil rights and against the war as well as do concrete things in the real world. Inside the government, I felt sure I could make a difference.

At city hall I had observed many elected officials — council members, state legislators, congresspeople — up close. I listened to them, assessed their capabilities. If they could get elected, I thought, why couldn't I?

I remembered Mrs. Marcus's comment and considered the idea of running against Celler. One day I dropped by the office of

Eddie Costikyan, the former head of the Manhattan Democrats. In my eyes Eddie personified a serious, grown-up politician, as well as a respected lawyer. I wanted his opinion about my taking on Celler but worried that he might tell me I was crazy. I explained my idea. He sat quietly, expressionless, for quite some time. Then he broke into a smile. "I think you can do it," he said. That made four people: my dad, a friend of a friend I had lined up as my campaign adviser, me — and now Eddie Costikyan. If he thinks I can do it, maybe I really can, I thought.

Unfortunately, when the firm members heard that I was thinking of challenging Celler, they presented me with a choice. I could either work for the firm or run against Celler. The firm apparently had once represented Celler. Faced with the alternatives, I was lucky that my parents were willing to take me in. I was soon without a job and on a political journey. I had decided to run for the U.S. Congress.

My love of organizing became handy immediately. Setting up a campaign meant analyzing the tasks that needed to be accomplished and finding the people to help do them. I needed to get on the ballot, which meant having petitions printed and petition carriers to collect signatures. I needed lawyers to make sure I complied with the election laws. I needed campaign literature to get my message across. And my message needed to be well informed. I also needed to be aware of the flaws in my opponent's record, all of which meant I needed a researcher. Even going out and shaking hands with voters required a plan — where to go, when, with whom.

My parents' house became a center of campaign activity. The same basement where my brother and I had planned our high school "Win with the Twins" victory now became congressional campaign headquarters, at least until we could afford a real office in a vacated Sneaker King store near Brooklyn College.

I reached out for help, finding people who shared my commitments to peace and civil rights. Coworkers from Lindsay's campaign, along with friends from high school, college, and law school, all pitched in.

We had virtually no campaign money. I raised $32,000 and borrowed $4,000 — a pitifully small amount for a campaign in

New York even then, and absurdly low compared to the enormous costs of a campaign today. We didn't have enough money to buy media time, so we used ingenuity and footwork. I went everywhere I could to meet as many people as possible.

We had a very short time in which to work — from March until the primary in late June. Not having a job proved to be an asset: I could campaign full-time. Beginning at 6:00 A.M., I stood at subway stops to greet riders. After the morning rush hour, a campaign worker and I hopped into my silver Camaro and drove to the supermarkets in the district. I walked down the aisles and shook hands with prospective voters. Supermarkets were great places to campaign, if also a bit treacherous. A vote won by the fruits and vegetables vanished by the cottage cheese and eggs if I failed to remember that I had already introduced myself to the same shopper. I trained myself to snap a mental picture of people I met. If we crossed paths in a different aisle, I nodded with a nonchalant "Oh, hi again."

In driving from store to store with a campaign worker, whenever we saw a crowd — we considered more than one person to be a crowd — we stopped the car. My campaign worker and I parked, got out, shook hands, and asked for their votes. In the evening I hustled back to the subway, then to the movie lines and bingo games. The schedule raced forward, but my campaign workers and I thrived on the challenge.

My brother Robbie jumped in, finding special pleasure in campaigning for his little sister. A doctor by now, he spent his free time putting up posters along Ocean Avenue and going door-to-door, urging voters to get out and vote for me in the primary. My father promoted me with gusto to every person in every courthouse in the city — no matter what district they lived in, according to what people later told me.

To reach out to community activists, I convinced my mother to host teas. When I had first told my mother that I was thinking of running for office, she responded that politics was a dirty business. Now she pulled out the coffee urns used for her parties of Russian-language students and bought a big new set of china cups. Thirty to forty people at a time — heads of PTAs, community board members, school board members, precinct council members — arrived at my parent's house. We sat in the living room, passing tea around, discussing topical issues and ideas for reform.

About a month before the all-important primary day, my friend Mike Churchill arrived from Philadelphia to run the campaign.

From the outset, I focused on my central message. Issues — especially the war — separated me from Celler, a war hawk. One volunteer who later became a friend, Judy Ames, sought out our one-room campaign headquarters because her mother had gone to Washington to protest the war with the Women's Strike for Peace. Judy's mother had spoken personally with Celler. Celler brushed her away rudely, saying, "Oh, please, I don't need your vote." My speeches, by contrast, called for an immediate end to the war and assailed the military-industrial complex that kept it going. George McGovern's run for the presidency on a peace plank that year spotlighted antiwar concerns; to make sure that antiwar voters got my message, we coordinated efforts with his campaign.

To convince voters to select me over Celler, Marilyn Shapiro documented Celler's history of serious absenteeism and a congressional voting record that had peculiarities, to say the least. He backed special interests that had little to do with Brooklyn — peanut farmers, for example. Thousands of dollars in campaign contributions had been given to him by one of the major defense contractors in the war, Fishbach and Moore. Jack Anderson wrote a column castigating Celler for his ties to defense contractors and support for the war, which was a definite boost to my campaign.

"Double door" also entered our vocabulary. The term was new to me. The New York City Bar Association had criticized Celler's ethics for having a double-door law practice. Celler used a clever facade to skirt congressional rules. Members of Congress were not supposed to represent clients before federal agencies; yet Celler served both as a representative and as a member of a Manhattan law firm that represented many clients before federal agencies. He circumvented the ban by having two doors leading into his law firm. The doors were right next to each other, and both opened into the same reception area. One door listed the firm's name with "Celler" as part of it; the other door designated the firm without "Celler." If clients had federal business, they were supposed to go through the door without Celler's name on it; if they didn't, they went through the door with his name on it.

All of our information about Celler needed to be crunched into an effective campaign flyer. Carolyn Herron, a college classmate with a master's degree in comparative literature, helped me find the right words to contrast Celler's weaknesses with my strengths. As we crafted the language, we kept coming back to Celler's absentee record. It spoke loudly about the drawbacks of having someone so senior compared to someone fresh. We didn't want to say that he was too old, but we wrote, "At 84, Celler is too *tired.*" The theme resonated with the voters. When we called likely primary voters, one elderly woman with a Yiddish accent said, "Darling, I am eighty-four. If Celler feels anything like I do, he has no business being in Congress."

I faced one enormous hurdle — the Brooklyn machine. I ran as a reform candidate. Reformers took aim at machine politics, including the powerful Brooklyn political organization. Machines dominated much of the politics in New York City; the machine bosses picked the candidates and won primary elections by trotting out large numbers of loyal voters. Practically all the campaign workers also held government jobs. In one district, I saw the political captain actually walk into the voting booth with several voters. The system was rife with corruption. By the mid-1980s almost all of the old-time political bosses were out of office because of the successes of the reform movement and a series of corruption exposés that sent several machine bosses to prison. Meade Esposito, the boss of Brooklyn when I ran for Congress, was convicted in federal court in a bribery scandal in the 1980s.

Being elected by the machine trapped candidates. They soon found themselves in the position of Persephone in Greek mythology, who, because she ate six seeds of the pomegranate while in Hades, was forced forever after to spend six months of every year there. If candidates fed off the machine, they ended up doing the machine favors. The initial connection with the machine might seem slight, but once obliged, candidates became obliged forever.

The machine made it hard for anyone to challenge the status quo. In running for Democratic state committeewoman in 1970 two years earlier, I declared myself a reform candidate and challenged the machine's incumbent. But I discovered a slight hitch. By law, incumbents had the first position on the ballot. Being first gave an advantage; studies showed that voters who were not familiar with the candidates cast their vote for the person in the first position. The machine placed most of the incumbents in office and naturally supported the law that placed the incumbent in the first position. To the machine's great delight, challengers faced a big disadvantage.

I rebelled against this ballot design and decided to go to court. I won, and the practice was halted. The lawsuit was called *Holtzman v. Power.* Power headed the Board of Elections, but I found the name ironic. On this occasion Power lost. I later engaged in other struggles against power, and unfortunately power didn't always lose.

In my congressional race in 1972, the Brooklyn machine tried a few other tricks. For example, a strong anti-Celler feeling existed among Irish voters because two years earlier a redistricting had pitted Celler against the pride of the Irish community, Congresswoman Edna Kelly. Celler defeated her, and her supporters didn't forget. To assure that this Irish vote would not go to me, the Brooklyn machine put up a third candidate in the primary, Robert O'Donnell, characterized by the *New York Post* as the "Howdy Doody candidate." Putting up third candidates was a ploy often used in New York politics, and one I encountered later running for the U.S. Senate.

Brooklyn boss Meade Esposito did not like me. Referring to me as "the broad running against Manny Celler," he complained to writer Jimmy Breslin, "(T)his girl, she's got all kinds of young girls running around for her. Indians. Freaking squaws. I've tried to talk her out of the race, but it looks like I can't do it."

Despite Esposito's cracks, being a woman helped. A woman cut a different figure from the image of a politician as a cigar-smoking man, and at five feet, three and a half inches, I provided a definite contrast. So few women campaigned for office that whenever people met me, they remembered it.

No pundits gave me a chance. Celler called me "a toothpick trying to topple the Washington Monument." The press reported very little on the race. Finally, in the last week before the voting, a couple of TV stations did short segments. A televised debate on a rainy Sunday boosted my visibility. The *New York Times* came out criticizing Celler for his double-door law practice and endorsed me.

When the polls closed on the night of the primary, June 20, the first returns showed me ahead. Our excitement rose. The campaign people suggested I go to Cookies, a neighborhood restaurant with red leather seats, to wait for the rest of the returns with supporters. I got into the car and hit the dashboard with my fist, saying, "Well, at least we gave them a run for their money."

At Cookies, our attention turned to the television screen. Each flash of the returns showed me ahead. Most of the TV reporters concentrated on well-known personalities, such as Bella Abzug and Allard Lowenstein, both of whom lost. Then finally, late that night, the broadcasters projected me as winner. A mere 635 votes, out of a total of about 35,000, put me on top.

Our celebration didn't last long. I spent the night in tense strategy meetings with my campaign advisers. Because of the narrow victory, we wanted to secure all the voting machines that night to prevent any tampering. In the wee hours we tracked down a judge — a Republican not afraid of the Democratic machine — who signed an order impounding the voting equipment.

The Brooklyn machine did not take the loss of Celler's seat quietly. In fact the machine sued, trying to block my victory. The machine controlled the election mechanics, since all the Democratic inspectors worked for it. Nonetheless, the machine dragged me to court, claiming there had been irregularities in the voting. The judge didn't buy the argument, especially after hearing the testimony on my behalf by the head of the mathematics department at Columbia University. He said that even if all the irregularities could be attributed to me, the possibility that they would have changed the outcome of the election was minuscule, less than the fraction one over the number of grains of sand on all the beaches of the world. I won. Even so, I began to think of this lawsuit as the very definition of chutzpah. The machine politicians controlled the process, and then if it didn't work in their favor, they blamed the other side. The attempts of those in power to shift the blame and deflect attention was something I would learn much more about in the years to come. I never tried to make amends with the Brooklyn machine. Typically, once they were elected, candidates who ran against the machine tried to smooth things over, patch up any disagreements, show that they could be counted on.

Not everyone understood my position. Shortly after I won the congressional primary, I received a call from a woman. "Am I still on the payroll?" she asked. I didn't know her. "What do you do?" I said. There was a silence. "I hand out political literature," she responded. I guessed she held a spot as a "no show" worker — people sponsored by the machine who were carried on a government payroll in vaguely defined jobs. I told her to send in her résumé. I never heard from her again.

In December 1972, as I planned stepping into my new congressional seat, the Watergate break-in and cover-up seemed still remote. The big breaks in the case lay months away. At the moment I had to find places to live in Washington and Brooklyn, open a district office, hire staff for offices in both cities, and get settled into the office provided to me by the House of Representatives.

On one of my first forays to Washington, Marilyn Melkonian, a friend from Brooklyn, gave a party for me. She owned a house in Washington, and I thought how much I would love to own one, too. I welcomed my new salary, which at $42,000 doubled what I had earned in my last job as an associate at a law firm. But I didn't have the money even to consider buying a house.

Instead I rented a partly furnished apartment near the Capitol in a high-rise building on I Street. The apartment never felt like home. Except for a bed, I owned none of the furniture. I kept almost no clothes there. And I had very few books in the apartment. But I also moved into a new apartment in Brooklyn at the edge of my congressional district, not too far from my parents. (My parents' house was actually cut out of the congressional district at the last minute, when Celler had the lines redrawn to suit him.) Although it only had one bedroom, my Brooklyn apartment accommodated my furniture, belongings, and yes, books. This was my home.

My shuttling days began. From Tuesday morning through Thursday evening, I stayed in Washington. I flew to New York on Thursday, and Thursday night through Monday evening, I lived in

Brooklyn. Living in two places had significant drawbacks. The milk inevitably turned bad in both places, and I constantly found myself searching for blouses left in the other apartment.

As my first official act I opened a Brooklyn office. Celler hadn't bothered to have one in nearly half a century. To run the district office I hired Tony Freedman, a Stanford law graduate with a jovial manner and a head of bushy hair that looked like an Afro.

The district office had one central mission — to help constituents with problems. Volunteers and paid staff bustled to tackle problems, whether veteran's benefits or reunifying a Chinese family. At first the people coming in apologized that they weren't registered Democrats or had no money to pay. Tony patiently explained that neither was a prerequisite. When our office had helped them with whatever problem they had, many grateful constituents wanted to give a gift — money, jewelry, clothes. Tony and I formulated a simple rule: gifts were forbidden. Not long after, a woman we had helped on a social security problem arrived bearing a steaming plate of homemade blintzes, and we were all perplexed. Was this a gift? Should the old woman be thanked and sent away? You couldn't really send blintzes back. We instantly formulated a new rule: if a constituent brought food that would spoil unless devoured then and there, it was okay to accept it.

I greatly enjoyed being in a position to assist people. Every weekend I met with the district staff, gave speeches to various community associations, held open-office hours on Sunday, giving constituents a chance to come in and see me without any appointment, and on Monday headed back to Washington. A whole day off became a luxury that almost never happened.

In Washington I moved into my official quarters on the ground floor of Longworth, a House office building, where the ceilings were low and the rooms dark. I had a reception area, a staff room, and two offices, including my own. When I sat in the huge padded-leather "congressional" chair provided for my office, my feet could barely touch the floor. But I discovered nice surprises, too: a red leather set of the U.S. law code with my name embossed in gold, and fresh flowers from the Botanical Gardens, which arrived once a week.

Longworth was connected to the Capitol by long, gray tunnels. On one of my first trips through them, a guard stopped me.

"Where are you going?" he asked. Without breaking my stride, I said "To the Capitol; I'm a member of Congress." I guess I didn't look like one. The guard reached for his gun. "You'd better stop now," he said. I saw his gun; I stopped. Handing him my identification card, I stood by as he read it, looked at me, and read it again. Finally he put away his gun and allowed me to proceed.

Marilyn Shapiro agreed to head up my Washington office. I knew she would bring superb political judgment and a calm, pleasant demeanor to the job. She and a group of advisors with extensive political experience met with me to narrow down my preference for committee assignments in the House of Representatives. We bandied about the committee choices, trying to decide the political advantages of each. Because Celler had been on the House Judiciary Committee, it would be natural for the House leaders to replace him with me, especially since I had a law background. I liked the committee's civil rights jurisdiction. On the other hand, my advisors pointed out that Celler had not only been on the committee but had been its chair. Committee members might resent me. A consensus quickly emerged: I should try to make my mark in a different area and avoid the House Judiciary Committee. I wanted to be on the Commerce Committee, which dealt with many health and urban concerns.

No one — not even the most politically savvy among us — envisioned at that point the possibility that the Watergate break-in would trigger a constitutional crisis, and that the House Judiciary Committee would sit at the center of history.

To secure a slot on the Commerce Committee, I undertook my first legislative effort in the House. I visited every Democratic member of the House Ways and Means Committee, which in those days picked the committee assignments for Democrats, and asked not to be put on the Judiciary Committee. My request did not elicit great enthusiasm, to put it mildly.

One meeting, with Philip Landrum of Georgia, a tall, stately southerner with a distinctive drawl, discouraged me considerably. I knew he was associated with regressive labor legislation. Landrum felt obliged to give me some fatherly advice about what to expect in Congress. "Now, don't worry," he said, "just because you are a Jew and a woman." At once, I knew I was in trouble.

I entered office as the youngest woman ever elected to the House. At the time women comprised about 2 percent of the membership and did not have all the benefits that men did. The gym for members of the House of Representatives, for example, excluded women. I thought it unimportant until I realized that deal making and workouts seemed to go together. Power lifting had a special meaning in the House gym.

At the time I spoke to Landrum, the anti-Semitism struck me more than the sexism. Not surprisingly, I encountered other instances of anti-Semitism in politics. One episode occurred with George Bush, who at the time served as head of the Republican National Committee. We were both part of a televised debate in Independence Hall in Philadelphia about the Constitution. Panel members discussed the right of the president to declare war without congressional approval. Mindful of the Vietnam War and the president's unauthorized bombing of Cambodia, I strongly opposed the idea of any president usurping war-making powers, and explained why. Bush, a hawk, looked over at me and sneered, "You would never be saying this if Israel were involved." This thinly veiled anti-Semitism enraged me. Sinking to a level of debate that required him to draw upon my religion, Bush was suggesting that as a Jew I had a dual loyalty.

In my determination to be placed on any committee except the Judiciary, I completed full rounds of Capitol movers and shakers. I waited for the results, only to learn that I had failed in this lobbying debut. Despite my efforts, I was placed on the Judiciary Committee.

Very quickly, my life began to intersect with Richard Nixon's presidency. Reelected by the largest margin ever, President Nixon issued a White House invitation to greet all the new members of the House. The Christmas bombing of Hanoi had just taken place. Nixon escalated the war and dropped bombs on civilians in violation of basic international rules.

How then was I to react to the invitation to the White House by President Nixon? Entertainer Eartha Kitt was ostracized in some circles after she stood up at a White House dinner and criticized the president on the war. The idea of a White House ceremony attracted me — the pomp and circumstance, the high-powered introduction to Washington. But I couldn't bring myself to do it. I hoped I could get several others to join me in refusing to go. I called House colleagues elected with me and asked them to stay away as well. None would. I didn't go, but I didn't make a public stand of it. On the evening of the reception, Washington felt rather lonely to me.

## WATERGATE

Watergate snapped into public consciousness in the early months of 1973, as I was still learning my way around Washington. Indications that Watergate could turn into something bigger than a case of breaking and entering (actually there were two burglaries, since the first one failed to place wiretaps successfully) came from Judge John Sirica in early February 1973. Judge Sirica had presided over the criminal cases of the seven Watergate defendants that had ended in January. Although a conservative Republican, Sirica announced his dissatisfaction. He didn't think that the trial had disclosed the full story and let it be known that he planned to sentence the burglars to long jail terms. Pressure mounted for the defendants to talk.

My first personal involvement with Watergate came almost at the same time. I had a tip about an obscure issue before the House Judiciary Committee, which ultimately helped to block Richard Nixon's cover-up of illegal activities related to Watergate. The lead — about an official secrets act hidden in rules before the subcommittee on criminal justice to which I was assigned — grabbed my attention, and soon that of other subcommittee members as well.

The subcommittees were carved out from the thirty-eight-member Judiciary Committee. Assignments came from its new chair, Representative Peter Rodino of New Jersey, a liberal with a very deliberative style who with the defeat of Celler had ascended to the head of the Judiciary Committee. As it turned out, Rodino lived on the same floor in my Washington apartment building, and he and I met occasionally as we took our garbage to the incinerator.

In addition to being untested himself, Rodino had many new members — including me. At a meeting at the Rayburn Office

Building shortly after I was sworn in, I sized up my fellow committee members. All of us were lawyers, and many of my colleagues
impressed me with their legal skill. Possibly because the Judiciary
Committee didn't fall under the category of a pork-barrel committee with money to hand out, many members seemed to enjoy abstract ideas. Diversity was great. We had a number of southerners,
including Jim Mann, a thoughtful conservative from South Carolina. The committee had three black members and two women —
the other woman was Barbara Jordan of Texas, also new. When the
full committee met, I sat next to Wayne Owens, a Mormon from
Utah, and became friendly with Ed Mezvinsky, a Jewish member
from Iowa. Several members had liberal track records — Bob
Kastenmeier, Don Edwards, John Conyers, Father Robert Drinan.
Old-timers were on the committee, too. Paul Sarbanes, a former
Rhodes scholar, consistently showed himself to be extremely smart,
and the colorful, wisecracking Jack Brooks from Texas enlivened
our sessions.

The criminal justice subcommittee was led by Bill Hungate of
Missouri, a Democrat with a relaxed sense of humor. Our first meetings, all about the federal rules of evidence, seemed tedious to me
until I had a visit from George Frampton, a young lawyer working
for a public policy organization.

Frampton had a sense of urgency. There was a problem with
the rules of evidence, he said, specifically Rule 509. Rule 509 had
been sneaked in by the Nixon Justice Department after public hearing and comment. Its content was explosive — Rule 509 potentially
allowed the government to prevent any evidence from being introduced in court if the government claimed that the information was
a state secret. The government didn't have to show that the disclosure would harm national security or even government operations;
it merely had to assert a right to secrecy. Rule 509 created the equivalent of an official secrets act.

I realized at once that under Rule 509 the government could
put documents about the Vietnam War under wraps for good, as
well as any secret activities of Richard Nixon. Included would have
been the Oval Office tapes that ultimately unraveled Nixon's par-
ticipation in the Watergate cover-up. I knew nothing about the
tapes at the time — but Nixon did. I suspected the motives of

Nixon and the Justice Department in trying to slip in this rule. Was the purpose to hide other documents about the war — materials similar to the Pentagon papers released by Daniel Ellsberg? I thanked Frampton and got to work with my top legislative assistant, Michael Greenberger.

We were faced with another problem. Rule 509 would become law automatically within ninety days of its presentation, unless Congress took direct action to stop it. This procedure resembled that of a book club — you got the book, or the rules in this case, unless you sent in the card, or passed a law, saying you didn't want it. Mike and I didn't waste time. But both houses of Congress had to act quickly to stop the official secrets provision. Senator Sam Ervin of North Carolina, the leading constitutional lawyer, wanted to extend the ninety days to allow Congress more time to consider the rules.

Mike and I believed that merely extending the time might not work, since a serious analysis of the rules could take substantial time. If either the House or the Senate missed the extended deadline, the official secrets provision would become law. I had an idea: Congress could block Rule 509 by stepping in and declaring that only the rules specifically approved by Congress could take effect.

Michael and I wrote the bill, my first to be introduced, and I wrote a short speech to give on the House floor. It was imperative that I sound completely professional and calm. On the day of the introduction — March 19, 1973 — my whole Washington staff trooped to the House gallery to hear me. Some friends even flew into Washington for the occasion. The bill went through the House without a hitch, and Senator Ervin passed it in the Senate.

Our strategy worked. Congress never allowed the official secrets rule to take effect. Smuggling in the provision, or trying to, was another of the Nixon administration's attempts to amass power for itself. The blockage of the act signaled an alert House Judiciary Committee willing to take a stand against Nixon. I later understood the full implications of our action when Nixon fought tenaciously to keep secret the White House tape recordings that revealed his direct complicity in illegal activities. He lost. But if Rule 509's official secrets provision had become law, Nixon would probably have succeeded in keeping the tapes concealed, according to an appellate judge on the case. The tapes would never have become public.

Congress acted in the nick of time. A few days after my speech on the House floor, Judge Sirica read in court the letter from Watergate burglar James W. McCord Jr. describing a cover-up that pointed to the White House and other top officials.

Suddenly the Watergate case broke wide open, revealing a vast catalog of illegal activities. More disclosures, abrupt shifts and turns, filled the daily headlines of the newspapers coast to coast. At the end of April President Nixon's top advisors, John Ehrlichman and Bob Haldeman, both resigned. The Senate began hearings on May 17, with Senator Ervin in charge. The atmosphere crackled with tension. I got a little five-and-a-half-inch black-and-white television for my House office so that we could watch the hearings. Ervin's firmness and courtesy were impressive. Some Republicans stood out, too. I liked Lowell Weicker's independence. Howard Baker's refrain — What did the president know, and when did he know it? — started as a way to bait those seeking to attack the president and ended up focusing the evidence on him.

White House lawyer John Dean said that he had discussed the cover-up of Watergate and payoffs of the burglars with the president and told the president about a "cancer on the Presidency." He described the president as nonchalant about the cancer and complicit in the payoff. About this time impeachment became more of a concern, and that would involve the House Judiciary Committee.

The first call for impeachment from a member of Congress came from Father Drinan, a former law professor and Jesuit priest who had been elected two years earlier than I. In response to the disclosure that Nixon had secretly bombed Cambodia, Drinan took to the floor of the House and introduced a resolution of impeachment against Richard Nixon. Since I had been fighting in court for a ruling stating that Nixon had no constitutional right to bomb Cambodia, I applauded Drinan's action and told him so. I wanted the Judiciary Committee to act on Drinan's resolution. So did others; Conyers, Edwards, and Kastenmeier began to call for action, too. Committee chair Rodino seemed in no hurry.

Then came the Butterfield revelations. In late July Alexander Butterfield, a former deputy assistant at the White House, told the

Senate committee that a daily taping system existed in the president's Oval Office. I, like many in the nation, immediately understood the significance of this bombshell. The tapes could verify — or disprove — the testimony of Dean and other individuals, each of whom the White House had tried to discredit. What did the president know, and when did he know it? The tapes could tell.

The Senate committee demanded the tapes. Archibald Cox, who had been named as the Watergate special prosecutor by Attorney General Elliott Richardson, also demanded the tapes, and later subpoenaed them. In late August Judge Sirica ordered the president to turn the tapes over to Cox. Nixon appealed. The higher court agreed with Sirica that the president had to release the tapes. A showdown followed: would the president obey the court order or not? The answer was not at all clear.

Then came the shock of Saturday night, October 23, 1973. I was spending the weekend in New York. Relaxing on Saturday night, I enjoyed a dinner with my friend Becca and her mother. Later that evening we turned on the television in their library for a recap of the day's events. The news alarmed us. Watergate Special Prosecutor Archibald Cox had been fired on orders from Richard Nixon. How could this happen? Attorney General Richardson had given his word to the Senate at his confirmation hearings that the special prosecutor would have full independence to do his job, but earlier that evening Nixon had passed orders to Richardson to fire Cox. Richardson refused, resigning immediately. Deputy Attorney General William Ruckelshaus received the orders next. After refusing to fire Cox, Ruckelshaus had resigned as well. An obscure Justice Department official, Robert Bork, the solicitor general, was the one who did Nixon's dirty work. In what came to be known as the Saturday Night Massacre, three top officials had been summarily eliminated.

I felt as if I were living in a banana republic. The president claimed to be beyond the reach of our laws. The Justice Department had fallen into shambles. Prominent Republicans — Richardson and Ruckelshaus — had resigned rather than go along with improper presidential orders. I wondered if this meant an overthrow of our government as we knew it. How would other Americans react? Soon the public's outrage expressed itself in an avalanche of phone calls to the White House, urging the rehiring of Cox and the president's obedience to the subpoena.

With the country galvanized, I returned to Washington. Now, I thought, the House Judiciary Committee had no choice but to act on impeachment, get an investigation underway. Rodino was still moving slowly, giving no sign of what he intended. Why was Rodino taking so long?

Behind the scenes, I later learned, important decisions were under way. A critical procedural issue that affected the landscape of Watergate needed resolution. Carl Albert, Speaker of the House, needed to decide exactly which committee should handle the inquiry into impeachment. Under existing House rules the Judiciary Committee had jurisdiction, but Albert could create a special committee, the mechanism used later in the Iran-Contra hearings. Forming a special committee would give Albert the opportunity to select its members and add more senior Democrats. But if a special committee voted to impeach the president, it would be vulnerable to the charge that a Democratically controlled House had hand-picked a committee just for the purpose of impeaching a Republican president. Using an existing committee would eliminate that argument. Still, the Judiciary Committee presented a risk because it had so many new members and a new chair. How would we handle a matter of this sensitivity? Albert finally decided to put his trust in the existing committee.

Speaker Albert referred impeachment resolutions to the House Judiciary Committee. Finally the committee announced it would take up the question of impeaching the president. Despite the fact that I had not asked to be there — I was thankful now my efforts to join the Commerce Committee had been rebuffed — I was fully aware of the historic stage on which I was standing. For the first time in almost one hundred years, since the attempted impeachment of President Andrew Johnson after the Civil War, a president of the United States was going to be the subject of an impeachment inquiry.

Toward the end of December 1973 Rodino made his first outward step, selecting John Doar — a Republican who had headed the Justice Department's Civil Rights Division under Kennedy —

as Democratic majority counsel. The committee Republicans picked Albert Jenner, a Republican lawyer from Chicago who sported bow ties. The selection of John Doar actually signaled the seriousness of purpose and the high level of political sagacity at work in the House. Rodino understood that impeachment would never succeed if it were seen as a partisan effort by Democrats. From the beginning, Rodino planned to bring the Republicans along to the fullest extent possible. In fact, Rodino's style contrasted starkly with Celler's. According to those who preceded me, Celler as Judiciary Committee chair was highly partisan, and partisanship would have undermined the credibility of an impeachment hearing. Once, as the demands of the impeachment proceedings escalated, Rodino called me on the phone. "I've got you to blame for all this," he teased, implying that if I hadn't defeated Celler, his life would have been much calmer than it was as Celler's successor to the chair.

The process of presidential impeachment was completely new to everyone. I remember pulling out the thin pamphlet of the Constitution that I kept in my office. What should a presidential impeachment hearing look like and sound like? What type of evidence should be used? We had no role model. Although it is a constitutional safeguard against serious presidential misconduct, impeachment is in its own way antidemocratic. After all, Richard Nixon had a landslide victory in 1972; who were we to suggest throwing him out?

I had never liked Nixon. He had gotten elected by vicious and baseless red-baiting of his opponents, including Helen Gahagan Douglas, and whipped up anti-Communist sentiment to secure victory after victory. He won the presidency in 1968 by promising to end the Vietnam War, a hollow claim. He had invaded Cambodia illegally. On the domestic front he dismantled social programs and concocted a new practice called "impoundment," claiming the unilateral right to cut funding from programs. His ethical standards, going back to the years when, as Eisenhower's vice president, he groveled to the American people in his famous Checkers speech, had always been questionable. During Watergate I was particularly struck by the speech in which he felt compelled to declare, "I am not a crook." How pitiful, I thought, that the president of the

United States has to stoop to such depths. But when it came to impeachment I tried to put my personal feelings about Nixon aside. Whatever each of us felt about the man, we couldn't lightly overturn a presidential election.

Our only precedent for presidential impeachment — the post–Civil War attempted impeachment of Andrew Johnson — had been a mess. History recorded it as highly partisan and unjustified. What *was* justified? I buried myself in dense books. The Constitution said that a president may be removed from office for "high crimes and misdemeanors." What did those words mean? Did they mean criminal conduct, or something else? Nixon's people wanted to keep the scope narrow, only to crimes or their equivalent. I concluded that the scope of conduct covered was broad — the serious abuse of presidential power. The term "high crime" meant a constitutional infringement, a political crime.

Impeachment began in earnest in January 1974, barely a year after I had moved to Washington. I felt the weight of that responsibility. My committee had to listen to and evaluate all the evidence against Nixon and make a decision not only for all 435 members of the Congress but for the entire nation. As a member of the Judiciary Committee, I attended daily sessions. At the culmination of each, I would be asked to vote yes or no on a recommendation of impeachment. I dug in. I wanted to know all the facts, all the law, everything I could get my hands on. Even without the impeachment hearings, I worked late most nights, reading mail, studying the bills coming up for vote, working on my own legislation. Once the impeachment started, the workload multiplied exponentially. I stayed in the office until midnight and, then a smoker, lit cigarette after cigarette.

Letters from across the nation poured into my office. A member of my staff, Anne Stone, was the one who opened the mail. The majority of writers supported the committee's work; others sent vile tirades, accusing me and other members of all sorts of improprieties. Some envelopes even included feces. Liz Schroeder, a nineteen-year-old student from Oberlin College working in my office for the year, told my mother about the awful things that some people would write. My mother was stunned.

The committee worked all day in closed sessions. Behind

closed doors, all thirty-eight of us still took our formal seats, Democrats on one side, Republicans on the other. I sat in the center, and the row ended to my right. Next to me on the left sat Wayne Owens.

I and the other committee members all received a large set of black three-ring, loose-leaf notebooks, which were confidential. I locked the black books in a safe in my office. Each notebook contained evidence against Richard Nixon. A cover sheet held a statement of fact on one page, with material supporting the statement on backup pages. Our role as committee members turned into a quasi-judicial function. John Doar and his hundred-member staff (including Hillary Rodham) gathered the information. Doar presented it to us, reading the statements of fact aloud, usually one paragraph at a time. Committee members could ask questions. Rodino took no chances that any committee member would say at a later point, "I never knew this," or "You never explained that."

This procedure continued day after day after day in a slow, deliberative process. After several weeks, I felt as though I were sinking in quicksand. The evidence against Richard Nixon was massive; I saw no bottom, no limit in sight. The black books clasped thousands of pages of evidence, with descriptions of a total of 243 incidents.

The extent of illegality and immorality in Watergate was overwhelming. At the top of the list we found the president obstructing the lawful investigation of criminal activity by ordering the CIA to have the FBI stop investigating. We heard about the cover-up, the hush money, the payoffs made by the president's attorney, Herbert Kalmbach, to the Watergate burglars. The committee examined the misuse of the IRS to audit Nixon's enemies, the White House "plumber's" break-in at Daniel Ellsberg's psychiatrist's office, the unlawful wiretaps of reporters and White House staffers, the payoffs, Nixon's falsified taxes. Watergate as we saw it unfold entailed much more than a break-in. It was a true constitutional crisis, a frightful attempt to implode a democracy like none America had ever seen before.

Rodino bent over backward to be fair to the president. In our closed sessions we heard many witnesses, including John Mitchell and John Dean. The president's counsel, James St. Clair, was allowed to sit in, too. Sometimes I thought Rodino had gone too far, although in retrospect he was right. Certainly no one could claim that the hearings sandbagged Nixon. Democratic committee members met regularly in a caucus. Provocative discussions arose. One dealt with milk. Nixon had received a very substantial contribution from the dairy industry after a personal meeting with its association's representatives. The evidence showed that shortly afterward, Nixon agreed to raise dairy price supports. Although tapes of the conversations could have shed light on whether he agreed to do a favor in exchange for a contribution, or some other quid pro quo, Nixon refused to turn over the tapes. The committee was left to decide what course of action to follow.

Committee members felt very uncomfortable. Many of them had also received contributions from the dairy industry. Nixon's people — in an effort to embarrass the committee — had made this public. Fortunately, I had escaped the list: Just after I won the primary I had received a $1,000 contribution from the dairy people — and $1,000 was a substantial amount, given my campaign finances. I didn't know why the dairy association had sent it to me. I had never communicated with the dairy association; in fact, I had never even heard of it before the check arrived in the mail. There were to my knowledge no cows in Brooklyn. I sent the check right back. They wanted to curry favor with me, but I had no reason to want to be curried by them.

Dairy contributions alone did not account for my colleagues' unease. Finally one committee member — I don't remember who — asked, "How can we hold Nixon responsible? This is just politics." And to my dismay, the matter was dropped.

I became intensely involved in another issue that John Doar and the committee refused to pursue in depth: the bombing of Cambodia. I believed strongly that in doing so the president had exceeded his war powers. In bombing Cambodia, Nixon had acted secretly, keeping two sets of books — one for Congress, another for the White House — in order to conceal his actions. Congress never authorized the bombing.

I came to believe that the secret bombing, and leaks about it early in Nixon's administration, formed the original impetus for much of the illegality that corrupted the Nixon presidency. Nixon had been so furious about leaks in the newspapers that, at Secretary of State Henry Kissinger's behest, he had authorized wiretaps of White House staffers and newspaper reporters. These wiretaps were illegal. Later a top Justice Department official, Robert Mardian, obtained the records of the wiretaps for "safekeeping" and then turned them over to the White House at its request. In many ways this scheme repeated itself again and again in Watergate — illegal activity, compounded by wiretaps, compounded by high-level government officials participating, wittingly or less so, in covering up the activity. To impeach Richard Nixon and leave out the war seemed wrong to me. How could you deal with the symptoms and not the cause?

Other members of the Judiciary Committee, including Father Drinan, Bill Hungate, and Don Edwards, also felt ardently about this. I pressed Rodino, also a war opponent, about looking into the issue, and he agreed that the staff would do so. But he assented reluctantly, and in a meeting with John Doar I criticized the superficiality of the staff work. I wanted him to seek more information about the Cambodia bombing; he refused.

Doar waved some document suggesting that a few members of Congress knew about the Cambodia bombing, that the bombing actually hadn't been concealed from Congress. I pointed out that his investigation had stopped short of asking the named members of Congress whether they had in fact been informed, and if so to what extent. Even assuming they had been *fully* informed, what difference did it make under the Constitution if a few friendly members of Congress had received a confidential message from the president disclosing his bombing of citizens in a foreign land? This was not what the Constitution called for.

Although polite, Doar became a brick wall on the subject. The committee wasn't going to draft an impeachment resolution on Cambodia. Here, I believed, one of the most vital issues of our times, involving the improprieties of the Vietnam War, the loss of thousands upon thousands of lives, and the executive branch's grab for power, had been summarily dumped. I talked with my neighbor on the committee, Wayne Owens, who said he would consider voting for an impeachment resolution on Cambodia if it were focused only on the concealment of the bombing from Congress.

I decided to go ahead and draft a resolution myself. The idea energized me, but a lot needed to be done. I had to gather facts, write the precise resolution, and prepare my statements in support of it. I asked Tony Freedman from my district office to join me in Washington. At one point Sy Hersh of the *New York Times* came to talk to me about the resolution. Afterward Tony went to Sy's office, and Sy pulled out a drawer full of State Department cables. Using the information we collected, Tony and I wrote a fourth article of impeachment. I thought someone more senior should introduce the Cambodia impeachment resolution at the public hearings, and asked John Conyers if he would do it. He agreed.

Outside of the impeachment proceedings, my other initiatives went on full speed, and then an entirely new one developed: I uncovered information that Nazi war criminals were living in America. I felt strongly about this issue; one aide, Aviva Futorian, immersed herself in it. The pressure in my office grew as I took on the Nazis and impeachment simultaneously.

The committee met daily for months. One day I and the other members were handed headsets so that we could listen to the White House tapes. Nixon had danced around the tapes issues with a plan a day to avoid turning them over. But Rodino held firm. He wanted the tapes. I remember watching Nixon on television when he decided to present us with transcripts, instead of the tapes themselves. Nixon stood behind a table of transcripts bound in black three-ring notebooks of the type we had on the Judiciary Committee. The pile, enormous, filled the table. Waving his arms dramatically, Nixon claimed this was the largest disclosure that any president had ever made. To me, he simply looked foolish.

Ultimately, when we got the actual tapes, the committee saw how Nixon, despite his arm waving, had doctored the transcripts. Nixon's release of the doctored transcripts became one of the grounds for impeachment, part of his cover-up. And bowdlerizing the transcripts amounted to one of Nixon's worst political mistakes. In eliminating all of the uncouth and vulgar phrases and replacing them with "expletive deleted," he inspired the nation's comedians to make a hundred "expletive" jokes.

Accurate transcripts, prepared by Doar's staff, lay in front of us as we listened to the tapes. I had to strain to hear through the earphones. The tapes were scratchy, the sound quality terrible. But the worst part was when I *could* hear. I wanted to block my ears. The tapes revealed endless hours of scheming and plotting by the president and his staff. I hadn't imagined the gutter level to which both the president and people inside the Oval Office had sunk. They sounded like the speakers in tapes transcribed from secret hideouts that I later encountered as district attorney in Brooklyn — ordinary gangsters plotting to avoid detection. Wiretapping and money laundering, break-ins and covering up, were everyday events, a way of life. Never once in those tapes — or for that matter in any piece of evidence we had — did the president or his associates ask what was the right thing to do, what was good for the country. They acted with such total disregard for the office of the presidency and for the American people that at times all I wanted to do was to take off the headphones and leave: I didn't want to know this sordid information about Nixon; I was reluctant to carry this devastating evidence in my consciousness. Emotionally, it exhausted me.

We had completed much of the absorbing and sifting through the evidence when the press, impatient, accused us of dillydallying. Perhaps this was a White House gambit — to push us into action before we were ready. Rodino handled the criticism perfectly: he ignored it, insisting that we proceed at our usual deliberate pace. The professionalism of the result meant more than momentarily placating the press.

As we neared the time for final presentation of the articles of impeachment and debate on them, Wayne Owens suggested in the committee's Democratic caucus that the hearings be televised. Rodino immediately opposed the idea. Rodino didn't often express his opinions so quickly. But Wayne persisted, arguing passionately for televising. I didn't really understand much about the media in those days. Television had barely covered me during my race for Congress. Wayne's insistence on the value of televising impressed me, and since I liked and respected him, I supported his proposal. The other three newcomers to the committee argued for televising the hearings, too. Finally Rodino gave in.

Televising the hearings worked better than anyone expected. With the assistance of the camera, the public sat in on one of the great dramas of American politics; Americans across the land could see and appreciate the seriousness of the process.

By now I had switched everyone on my legislative staff to working on impeachment. Bob Sheehan and Aviva Futorian divided the three major impeachment resolutions for analysis. Tony Freedman concentrated on my own impeachment resolution on the war powers, which Bob thought was beside the point. In a pragmatic way, Bob felt the committee members should focus on the strongest evidence and not be diverted. At any rate, no lawyer on my staff had the time to spend on the normal legislative calendar. I drafted college intern Liz Schroeder. Her job notched up several levels to analyzing the bills coming up for a vote in Congress and briefing me on them.

Shortly before the committee planned to begin the televised debates on the articles of impeachment, I received a call from a college friend of my brother. Through his connections in the jewelry business, he had just learned about the purchase of a pair of $5,000 diamond and platinum earrings for Pat Nixon. The earrings cost the same as a moderate-sized car. Something seemed strange about the transaction, the friend said. I probed, and it turned out that the earrings had been purchased with money furnished by Bebe Rebozo, a Nixon friend. In fact, to pay for the earrings, $5,000 had been taken out of Rebozo's bank account and, in an unusual banking transaction, went through five other accounts in one day. This seemed like the kind of Watergate money laundering with which the committee had become familiar. Was it an illegal contribution to the president? I mentioned this to Jack Brooks, a partisan Democrat if ever there was one. With a touch of glee, Jack asked for an investigation of the earrings, but the committee declined. He then helped develop a fifth article of impeachment for introduction by Ed Mezvinsky on Nixon's many financial improprieties, earrings included.

Each of the articles of impeachment began with a single paragraph. It proclaimed that President Richard M. Nixon had acted contrary to his constitutional duty and oath of office, and went on to specify how he had done so.

After seven months of research and analysis, the committee found substantial evidence to accuse Nixon. He was charged with obstructing justice — the equivalent of a crime — by covering up the Watergate burglary and arranging for the CIA to interfere with the FBI investigation. The president stood accused of abuse of power and failure to enforce the laws, and we charged him with disobeying the committee subpoenas and subverting the constitutional process of impeachment.

Altogether, three resolutions cited some fifteen activities: making false statements to investigative officers; withholding material evidence; approving false testimony of witnesses; interfering with investigations by the FBI, the special prosecutor, and congressional committees; approving hush money to witnesses or defendants; misusing the CIA; passing on information received from the Justice Department to the subjects of investigation; making false public statements to deceive people about misconduct; telling defendants they would receive rewards for false testimony or silence; using the IRS to audit and harass political enemies; placing illegal wiretaps on private citizens; authorizing the break-in of Ellsberg's psychiatrist's office; maintaining a secret investigative unit that used CIA resources and undertook illegal activities; refusing to turn over papers and documents; and impeding lawful inquiries.

Each of the three articles of impeachment ended with a simple line: "Wherefore Richard M. Nixon, by such conduct, warrants impeachment and trial, and removal from office."

The final step in the process was upon us. In public, I would be called upon to vote on the articles of impeachment, a process now to be televised. I, like most committee members, felt nervous but confident.

I didn't make a public announcement of my position on the impeachment resolutions before the final hearings, although some of my colleagues did. I didn't want to suggest an unwillingness to listen to all the evidence and the arguments on both sides.

The hearings started in the evening so the public could watch. My brother and mother came from New York to join the audience. Other committee members had invited their families as well. Heading for the hearing room, we were ordered to stand back. A bomb threat had been received, and we had one more delay while German shepherds sniffed the premises.

The bomb scare ended without a bomb, and we filed in, met by a multitude of press, television cameras, photographers. The room reverberated with anticipation. I took my place just below Rodino, next to Owens. As the hearings began at last, the atmosphere shifted perceptibly to one of solemn reflection. I kept thinking about my parents and grandparents. All of them came to the United States as immigrants. My brother and I made up the first generation born in this country. And now, in my first public office, here I sat, passing judgment on the president of the United States.

Rodino framed the debate, sounding dignified, serious, and pleasant at the same time. Being so junior, I had to wait until near the end to give my remarks. I gave a straightforward recitation of the central facts of Nixon's involvement in Watergate, using the opportunity to describe the extensiveness of the evidence against him. Barbara Jordan spoke more philosophically and memorably about the Constitution, reminding Americans that as an African-American and a woman she had been excluded at its inception.

The first day of the hearings went badly. The Republican defenders of the president demanded specifics on each charge. The committee wasn't organized sufficiently to respond. That evening, the Democrats scurried to reorganize. Paul Sarbanes, with a deliberate and thoughtful style, became specificity czar. He led the debate for the Democrats and helped organize the response for the remaining hearings.

On the whole the hearings proceeded without grandstanding. Both sides acted with extraordinary decorum. During the debates on the articles, many members bared their souls, particularly the Republicans. Tom Railsback, for example, expressed his agony about voting. The facts were overwhelming, but I think that in the end the public was persuaded most by the sincerity, decency, and intelligence of members of the committee. Via their television sets, the public witnessed neither a traditional debate nor a traditional trial. They observed up close the people who struggled honestly with the decision.

I did feel disappointed during the debate on the Cambodia article that I had drafted and turned over to John Conyers to introduce. The arguments of my colleagues troubled me. Bill Cohen disingenuously argued that Congress had approved the bombing of Cambodia. While I knew the resolution wouldn't pass, I thought the debate would be more enlightening. Although a majority of committee Democrats supported it, the resolution went to a resounding defeat.

The vote on the first article of impeachment took place on July 27, 1974. The members of the Judiciary Committee were called upon to state their votes, and a hush fell over the committee chambers, despite the normal bustle of the audience and the media. The moment was historic; we all knew it. When my turn to vote came, to my surprise a feeling of deep sadness washed over me. I had to judge; I couldn't turn away from it. Richard Nixon was contemptible, but I still found it painful to vote in favor of the impeachment resolution. I realized the enormous difference between voicing a personal opinion and issuing a formal judgment of condemnation. And I could hardly ignore all the weighty consequences of this judgment. As the head of the committee staff read off the names of committee members, I recognized the same somberness and anguish in everyone's voice.

I voted for all five impeachment resolutions. Two — on Cambodia and Nixon's taxes — weren't adopted. The other three passed with substantial Republican support. The committee had huge public support, as well. The full impeachment process would entail more steps — a vote in the full House and a trial in the Senate. But they were not to be. The Judiciary Committee action stood so solid that even the president, who had been belligerent and engaged in stonewalling, began to cave in. The Supreme Court ordered Nixon to relinquish the tapes, and in a few days he finally released the "smoking gun" tape, in which he could be heard conspiring to obstruct the FBI's investigation. At this point the holdout Republicans joined every other representative on the Judiciary Committee in calling for Nixon's impeachment.

In a way, the drama of the committee obfuscated another drama — that of a president grappling with the growing realization that he would have to give up his office. Until the committee hearings, people didn't know that Nixon would be forced out of office. The dignity of the hearings and weight of the evidence made it clear that there was no other course of action. We hadn't noticed if or how Nixon changed. We were absorbed in the hunt, in setting a trap for a dangerous person. We weren't thinking about how he felt as the trap held him tighter and tighter. Within two weeks, the inevitable happened. Nixon resigned from office.

I didn't experience the slightest surprise when I learned of Nixon's decision to resign. I watched him on our television set in the Washington office. The spectacle stretched credulity. He resigned in disgrace, and yet we saw him making a fond farewell speech to the White House staff and stand on the top of the steps of Air Force One giving his famous campaign wave. Nixon defied the reality of his situation and put on this bravura performance at the moment of his greatest humiliation.

I felt deeply relieved to see him go. All the hard work we put in, the countless hours of reading briefing books and absorbing the thousands of pages of evidence, had paid off. Democracy had been restored; the rule of law prevailed. The threat he posed to the country had finally ended.

Today, Watergate has come to be associated with the beginning of public cynicism about government. But from the inside, I saw something else: a system that worked, and worked amazingly well. An out-of-control president had committed crimes, abused his powers, spied on his political enemies, and retaliated against ordinary people who disagreed with him. And he was stopped. The balance of power was reasserted, in a professional, convincing manner.

Why did Congress work so well in Watergate? I've continued to think about this over time, particularly as I have seen Congress fall flat on its face in the Iran-Contra matter or in the confirmation of Clarence Thomas. Each of those hearings bogged down into a morass for various reasons. They were bent to respond to the press and not the needs of a professional inquiry. The committees approved artificial deadlines that short-circuited the investigations, giving witnesses an incentive not to produce material and to wait for the deadline to pass. The committees entered the public arena before they were prepared.

What made Watergate different? Outside the executive branch, all the systems of government lived up to their duties. The courts and justice system worked — even though Nixon tried to interfere. Judge John Sirica smelled something fishy and refused to back down. Attorney General Elliott Richardson and Deputy Attorney

General William Ruckelshaus acted with courage and honor. Archibald Cox refused to be intimidated. The Supreme Court did its part, too. The chief justice and three associate justices had been named by Nixon. All the justices, including those Nixon appointed, ruled against him and held that the president had to comply with the subpoena to produce the tapes.

The Senate Watergate Committee used professional, determined inquiries to seek the truth, and then the House Judiciary Committee painstakingly reviewed the evidence for impeachment.

Congress, despite what I saw as blindness on the issue of war powers and the bombing of Cambodia, performed magnificently. In hindsight, I understand why Rodino did not delve deeply into the Cambodian bombing on impeachment. He desperately wanted to hold together a bipartisan center. The Vietnam War provoked heated disputes. The article of impeachment on Cambodia may have seemed too much like punishing the president for a policy dispute over Vietnam, rather than protecting democratic decision making in the area of war making. Still, in my view the decision not only was wrong but proved costly, allowing other presidents to transgress in similar ways.

Watergate arose against the backdrop of imperious acts by the president. People were concerned, even scared. The president had arrogantly overstepped the powers of his office: he had continued a war that the vast majority of people wanted to end, and he had claimed that he could unilaterally refuse to spend money appropriated by Congress for programs he didn't like and that he could dismantle government agencies. Combined, these assertions of power suggested a presidential coup.

I came to the conclusion that the president had not only covered up the Watergate break-in but had ordered it as well.

In the Watergate hearings, the constitutional system asserted itself against a president run amok. But it only worked because, in the end, we discovered as Americans that we shared basic values — that more important to us than any president was the survival of our constitutional system itself.

# 3

# System Failure: The Ford Pardon

*O*N SUNDAY, SEPTEMBER 8, 1974, a mere thirty days after Richard Nixon resigned in disgrace, President Gerald R. Ford issued a full pardon to his predecessor. The pardon, unconditional, covered all crimes that Nixon may have committed during his presidency.

I got on the phone immediately and called staff members and colleagues. Ford had undone the normal legal process. Worse, he protected Nixon from accountability under the law. Leon Jaworski, the special prosecutor, hadn't even yet announced if Nixon would be prosecuted. What could we do?

On one level, I couldn't claim surprise: the pardon explained Nixon's resignation. But I reeled at its sheer audacity. In a single act Ford had demonstrated a combination of disdain for public opinion, rejection of constitutional norms, and disregard for the rule of law.

I came to believe that the pardon of President Nixon cut a swath of deep and long-lasting harm. Congress aggravated the situation by failing to act strongly and effectively in response. And that in turn set a dangerous precedent for how Congress would act — or fail to act — when new travesties arose during Irangate and future scandals. What happened in Washington in those months fostered a fundamental, and damaging, shift in the separation of powers.

When people say that Watergate left a stain on the American

consciousness, I have a slightly different view. During the Watergate hearings Congress climbed to unexpected heights, demonstrating real backbone and character. Congress stopped the abuses of a president, refusing to allow the Constitution to be ignored. But when Congress confronted Ford's pardon, it slid back to business as usual.

Nixon's resignation left many unanswered questions, including whether he should still be impeached. Congress could impeach him despite the resignation. As it was, Nixon received the perks of the presidency — a pension, staff, Secret Service protection. Impeachment would have cut off those benefits and made the verdict on his conduct clear for all time. Emotionally, I leaned in that direction. But I concluded that the public might believe that an impeachment after Nixon's resignation was vindictive, and further proceedings would be too risky.

Ford's pardoning of Nixon kindled altogether new questions. Ford became president in 1974 without a single vote of the American people electing him to national office. The Twenty-fifth Amendment to the Constitution, ratified in 1971, gave the president the power to name a vice president when the office was vacant. The House and the Senate had to approve. When Vice President Spiro Agnew resigned amid a bribery scandal in October 1973, Nixon nominated Ford, a Republican party loyalist who had served as House minority leader. Ford's prior role in the Watergate affair had been to play along with the president and squelch any hearing by the House Banking Committee prior to the November 1972 presidential election.

I didn't like Ford's record on civil rights and the way he had blindly supported the Republican party agenda to attack Supreme Court Justice William O. Douglas. Ford went to the floor of the House and called for Douglas's impeachment, something that seemed shameful and dishonest to me. Douglas had done nothing to warrant impeachment except annoy the Republicans by being such a fierce and independent liberal. I also thought there were serious unanswered questions about Ford's finances. I voted against Ford, one of a handful of representatives to do so.

By and large, vice presidential confirmation hearings in November 1973 sailed smoothly for Ford. Congressional colleagues treated him gently in confirmation hearings. Still, keen observers already believed that President Nixon might not finish his term — he might be impeached or forced to resign. If so, Ford might become president. And if there weren't a vice president, impeachment would be politically impossible since next in line to the presidency was the Democratic speaker of the House.

If Ford were president, the Constitution gave him the "power to grant reprieves and pardons for offenses against the United States." Several members of Congress, questioning Ford as he was being considered for vice president, wanted to know: What would he do? Would he consider a pardon? Ford responded. He did not believe that the American people would tolerate a pardon, he said. Yet by stating what the American people would tolerate and not what he would actually do, Ford had adroitly sidestepped the issue. Reporters and participants believed Ford had said he would grant no pardon, should the issue arise. Congress confirmed Ford as vice president, and he took the oath of office on December 6, 1973.

Eight months later following the Judiciary Committee vote and the release of the "smoking gun" tape, Nixon resigned in the face of certain impeachment. On the next day, August 9, 1974, Ford became the thirty-eighth president of the United States.

Watergate had more chapters to go. Criminal investigations continued, and criminal trials awaited numerous people who had worked for Nixon. Nixon left office, but why should he too not be indicted for his role in various illegal activities? Nixon had unquestionably committed crimes; he had been named by the Watergate grand jury an unindicted coconspirator on obstruction of justice. The grand jury was obviously disturbed by Nixon's conduct but followed instructions of the special prosecutor to the effect that his status as president shielded him from indictment. No shield, however, protected a former president. Why not prosecute him as any other criminal offender? Even some of Nixon's friends, such as California's Charles Wiggins, reportedly said that Nixon should pay for his misdeeds even if it meant he had to go to prison. No person should be above the law, said Wiggins and others.

The legal system seemed ready to work as it should. A little more than two weeks into his presidency, Ford held his first press conference. He said that he hoped President Nixon would find peace, and that until there was any legal action against Nixon or decision by a court, it would be "unwise and untimely to make any commitment" about a pardon. Although Ford evaded questions, reporters were convinced that the new president would not make a snap decision, according to writer Clark Mollenhoff.

And then suddenly, only eleven days later, Ford announced the pardon. Investigative actions against Nixon, still incomplete, screeched to a halt. Ford didn't stop there. He also gave Nixon control of the controversial White House tapes, many of which held the secrets to illegal activities. Why the turnabout? Ford first offered medical grounds, stating that Nixon suffered from phlebitis, which endangered his life. But phlebitis wasn't life threatening. The country couldn't handle the spectacle of a prosecution of Richard Nixon, Ford said. But I thought the country could take anything except lies and usurpation of the system.

Public alarm sounded again — not as great as after the Saturday Night Massacre, but strong and loud. For many, including me, the pardon rang of a dual standard of justice — one for the powerful and another for everyone else.

To me, the pardon smacked of a deal. Did Ford, in order to gain the presidency, put Nixon beyond the reach of the law? But suppose there had been a deal? Could you undo the pardon? I asked my staff to do some research. Digging back through the old cases, the answer seemed to be yes. A pardon could be reversed. The president's pardon power paralleled that of many state governors, and we found a case in which bribery voided a governor's pardon. No governmental power in our system reigns absolute. The pardon power had its limits: bribery was one.

Our findings emboldened me. If there were a deal over the pardon — if Ford, in return for Nixon's agreement to resign, offered a pardon either when nominated by Nixon for vice president or later when Nixon made a decision about resignation — that could nullify the pardon. How could we find out about it?

Not everyone opposed the pardon. Judge Sirica, for example, said that the pardon might heal the country and put Watergate behind us. Nixon's acceptance of the pardon implied his guilt, Sirica believed at the time. Later Sirica changed his mind, calling his support of the pardon a mistake. In his book *To Set the Record Straight* Sirica wrote that the evidence of criminality against Nixon had been overwhelming and compelling, and that the pardon left an air of incompletion. Nixon had shown himself to be ruthless, self-serving, arrogant, and false, and the pardon allowed him to stand above the law and claim he had done no wrong. "I feel it would have been better for the country if the legal process had been allowed to run its course," Sirica wrote. Nixon should have been tried, he felt, either in a Senate impeachment trial or through the courts.

In Congress members called for an investigation. Some Democrats introduced "resolutions of inquiry" on the pardon. Resolutions of inquiry are ancient parliamentary devices that allow the authors to demand a vote by the whole House of Representatives on the resolution at any time, a powerful tool. To deflect an immediate vote on these resolutions on the pardon, they were referred to the House Judiciary Committee, and in particular to the subcommittee on criminal justice, on which I sat.

I wanted to get to the bottom of the pardon, possibly one of the biggest cover-ups of all. Everything about it made me wary. Ford had bypassed the regular pardon process. Presidents can and do pardon people, and a well-established procedure existed to facilitate pardons. Pardon applications went to a Justice Department pardon counsel, who considered them and made a recommendation. The attorney general then reviewed the recommendation. By the time the Justice Department sent any proposed pardon to the president, it had been fully analyzed, scrutinized, evaluated. Why did Ford circumvent this process? The only reason, I thought, was because he didn't want the pardon application to be reviewed. Suppose the pardon counsel or the attorney general had said no? Ford didn't want to tempt that possibility.

Other Watergate criminal cases were on deck, waiting to be completed. A pardon of Nixon could have adversely affected the trials of Bob Haldeman, John Ehrlichman, and others — all still pending. Juries could wonder why they should convict the small fry if the big fish was let go. Ford didn't consult with Leon Jaworski, who handled those cases. Again, I thought, Ford worried that Jaworski might say no.

The issue of the White House tapes constituted one of the worst parts of Ford's action, in my opinion. What better way to cover up all the crimes of Watergate and other misdeeds than to make sure that Nixon himself had full control over the tapes and their future fate?

To decide how to handle the congressional resolutions inquiring into the pardon, the chair of the subcommittee on criminal justice, Bill Hungate of Missouri, called a meeting of the Democrats. There were three options: the subcommittee could hold hearings on the pardon resolutions, do nothing, or send the resolutions back to the House without any hearings for an up or down vote. Holding hearings seemed the only responsible course of action. President Ford let it be known that, if hearings were held, he would testify.

What kind of hearings would they be? Not all hearings are alike. Not all are effective. The process to follow seemed entirely obvious to me. Before any public hearings, all documents relating to the pardon should be subpoenaed, and then all the people involved should be questioned. What did Ford know, and when did he know it? Who had met with Ford, and what had they said? The public wanted to know if there had been a deal. With full preparation, the questioning of President Ford could be accomplished in a focused manner. I'm not sure if I understood this because I had only recently left the practice of law at a large New York City law firm, or because of pure common sense.

At the first meeting of the Democratic caucus of the subcommittee, I suggested a pragmatic plan. Let's subpoena the documents and question the witnesses. Let's do a real investigation. I received a frank response. Of course, subcommittee members said.

But nothing happened. No witnesses were questioned; no documents were requested, much less subpoenaed. Another caucus took place. Again I made my proposal and said that without preparation beforehand, we could not find the truth about the pardon. Again I heard an encouraging round of Yes, we should do it. But time wore on. Returning from the subcommittee meeting, I exchanged comments with Aviva Futorian, one of my legislative aides. The subcommittee had undertaken no investigative effort; none was planned, I said.

Not intending to give up, I decided to seek a change in the rules for the hearing. Under normal House of Representatives rules on a hearing, each representative has a right to question a witness for just five minutes. With only five minutes, especially if the witness gave long answers or stalled for time, it would be difficult to raise serious questions, and impossible to get them answered. At least, I urged, let's change the rule and expand each member's time for questioning the president to ten minutes. The subcommittee flatly rejected the suggestion. The five-minute rule would remain in effect.

Only later did I suspect a reason for the recalcitrance. What if we found out a deal did exist? Then the House might have to act to impeach Ford, and few representatives wanted to risk that possibility.

The hearings were quickly placed on the calendar for October 17, 1974. The day before the president planned to testify, I saw clearly that the hearings would be a mockery — simply an opportunity for the president to make his case, without any serious search for the truth. President Ford would get a platform to appear open and candid, while saying nothing. It was a public relations event.

Given the five-minute rule and the lack of any preparation, the hearings were not designed to uncover the truth.

I struggled with what to do. Five minutes wouldn't give me the time to get answers to basic and troubling questions about the pardon. But the hearing would be the sole opportunity to do so. I told my legislative aide, Aviva, that when President Ford came before the committee, I planned to mention that there were many questions that had not been answered. Specify the questions, Aviva counseled.

I closed the door to my office and wrote out in longhand the specific questions that Ford should be asked, considering the most disquieting issues about the pardon. Why the hurry? Why not consult with the new special prosecutor, Leon Jaworski? Why block the release of the tapes? Was there a deal? I had a thought: if I used all my time running through the questions, the subcommittee would still allot the president the time to answer.

I went over the questions I had written with Aviva and the rest of my staff, and then reviewed them myself. Was this the right thing to do? I didn't relish the idea of asking the president of the United States if he had entered into a deal over the pardon. I called trusted friends and asked for their views. Everyone agreed with my course of action. One friend initially refused to give me an answer, saying she didn't want to have to weigh in on a decision that she perceived as having such great import. In the end, though, she too agreed. No one I spoke with dissented.

During this time I developed terrible bronchitis and lost my voice. Knowing that I would have to question the president of the United States, and in such a public way — the hearings were to be televised — I wanted my voice back. I put in an emergency call to my doctor in New York. Stop smoking, he said. I did, and never started again. At least I have Gerald Ford to thank for that.

The day of the hearing arrived. I felt very tense; not smoking only made it worse. The hearing started. The members of the subcommittee complimented the president again and again on his appearance — the first time in history that any president had testified before Congress. Most of the subcommittee members spent their five minutes congratulating the president. Perhaps because of his status as a former colleague, they were particularly genial. I kept listening, pen at hand. My name came last on the roster of Democrats, and I thought that senior colleagues would surely ask Ford at least some of the questions that I had written out — and probably all of them would be asked by the time my turn had come. But no one asked even one of them.

My turn came. I hesitated. I really didn't want the confrontation. I thought about the calls to my friends, the advice I had solicited and received. I thought about the piles of letters that ordinary people had sent to me. I looked around and realized if I didn't ask the questions, no one would.

By then I had the questions virtually memorized. I explained that the five-minute rule wouldn't permit me to ask the president each question and allow him to answer one by one. I said that the resolutions that prompted the hearing resulted from dark suspicions that had been created in the public's mind, and that they needed to be addressed. These were some of the questions most Americans wanted answered. The suspicions, I said, were brought about by the circumstances, the secrecy, and the implausible reasons given for the pardon, which caused people to question whether there was a deal.

The president sat silently until I said the word "deal." Then he interrupted to say there was no deal.

When he finished, I continued. People, I said, were asking specific questions about the pardon, and from my mail I had gleaned several. How could he pardon Richard Nixon without specifying any of the crimes for which he was pardoned or obtaining any acknowledgment of guilt from him? Why did Ford fail to go through normal channels or consult the attorney general? What was the reason for the extraordinary haste with which the pardon was decided? Didn't the agreement about the tapes hamper the ability of the public and the special prosecutor to know the full story of misconduct in the Oval Office? Why had he negotiated the tapes agreement using an attorney who was under criminal investigation? How could he explain not having consulted the special prosecutor before approving the tapes agreement? Would Ford be willing to release the tapes to the subcommittee for review, in order to alleviate any suspicion that the simultaneous pardon and tapes agreement was to protect recordings of conversations between himself and Richard Nixon? Relief filled me as I reached the end of the list. Directing these difficult questions, in person, to the president had been much more of a strain than I had imagined, but I got the questions out in the public arena, where they could be aired.

After I concluded, the president made a fumbling reference to the tapes, saying that according to the attorney general, they belonged to Nixon, but that they were being held for the special prosecutor and would not be destroyed. Other than that, the president had no answer. And to this day those questions have still not been answered.

Once the hearing ended, I didn't know what to expect. What reaction would I get? Would this be the last of my career in Washington?

The next day New York's *Daily News* attacked me editorially for having the temerity to question the president and for daring to call him Mr. Ford instead of Mr. President. (In fact I had called him Mr. Ford once, and Mr. President twice.)

The North Carolina press, at least, had a more humorous view. A cartoon showed smiling subcommittee members gratuitously patting and praising the president, while a phantom enforcer covered my mouth to shut me up. The drawing so captured my own sentiments about the subcommittee response that I contacted the artist, Larry Barton, who sent me the original.

But how would my constituents respond? That weekend I came back to New York, as I usually did, and took a few moments to go into Doubleday's bookstore on Fifth Avenue. All of a sudden people walked up to me, grabbed my hand, in a few cases hugged me, and thanked me for asking the questions. My trepidation eased: my asking tough questions of President Ford would not cost me my seat in Congress.

In another way, though, my optimism about Congress had been shattered. Yes, Congress could do what was right — but only some of the time. Could it be counted on only when the country was in a crisis? I kept agonizing over the hearing. Later, in watching the botched Iran-Contra hearings and the Clarence Thomas confirmation hearings, I recognized how much people wanted to feel that matters were fully aired and that the representatives and senators conducting the hearings were not purposefully avoiding tough issues, even if answers were not forthcoming.

Of course, Ford himself paid a price. He lost his bid for reelection. But I've never had a good explanation for why the subcommittee (and Congress) abdicated its duty to find the answers about the pardon.

I still turn the question around from time to time. Perhaps, I've thought, the leaders of Congress were involved in the deal over the pardon. That doesn't seem such outlandish speculation. Key Republicans had an interest in Nixon's leaving office quickly to keep him from dragging the whole party down. November elections were just around the corner. Democrats and Republicans may have felt Nixon couldn't really lead the country anymore, and with the cold war still on, a full-time president was needed. Some worried about Nixon's mental health — at one point, a rumor spread that Nixon was going to call out the army to occupy Washington.

On the twentieth anniversary of the pardon, I went back and reviewed the record. Facts had emerged that suggested very clearly that if a real investigation had taken place, much more would have been found. The record showed that Ford had not told the whole truth at the hearing.

Had Ford made a deal to pardon President Nixon? Prior to Nixon's resignation, then–vice president Ford had conversations with Alexander Haig, Nixon's chief of staff. What did they say in those meetings? The meetings took place at Haig's request shortly after the "smoking gun" tape became public. Ford's top aide, Robert Hartmann, insisted on being present when Haig first met with Ford. In a perfunctory conversation, they discussed little of substance. Then Haig called and asked for a private meeting, and Ford agreed. Ford acknowledged some, but not all, of the conversations with Haig. In at least one conversation Haig reviewed the options under consideration by Nixon. Many options included a pardon: Nixon would pardon others and himself and then resign; Nixon would resign and be pardoned by Ford. At no time did Ford *reject* the idea of a pardon. More private telephone conversations occurred the same or the next day between Ford and Haig. At the time of the House hearing, we didn't know about all of those conversations.

Why was a deal likely? Ford, a loyal Republican, followed orders. Leading the impeachment drive against Justice Douglas was an example. Ford also demonstrated his readiness to assist the party during the first flaps about Watergate by cutting short the efforts of the House Banking Committee, which wanted to trace the money passed to Watergate burglars by subpoenaing officials of the Committee to Re-elect the President (CREEP), including Maurice Stans and John Mitchell. Virtually all of the potential witnesses on the list were later convicted of crimes in connection with Watergate. If any of them had told the truth, the election of Richard Nixon could have been in real jeopardy. To put off the House Banking Committee, John Dean, the White House counsel, asked Ford, then the minority leader, to make sure no subpoenas were issued; and they never were. Stopping those hearings dead in their tracks was a key element of the Watergate cover-up — and even though I don't believe that Ford knowingly obstructed justice, that was the effect of his actions. Gerald Ford could be counted on to do what he was told.

In the end the pardon, and what I believe was a deal to grant it, hurt America. The pardon had a corrosive effect on the public's belief in a single system of justice and equality under the law. Watergate was a high-water mark for American political justice; the pardon defined its low point.

The Ford pardon had long-lasting ramifications, paving the way for President George Bush to pardon the officials who violated the law in the Iran-Contra scandal. The message of the unpardonable pardon is that when the executive branch wrongfully fails to follow the law, and when Congress doesn't right the wrong, the public is left with a taste of ashes.

# 4

## Individual Action:
## Opposing the Vietnam War

*W*ATERGATE AND THE FORD PARDON DEMONSTRATED HOW WELL —
and how badly — the system of checks and balances could work in
the face of serious presidential abuses. The Vietnam War measured
us similarly. The war ran like a fault line through our country. It
ripped apart our society, pitting doves and hawks against each
other. National guardsmen gunned down students at Kent State;
police beat protesters at the Chicago Democratic Convention and at
demonstrations elsewhere. Antiwar activists burned draft cards
and the flag; war resisters fled to Canada. And the war tore apart
our institutions of government, as well.

The effort to win the war in Vietnam also entailed far-ranging
abuses of power, among the most serious in our nation's history
and involving every branch of government, including the judiciary.
The war deeply corrupted our institutions of government and cor-
roded our nation's policies for decades to follow.

The rule of law is not self-enforcing, and the system of checks
and balances doesn't step into action automatically. Just as a car requires a driver who knows how to handle the vehicle, read the
highway signs, avoid obstacles, and obey the laws, institutions require individuals willing to sit in the driver's seat.

In three situations related to the Vietnam War, I saw that individual action within the system made a difference in how institutions behaved. I witnessed, in one case, two great liberals — Justice Thurgood Marshall and Justice William O. Douglas — issuing opposite and contrary judicial decisions. One shrank from using his power to prevent war abuses; the other did not.

When I arrived in Congress in 1973, public hostility to the war was intense. I campaigned against the war. Horrific numbers of Americans and Southeast Asians had been killed. Waging the war in Vietnam had produced major and well-documented abuses of presidential powers. Lyndon Johnson had lied about what occurred at the Gulf of Tonkin, claiming that the North Vietnamese had twice torpedoed an American destroyer. This distortion of the truth enabled Johnson to seek and win a resolution from Congress for support of "all necessary measures" to repel armed attacks, which he used to justify major escalations of the war.

Congress was a handmaiden to the presidential abuse of power. Only two senators opposed the Gulf of Tonkin resolution. In the House not one of the 435 members spoke out against the resolution, and it was placed on a calendar reserved for noncontroversial bills. Although Congress finally voted to end the war during my first term, the postwar stress on our internal government systems continued for many years. The United States didn't even establish a liaison office in Vietnam until two decades later, well after every other nation had done so.

The bombing of Cambodia brought about some of the most insidious abuses. The bombing, still going on when I first entered Congress in 1973, had begun secretly and illegally as early as 1969, without the consent or knowledge of Congress. The president was deceiving the public in colossal ways.

Within a month or so of taking my congressional seat, I was sitting in my office in Washington when a call came from Burt Neuborne, a law professor who worked with the New York Civil Liberties Union. I knew the organization because the Law Students Civil Rights Research Council (LSCRRC) had an office right next door when I helped run its summer program of sending law students south. Both organizations had rented inexpensive space in the then-untrendy area of lower Fifth Avenue. On the phone, Burt exchanged a few pleasantries and then got right to the point. Would I, he asked, join in a lawsuit against the secretary of defense to stop the bombing of Cambodia?

Article 1, Section 8 of the Constitution is straightforward. It gives the power to declare war to Congress. The framers of the Constitution had been through wars under the British king, and they wanted to place a check on war's human destruction and financial cost. The chief executive, the framers believed, had a natural tendency to want to make war. Some brakes were needed on war-making power to force those in the government to think through the consequences of putting such a heavy burden on the people. The system the framers designed makes the president commander in chief but gives Congress alone the right to declare war and provide funding for it. No unilateral war making by the president was to be allowed, excepting the emergency need to repel imminent danger to the nation.

Congress had made no declaration of war against Cambodia, nor had Congress consented in any way to bombing Cambodia. The bombing was a unilateral action decided by the president.

Burt Neuborne's proposal of using the legal system to challenge the illegal war activity appealed to me. At that time I had a bit more trust than I did later in the willingness of the legal system to rectify injustice. Working on civil rights cases in the South and with the NAACP Legal Defense and Education Fund, Inc., I was optimistic that the courts could be a tool for justice.

Burt explained to me that four U.S. Air Force pilots stationed in Guam wanted to bring the suit. The pilots were flying B-52 bombing missions over Cambodia, risking their lives with every mission. Yet they believed that their orders to bomb were unlawful and unconstitutional. Burt and another lawyer, Leon Friedman, planned to sue. But they thought it might be helpful to have a member of Congress as part of the suit, which was why they were calling me. If I joined, the lawsuit would argue that my constitutional right as a congresswoman to participate in the decision about making war against Cambodia had been usurped by unilateral presidential action.

At first I was flattered to be selected as a possible plaintiff. But I quickly realized the lawyers' only reason for calling me had to do with a quirk of geography — I lived in Brooklyn, where they wanted to file the lawsuit. Burt explained that a prior lawsuit had been brought against the Vietnam War in Brooklyn, asking that it be declared illegal because Congress had not declared war. The federal judge in that case, Judge Orrin G. Judd, ruled against the plaintiffs, saying that even though Congress had not declared war, it had approved the war by voting monies to fight it. It seemed clear from the judge's opinon that if Congress hadn't approved expenditures for the war, it would be unconstitutional for the president to wage that war.

This was exactly the situation with respect to Cambodia. Congress had never authorized any fighting in Cambodia or voted for any funds for fighting in Cambodia. In fact, Burt pointed out, in several laws Congress had explicitly prohibited any war-making activities in Cambodia. If the same judge heard the case, his own reasoning would require him to declare the war unconstitutional.

I had lots of questions. For example, how could we be sure our case would be assigned to that judge? Burt had an answer for all the questions. Under the Brooklyn federal court rules, he said that our case would be assigned to Judd because he had handled the Vietnam suit with similar issues.

We hung up. I was curious to know more. Did a member of Congress have a right to sue? Would my residency in Brooklyn be a sufficient basis for bringing the case there even though the pilots lived elsewhere and the defendants, including the secretary of defense, were located in Washington? I pulled out volumes of the U.S. law code that each member of Congress was given and did a little research myself. Burt was right that a member of Congress could be part of the lawsuit and that the suit could be filed in Brooklyn.

I was excited. I had come to Congress to end the war, and now I might actually get the chance to help do that. The tactics were unique, but I believed that you needed to exercise all the legitimate power you had to get the result you wanted. I joined the lawsuit.

The papers were filed in Brooklyn. The government tried to dismiss the case, but the NYCLU papers were extremely persuasive. They explained that a war couldn't be waged on presidential say-so alone.

Burt was right about the judge, too. Judge Judd was assigned the case and heard court arguments on June 6, 1973. And although he was a Republican, appointed by Richard Nixon, when he released his ruling on July 25, 1973, it was in our favor. He had the conscience and character to be the first judge in the history of the United States to issue an injunction against any presidential war making. It was a landmark decision, and it was right. He ordered the government to stop bombing Cambodia.

Of course, the government appealed immediately — within two days — to the U.S. Court of Appeals for the Second Circuit. The government demanded that Judge Judd's order be thrown out or put on hold through a stay. On July 28, 1973, the court of appeals issued a stay, preventing Judge Judd's order from taking effect. Until the court of appeals held a full hearing two weeks later, the bombing could continue.

So the illegal killings in Cambodia would go on — or would they?

We were not prepared to give up. The only court that could overrule the court of appeals was the U.S. Supreme Court. The lawyers decided that the first priority would be to try to get the Supreme Court to reinstate Judge Judd's decision banning any further bombing. The legal procedure involved asking a Supreme Court justice to issue a stay of the ruling of the court of appeals. This request would be presented to Justice Thurgood Marshall, who was the Supreme Court justice assigned to hear stay applications from New York courts.

This sounded like an excellent plan. Justice Marshall was a hero to me — a man who had been unafraid to take on the structure of segregation in America. As a lawyer, he had been the brains behind some of the most significant antisegregation lawsuits. After working one summer at the NAACP Legal Defense and Education Fund, Inc., which had been Marshall's home as a lawyer for so many years, I felt almost a personal connection to him. I admired his determination to secure constitutional safeguards, and had no doubt that he would rule in our favor. I knew he would have the fearlessness to restore the check to the illegal war-making acts of the president.

Our petition was presented to Marshall on August 1, 1973. The lawyers called later in the day to say that Marshall had refused our request. I was dismayed. Why was this justice, deeply attuned to the needs of disempowered people, unwilling to take on the president?

Because of Justice Marshall's decision, the illegal bombing of small Cambodian villages could continue. But all was not lost. Under Supreme Court rules, if one justice rejected a stay, the lawyers were allowed to ask another justice. In fact, all nine justices could be asked. The lawyers decided to try Justice William O. Douglas next.

There was one problem. It was summertime. The justices were on vacation. Justice Douglas had left Washington, D.C., for his summer home in Goose Prairie, Washington. An avid outdoors enthusiast, he liked remote country living during his time off. He didn't even have a telephone there. The lawyers moved quickly. They flew out, and I next heard from them on the following day when they called from the other coast of America. They were physically stationed outside Justice Douglas's cabin at 6:00 A.M. "He's home," one lawyer reported to me. "The front door opened, and a hand reached out to bring in the newspaper."

The lawyers decided to wait until a more reasonable time of day before disturbing him. They finally knocked on his door a few hours later. Justice Douglas, dressed in blue jeans and boots, came onto his steps, and they presented him with the papers.

Douglas immediately scheduled a hearing for the next day, August 3, in the courthouse in Yakima, Washington, about fifty miles south of Goose Prairie. The Justice Department sent the U.S. attorney from Spokane. On the same day Justice Douglas rendered his decision. He ruled in our favor, granting a stay against the Second Circuit Court of Appeals and allowing Judge Judd's ruling to stand. Now the bombing would have to stop, and the lawyers made plans to serve the order on the president and the Defense Department.

Justice Douglas's decision was remarkable. Clarity ran through it. It showed courage and prescience. He wrote that this resembled a death penalty case: people's lives were at stake. At that time the rules in death penalty cases held that the authorities had to delay execution until the court could review the merits of the case to see if it had been decided correctly. Of course there had to be, on the surface, a plausible argument. But it would be preposterous to refuse to delay the execution and find that the case had merit after the petitioner was dead.

For Douglas, the issue was clear. He said that if the bombing continued, lives — Cambodian or American — would be lost. The "stark realities" of the case, he said, involved "grim consequences." He agreed that the bombing was unconstitutional. Except in an emergency, to protect American lives, the president does not have unilateral powers to make war, the justice noted, and there was no emergency about the Cambodian bombing. Nor was there any indication that Congress had approved, authorized, or even acquiesced in the bombing. To the contrary, Congress had voted by majority to deny the president money for any continuation of the bombing.

When Douglas issued his decision, we were overjoyed. Finally, at the highest levels of our government, someone was willing to rein in the president's abuse of war-making powers. Michael Greenberger, one of my staff members, jumped into his Dodge Dart and drove to the Pentagon, with the goal of serving the order on the Defense Department. Our celebratory mood was, it turned out, premature.

Within a matter of hours, the Justice Department and the Defense Department ran back to Justice Marshall. We hadn't foreseen this. Under Supreme Court rules, when a single justice granted a stay order, as Douglas had done, it could be overturned by a majority ruling of the other justices. For this to happen, however, all of the justices had to meet together. A quorum was needed, and a majority vote; a single justice could not overrule another justice.

The Pentagon, the president, and the rest of the war makers panicked. The idea that four pilots, a congresswoman, and a Supreme Court justice could stop the bombing of Cambodia sent them into a tailspin, and they were alarmed at the possibility that the courts could curb their war-making powers. At their insistence, Justice Marshall issued a new ruling. In a pretense of following the court's rules, Marshall polled the rest of the justices by telephone. Saying that seven agreed, he put a hold on Judge Judd's order, thereby allowing the bombing to continue. There was no quorum present in Washington, as the laws governing the Supreme Court required, since most of the justices were away on vacation.

Justice Douglas expressed his fury, charging in strong language that the court itself had failed to follow the law. A telephone poll was not the same as the whole court voting in conference, where the justices could exchange opinions and debate, said Justice Douglas; Justice Marshall had completely contradicted the very rules by which the Supreme Court operates. "The Court . . . is as much bound by the law of the land as is he who lives in the ghetto or in the big white house on the hill. With all respect, I think the Court has slighted that law." Marshall's decision, Douglas said, was not lawful.

Nevertheless, Marshall's decision allowed the bombing to continue.

Why had the Supreme Court acted this way? I understood that it was difficult for at least some of the members of the court to interfere with ongoing military activities. From the refusal to interfere with Lincoln's suspension of habeas corpus during the Civil War to the refusal to interfere with Roosevelt's internment of Japanese Americans during World War II, the Supreme Court has taken a hands-off position on challenges to war powers. The court's action here fit into that shameful pattern. Had the members of the court followed their own rules, and had Douglas's decision taken effect, it would have marked the first time in history that the court interceded to block a president's abuse of war-making powers. The court was too timid, too frightened of its own power.

I was saddened, especially about Justice Marshall. The same Justice Marshall who could be sympathetic to the lives of U.S. prisoners on death row and people whose right to vote had been denied could not hear the cries of the victims of illegal bombing. And at stake were not only the victims of the illegal wars in Vietnam and Cambodia, including American soldiers, but those of future wars.

My sorrow deepened just a few days later. The grim consequences that Justice Douglas foresaw did in fact occur. The United States mistakenly bombed a friendly Cambodian village. "Civilians Bombed by Error, U.S. Raid Hits Friendly Town in Cambodia," headlined the *Washington Post*. Hundreds of Cambodian civilians allied with the United States died. "All day long, the wounded have been coming into the capital by air and by river," wrote the foreign correspondent. "At the hospital, a trail of blood led up the steps . . . others held their battered and bandaged children in their arms." Did the lost lives weigh heavily on the conscience of Justice Marshall? Or on other members of the court?

Later in August a panel of three judges from the court of appeals considered the issues in the case. I went to the oral argument. One of the judges, Judge William Timbers, a rather elderly man, couldn't sit still. I had never seen anything like it. He would repeatedly come into the courtroom, sit down in his chair, immediately leap up, and leave the room. He heard virtually nothing of the argument. That didn't stop him from joining with Judge William Hughes Mulligan — both judges were Nixon appointees — in ruling against us on every possible ground. They completely ignored Judge Judd's thoughtful analysis. They said a member of Congress had no right to sue the government; the pilots had no standing to sue the government; and Congress couldn't interfere with presidential war making. The third judge, Judge James L. Oakes, disagreed. After the ruling by the court of appeals, the Supreme Court refused to consider the case any further because the bombing of Cambodia had ended. The presidential usurpation of authority had been completely sidestepped by the court.

Justice Marshall's decision had a long-term consequence, as well. Presidents thereafter knew that the courts would not challenge them on war making. If judges had gone through such contortions to allow the Cambodian bombing to continue, when would they ever say no?

Congress ultimately stopped the bombing, but only because of a weakened President Nixon. Congress had a majority of votes to stop the bombing and voted to do it. Nixon maintained that he would veto any such legislation, an act that would turn the Constitution on its head. The override of a veto would take a two-thirds vote of the Congress. The president was in effect asserting that he could start and continue a war with a vote of simply one-third plus one of the Congress. As long as he could prevent an override of a veto of an antiwar measure, he could continue a war. The constitutional framers never understood Congress's role to be limited in such a fashion — if the United States went to war, there had to be a partnership between the majority of the Congress and the president. Under his theory, though, Nixon probably could have kept the bombing of Cambodia going in perpetuity. By the time Congress actually passed legislation to stop the bombing, Nixon gave in and signed the bill, agreeing to stop the bombing. The majority in Congress, and among the people, finally prevailed.

For me, the episode with Justice Marshall lingered. I found it deeply disillusioning. Having been trained at law school to revere the Supreme Court, I saw it flouting its own rules. This incident showed that the system of separation of powers wasn't fail-safe after all. And sometimes even heroes have feet of clay.

There was, of course, a flip side. Burt Neuborne and his associates had pressed their points with legal precision and persistence. We were going to stop a war; we almost succeeded. Douglas and Judd had shown that people of deep conscience could act decisively against massive governmental abuse. And their rulings provided a ray of hope that in some future case a judge would use the power of the Constitution to stop the overstepping of war-making power by a president.

Interestingly, the Pentagon never stopped bombing Cambodia even for a few hours, despite the injunction of a federal court judge and the ruling of a Supreme Court justice. I thought we should try to bring a contempt action against the Pentagon to show the public how the U.S. government itself disobeyed the law. The lawyers never moved forward on that.

The most upsetting coda of all, perhaps, was the fate of the four air force pilots who had come forward. Three were removed from their duties, and at least one faced a court-martial. Like so many who take a stand against institutional abuse, the pilots suffered personal retaliation. I felt chagrined at that. At one point I called the ACLU lawyers and asked if they could do anything to help the pilots. The lawyers said they would look into it, but I wasn't really sure that they planned to do anything. Abandoning the fliers to the punishment of the armed forces seemed terribly wrong. It felt as if we had taken advantage of them to try to stop the bombing and cast them aside when they no longer suited our needs. I blamed myself for not following up.

*     *     *

My concerns about Cambodia spurred me to take action again in 1979 when I saw on the television news starving Cambodian children in refugee camps. The children were bone-skinny, with gaunt arms and legs and sad, sad eyes. These images were of refugee camps across the border from Cambodia in Thailand but reflected a large crisis of starvation in Cambodia. The stories were appalling, particularly since the trouble stemmed in part from the refusal of the new government in Cambodia, now under Vietnamese rule, to allow food to reach the people in the country. I wanted to do something to alleviate the suffering.

The starvation and refugee problem of Cambodia followed a complicated series of political shifts. Cambodia's U.S.-supported leader, Lon Nol, had ascended in 1970, overthrowing Prince Sihanouk, who the United States thought was too supportive of Vietnam. Lon Nol was ejected in 1975 by the Chinese-backed Khmer Rouge, bestial rulers of Cambodia with a vicious leader, Pol Pot. The Khmer Rouge instituted a reign of terror, the period of the "killing fields," murdering an estimated one million people. A Vietnamese invasion in January 1979 ousted Pol Pot, pushing the Khmer Rouge to the Thai border. The Vietnamese victors installed their own ruler, a former Khmer Rouge commander who had defected to the other side. These turbulent years had forced many Cambodians to flee, but there was nowhere for people to go, and they ended up in massive refugee camps along the border.

Because the United States had suffered a military loss in the Vietnam War, it seemed unable to develop a sensible and rational foreign policy for the region. The war had corrupted our ability to judge the situation clearly, and it seemed that the United States was not willing to come to the aid of the people starving in Cambodia. In fact, I believed that our government had a special responsibility toward them. Humanitarian assistance by the United States and the rest of the world was urgently needed. None was forthcoming. I began seeking a way to circumvent government inaction.

What if an international effort of women parliamentarians made a direct appeal to the Cambodian government to allow food in to feed hungry children? Could not the most peaceful of means —

persuasion and an international show of concern — bring help to those in desperate condition? I discussed the idea of having a congresswomen's mission make a direct, in-person appeal, and my colleagues responded with real enthusiasm. Others agreed to go, including Pat Schroeder, Olympia Snowe, Barbara Mikulski, Millicent Fenwick, Peggy Heckler, and Lindy Boggs, all highly respected congresswomen.

I sent cables to elected women in various countries. This was not so easily accomplished. Merely putting together a list of elected women around the world was a major project in itself. The State Department had no such list. I suggested that it was time to make one, and with some grousing, the department did. We contacted every woman parliamentarian the State Department could locate. Eventually two women from Australia agreed to join us.

Speaker Tip O'Neill arranged for us to use an air force plane. We planned to fly first to Bangkok in Thailand, after a stopover in Alaska. We were to visit some of the refugee camps on the border between Thailand and Cambodia and meet up with the women from Australia. We would then head over to Cambodia and undertake our actual negotiating efforts to get food to the country.

We went straight to Bangkok in Thailand, where embassy officials met and briefed us. The next day we flew in two military helicopters to the refugee camps on the Thai border. When we landed, we witnessed in person what the television cameras had only begun to capture. The situation was far worse than we expected. There were children by the hundreds, wasted away beyond belief, and elderly people as fragile as rice paper. Concerned physicians, mostly from the French group Médecins sans Frontières, tended to people. When we spoke with the doctors, they dealt another blow. Most of the starving children had already died, they told us. And of those alive, many children were completely alone, without parents or relatives.

We walked through the camp, talking to as many children as we could. One older boy described seeing his parents killed in front of him. Another child was completely demented, jabbering nonsensically. We were told that this child too had witnessed his parents' murder, and it had driven him mad.

Another little boy, sitting in front of his tent, about twelve years old, captured my eye. He was a charming, smiling boy. He pointed inside his tent. There dozens of sheets of white typewriter paper were pinned to the walls, each sheet covered with bright colored paintings. He didn't know where his parents were, the boy told us calmly. Only the extraordinary art inside his tent revealed the depths of his despair. Intense emotion boiled over into each stroke.

I studied his paintings. Is this what art was about? I asked myself. Unstoppable, explosive emotions? Was the agony that made some people go mad the same as what was erupting in his paintings? What kind of extraordinary qualities of spirit made this little boy capable of translating suffering into beauty? The blinding sunlight shone through the white canvas of his tent, creating an eerie surrealism.

Standing on the dusty ground, peering into his tent, I knew I was in the presence of a remarkable young boy. I fantasized for a moment about rescuing him from the misery of his situation, of taking him home to America with me. A desire to do something rushed over me. But what of his parents? I wondered. Suppose his family could still be found, how could I take him away from the possibility of reunification? I stepped away, repressing my feelings. Later I was sorry that I didn't at least take his name, keep up with him. I often wonder what became of him. One day I will perhaps learn about some great Cambodian painter, and it will be he.

We soon encountered our own disasters. Millicent's pacemaker went out temporarily, and Lindy became ill. Since camp conditions were not conducive to the finest of health care, we decided that both should fly back to Bangkok at once, where they could have access to our medical people or at least rest in their hotel rooms. This plan worked out, and they later recovered.

After Millicent's and Lindy's departure, we were able to go inside the camps in Cambodia, just across the border. Instead of organized camps, they were more like big fields crammed with people. The remaining congresswomen wanted to go over, and the embassy officials agreed to drive us to the border in their jeeps, although they would not cross because the United States didn't recognize the Vietnamese-run Cambodia at the time. With only a couple of staff people, we walked into a sea of people, probably a quarter of a million. Men, women, and children pressed photos of missing relatives up to us.

Back across the border on the Thai side, we were led to yet another portion of the refugee camp. Here we saw no elderly, no children, as we had in the other tents. What we did see were men and women, eighteen to twenty-two years old, very fit, and obviously well fed. They were clearly the soldiers of the Khmer Rouge. As they retreated from Cambodia, the soldiers had rounded up the elderly and children as servants but kept all the food for themselves, leaving the others to starve. I recoiled at this display of inhuman selfishness.

When we met the military head of this Khmer Rouge contingent, I remember he pointed to a wristwatch he was wearing. Turning to me he said proudly, "The Americans gave me this watch." I was shaken to realize that American officials were helping the leader of the military contingent responsible for the cold-blooded murder of thousands of innocent people.

The irony was inescapable. While we, members of the U.S. Congress, had come to save the lives of a diminished and starved remnant of Cambodian children and elderly refugees, American officials were working at totally opposite purposes by supporting the leader responsible for the terrible physical condition of these refugees and the deaths of thousands like them. Something was dreadfully wrong with U.S. policy.

This experience brought the tragedy of Cambodia during the Vietnam War era into focus for me. As William Shawcross noted in his book *Sideshow*, the central event was Vietnam, and Cambodia had no importance unless it advanced our purposes there. But Cambodia was a sideshow for other nations with an interest in Vietnam — for the Chinese and for the Russians.

In the region, no country wanted to act against the Khmer Rouge. China controlled Pol Pot and was happy to see the Khmer Rouge countering Vietnam on its western borders, bleeding it. Thailand wanted to placate China so that China would limit its support for a Communist insurgency inside Thailand. The United

States also wanted to appease China as part of its anti-Russian policy. As a result, the U.S. supported seating the Pol Pot regime in the United Nations.

Even when Vietnam invaded and removed the Khmer Rouge from power, the cries of protest from many nations displayed deep callousness toward the people of Cambodia. The well-being of the Cambodian people was not the concern; the paramount interest was in "strategic global interests" — that is, how countries believed the change in power in Cambodia would affect the balance in the cold war. From conversations with dozens of refugees, I learned that, while the Cambodians did not like the Vietnamese occupiers, they welcomed the overthrow of the genocidal Khmer Rouge.

The United States led a worldwide protest when the Vietnamese invaded and booted out Pol Pot. Nations couldn't have cared less about the good of the Cambodian people. And many nations continued their support of the hateful Pol Pot forces after they were ousted from power in Cambodia. The Khmer Rouge continued to fight from protected enclaves along the Thai border and in the Cardamom mountains. I suspected that the United States covertly supported Pol Pot, as the man with the watch demonstrated. The Khmer Rouge could never have survived without the aid of Thailand. The United States had close ties to the Thai military but apparently never pressured them sufficiently to sever connections with Pol Pot. Perhaps someday the whole story of the United States' role in the survival of the Pol Pot regime will be told.

By the time the rest of us left the refugee camps and returned to Bangkok, the two women parliamentarians from Australia had arrived. One was a liberal, the other a conservative. They knew no one else on the trip, and I admired their spunk in coming.

The next day we started out early for Phnom Penh, the capital of Cambodia. Millicent's pacemaker was no longer on the fritz, but she wisely decided to forego the rigors of the trip. The flight itself was an escapade, since no American plane had landed in Phnom Penh since the end of the Vietnam War. And because we couldn't fly over Vietnam, we had to navigate a circuitous route. When we arrived, the pilots made one sortie over the airfield and then decided to land. It was a little tricky since there were bomb craters all around. The pilots, all military men, took out their weapons when we landed. They told us they would not leave the plane, and warned us to get back before nightfall. The radar at the airport had been bombed out, and it would be impossible to take off after sunset.

All of us were intensely curious about what we would find. The road to the city didn't quite prepare us for the city itself, which was still largely abandoned. There were no shops, just doorless spaces inside buildings. The streets were virtually deserted, although a few people here and there cooked food on small braziers on the sidewalk. Brahman cattle grazed in the grassy street dividers.

Although we were on a mission to alleviate hunger, for some reason our hosts decided that our visit to the city should begin with a banquet. The banquet probably signified the importance of the visit to the Cambodians. All of us were seated at a long, narrow table. Servants brought in the food; immediately a thick crust of black flies swarmed over it. None of us had ever seen that before. Food was put on our plates repeatedly, but I suspect not one of us ate a mouthful. How to be polite in view of all those flies was probably the biggest hurdle we had to overcome. We did learn one interesting thing during the lunch: there was an ample supply of Coca Cola. Pol Pot, despite his detestation of things Western, had a soft spot for Coke, so apparently, even though nearly all of Phnom Penh's inhabitants had been driven out, vats full of Coke syrup remained in the city.

After our welcoming banquet we were taken to see the foreign minister. Hun Sen was twenty-seven years old, although a long, scarred face made him look years older. A Khmer Rouge defector, he was now one of the most powerful figures in Cambodia and would ultimately become prime minister. Hun Sen received us politely. We had divided each segment of our presentation among ourselves. We explained why we believed he should allow more food to enter Cambodia. We wanted desperately to succeed. He listened courteously. When we were done, he just said, "Okay, whatever you want."

We were elated that our objectives seemed so easy to accomplish, although we would have to wait and see if he kept his word. We thanked him and left, making one more stop before we returned to the airport. Our hosts wanted us to see an orphanage so that we could understand the devastation wrought by the Khmer Rouge, who had left so many children without parents. The experience was overpowering. The children were between the ages of three and six. When we walked in, the children literally leaped on us. They grabbed at our arms, legs, and necks and hugged and hugged and hugged, voracious in their desire for simple affection and human contact. A little girl threw herself to my chest and just held on and laughed. Holding her made me long for children of my own. Again I wanted to ask about adoption, but soon we were back in our entourage.

When we returned safely to Thailand, we agreed to announce our results at a press conference the next day. But there was one hitch. Congresswoman Millicent Fenwick had heard stories from the embassy about the so-called yellow rain, which some claimed was a poisonous gas, being used by the Vietnamese against the mountainous Hmong people in Laos. Millicent wanted to use the press conference to attack the Vietnamese on the subject of yellow rain. I was very opposed to this. The yellow rain issue was not related to our mission of alleviating the terrible problems of hunger in Cambodia. And the Vietnamese controlled the Cambodian government, which had just agreed to our plan to allow more food to come in. Attacking the Vietnamese at this juncture might cause the Cambodian government to renege on its promise to us. No one had really identified yellow rain, much less determined if the Vietnamese were involved. (As it turned out, the yellow rain was later recognized as a natural phenomenon and not a form of biological warfare.)

The challenge was how to persuade Millicent to save her yellow rain attacks for another day. Since she was not a woman to be easily silenced, we decided that the only person with sufficient credibility to have an impact on her was the American ambassador to Thailand, Morton Abramowitz, a very savvy and experienced diplomat. Somehow we succeeded in prevailing on him, and he succeeded in prevailing upon Millicent. She said nothing about the yellow rain until we returned to the United States.

The trip paid off. Through a complicated series of arrangements, an air bridge and a land bridge for supplies were opened, better trucking improved the distribution system, and more food finally got to the Cambodians.

The failure to respond more effectively to the famine in Cambodia was only one example of our government's inability to deal with the aftermath of the Vietnam War. One of the war's tragic consequences was the massive exodus of boat people. When North Vietnam consolidated its power over the entire country of Vietnam, hundreds of thousands of Vietnamese fled. Most left by sea, often in small boats that could barely make the voyage to nearby shores — Malaysia, Indonesia, China, Thailand. The refugees' plight gathered sympathy around the world.

I needed to grasp firsthand the political and human dimensions of the problem. I chaired the immigration subcommittee in 1979, and any special admittance of refugees by the U.S. government had to be approved by Congress, which would rely on my subcommittee. Wanting to be fully informed, I went to Southeast Asia and visited refugee camps of Vietnamese boat people.

The refugees broke down into two groups. One group included those who had worked for the U.S.-backed South Vietnamese government. The other group consisted of Vietnamese people of Chinese origin who were being pushed out by Vietnam. I soon learned that the Chinese, who had settled in Southeast Asian countries a hundred years earlier, had become a despised target like the Jews in Europe before World War II.

People in the refugee camps had enough food to eat, and makeshift bamboo huts provided adequate shelter. But the stories I heard of their sea escapes hit me in shock waves. In the stories of escaping refugees were the echoes of my mother's family's flight from Russia. The perils for the Vietnamese were worse than I had imagined. Many boats had capsized. Those that made the journey had been preyed upon by Thai pirates, who stole everything. Women described being raped by the marauders; men and women saw family members killed. Something had to be done — not just to place refugees in new homelands, but to stop people from facing such fearful journeys in the first place.

The priority was on finding new homes for the boat people. Many nations agreed to accept boat people, and this great humanitarian rescue was quite a success. Still, reducing the danger of their escape from Vietnam gnawed at me. How could we get Vietnam to permit its people to leave without having to escape in rickety, dangerous boats? Even if we couldn't stop the Vietnamese from expelling their Chinese citizens, maybe we could persuade them to allow refugees to leave in an orderly way so they wouldn't have to risk their lives on the open seas. The U.S. government refused to make such a request. No one would talk to Vietnam. In that case, I thought, the immigration subcommittee should do it.

Several of us decided to raise the matter directly with the Vietnamese and planned a trip to Hanoi. Committee member Billy Lee Evans of Georgia, Jim Cline, the Judiciary Committee's staff director, and I decided to go.

We encountered our first serious obstacle before we even got to Vietnam. We landed in Bangkok on the way and ran into the rancor of the U.S. government, which tried to stop us from going to Hanoi. Aside from its normal anti-Vietnam stance, the U.S. government did not want our presence to suggest any support for Vietnam at that time because China had just invaded Vietnam. The United States supported China. The embassy refused us access to a government plane to take us to Hanoi. Undeterred, I instructed our staff director to charter a private plane, but the only thing available was a World War II–vintage Flying Tiger. A scheduled flight on Air Laos sounded safer.

When we arrived at Hanoi, the signs of the Vietnam War were everywhere. We saw old bomb craters, mostly filled with water, surrounding the airport. The bridge into Hanoi, which had been repeatedly bombed, still was not fully repaired. There was only a narrow lane that the car barely negotiated, moving very slowly.

People wore the familiar bamboo hats and pajama-like pants, but the extent of the poverty surprised me. Most of the people walked barefoot. A barefoot people defeated the mighty U.S. armed forces, I kept thinking. There were few cars on the streets; the telephone system was almost nonexistent. The only way to reach the outside world was through a telex at one of the Western European embassies. What, I asked my colleagues, had we gotten ourselves into?

We were probably the first American congresspeople to visit

Vietnam since the war. But our hosts never mentioned the Vietnam War. They received us very cordially and put us up in the official guest house. Although these were first-class accommodations for Vietnam, they were very simple. Plumbing was primitive. But the food, served in austere surroundings, was delicious.

We promptly set about our business and arrived for our meeting at a stately old building erected by the French. Phan Hien, the vice foreign minister of Vietnam, received us graciously, accompanied by a single aide. The room was starkly furnished with an old wooden table. We sat down, facing each other.

Luckily, Phan Hien spoke English well. After the introductions and pleasantries, I began to talk. The stakes were very high. Could I win him over? I began by mentioning my visits to the refugee camps, my conversations with the survivors of the pirates and leaky boats. I tried to depict the plight of the boat people clearly and simply. Then I asked whether Vietnam would agree to institute a legal departure program as a humanitarian gesture, to spare as many people as possible the trials of escape on the open seas.

The minister listened politely and even seemed concerned. Yes, he said, we will agree to do this. This was splendid news. We didn't know if the American government would take up the commitment, as well. But at least we had a beginning.

Billy Lee and I also raised the issue of the American soldiers missing in action and a man named Garwood who, some suggested, had been kept against his will in Vietnam. The foreign minister said that Vietnam would be willing to work with the Americans to locate the MIAs. He said that the Red Cross could talk to Garwood. Garwood, as it happened, left Vietnam not long after our meeting.

Now that we had completed our mission there, the Vietnamese made an unusual offer. Would we like to see the war with the Chinese? If so, they would be happy to make arrangements. Billy Lee and Jim quickly accepted. I demurred, thinking I would return to Bangkok. Given the complications in air travel, getting out of Hanoi proved not so easy, so I ultimately decided to go see the war, too.

My hosts — three government officials and a driver —

arranged to take me to the war in a small car. On a hot, clear day, I wedged myself into a space in the backseat. Our destination was the city of Lamson. The city, my hosts explained, was the largest city near the Chinese border, sitting directly on the major north-south route to China. I didn't feel apprehensive about going, believing my hosts wouldn't want harm to come to an American guest — particularly an American congresswoman — nor to themselves.

We were soon driving through the countryside, passing by rice paddies with women working in bamboo hats and loose black clothing. After a few hours, my hosts stopped at a picturesque hillside and took out a picnic lunch. The French influence was unmistakable — the highlight of the meal was a beautiful roast chicken. Sitting on the grass with a view of blue mountains in the distance, I enjoyed the silence and splendor of our surroundings. The idea of a war was remote, almost inconceivable.

We pushed off, continuing on our way. We stopped in front of a very high hill. Near the base, a hospital had been dug into the earth during the Vietnam War, making it virtually impregnable to bombing. Inside were persons wounded from the recent Chinese invasion. As we traveled further, I observed a curious sight. We had seen virtually no traffic on the road for most of our journey. All of a sudden I saw people coming toward us, utilizing every mode of transportation, including water buffalo. People were lugging wagons full of household items. What started as a trickle became a flood. I finally asked my companions what this meant. They shrugged and seemed as puzzled as I.

We arrived at the city of Lamson. All the doors and windows of the houses were shuttered up, the city abandoned. I thought to ask what to do next, but before I could, my escorts announced that we would go to the Communist party headquarters and find out what was going on. There, people were loading up a truck — their last truck. "We're evacuating the city," they said. My hosts, however, were determined to follow through on their instructions to show me the war, so we headed to the military garrison in town. The commander came rushing out. His gestures were emphatic. We were in artillery range. It was clear what he wanted us to do. He ordered us to get out of town. We climbed into the car and sped

back to Hanoi. Before we left the post, I picked up a piece of shrap-
nel. It reminded me of what I should have known to begin with —
the dangers of war left no room to watch safely.

When we got back to the United States from our trip, our government accepted the plan for refugees to leave Vietnam in an orderly departure program without having to flee in boats. As a
result, 50,000 people were allowed to leave Vietnam every year by
plane, each spared the life-threatening escape by sea. After a while
the Vietnamese stopped expelling people, and most of those willing to leave at any cost had left. If our government had acted more
responsibly from the outset, if it had not been so blinded by its hostility to Vietnam, perhaps the boat people phenomenon could have
been avoided altogether. For example, the U.S. might have persuaded Vietnam to end its brutal expulsion policies by proposing
to lift the American trade embargo, something Vietnam desperately wanted. Despite the State Department's inaction, private initiatives by even a handful of members of Congress had succeeded
in saving thousands of lives. I had learned one simple tenet: there is
rarely justification for saying nothing can be done.

# 5

## Fighting Nazis

*I*N 1973, AFTER I HAD BEEN A MEMBER OF CONGRESS for less than a year, a mid-level official with the Immigration and Naturalization Service made a confidential appointment to see me. I served as a member of the immigration subcommittee, but I had no idea why this man wanted to meet. Tony Freedman, head of my Brooklyn office, happened to be in Washington, and I invited him to sit in.

"There is a matter that is troubling me greatly," the man said to us. His voice tightened. "The Immigration Service has a list of Nazi war criminals living in America, and it is doing nothing about them."

Tony and I exchanged puzzled looks. Nazi war criminals in the United States? This seemed impossible. America fought Hitler in World War II; hundreds of thousands of Americans had died in the struggle. It made no sense for our government to allow Nazi war criminals to live here. If the man was right, the information was explosive.

My mind raced through stories of the Nazis and the Holocaust. When I was a child, my mother had told my brother and me about a deep ravine called Babi Yar, located not far from the place where her family had lived in Russia. My mother described how during World War II the Nazis had rounded up more than 100,000 Jews, marched them to Babi Yar, and shot them to death. (In 1976, on a congressional trip to Russia, I went to Babi Yar. I felt the ground swell under me; it seemed as though I were rocking on an ocean of bodies.) My mother had also told us about Josef Mengele, the Angel of Death, who stood at the entrance to Auschwitz deciding who would be sent to the gas chambers and who would be spared. Mengele, she told us, had undertaken sadistic medical experiments on twins, and my twin and I could not help but identify with the plight of those children. From these stories and those of the pogroms my family lived through, I knew the precariousness of Jewish survival.

Some Nazi war criminals had, of course, stood trial for their crimes. Adolf Eichmann, who had been captured in Argentina, had been tried in Israel for war crimes at the same time that I was in law school. I followed accounts of the case. Hannah Arendt's description of Eichmann's ordinariness, despite his responsibility for implementing Hitler's "final solution" of executing millions of Jews, made a distinct impression on me. She portrayed Eichmann as a faithful follower of orders, a good bureaucrat, anyone's next-door neighbor. But I had not considered that Nazi criminals could become "good neighbors" to unsuspecting Americans, too.

Before the man from the INS left, he explained that he was not Jewish but of Armenian descent. He felt deeply ashamed of the American government for harboring Nazi murderers. He thought that perhaps I could do something about it.

I thanked the man for the information. Afterward Tony and I shared our reactions. The man seemed straightforward. But if his charges were true, why hadn't any others done anything about them? Many powerful Jews had served in Congress in the thirty years since World War II, including Senator Jacob Javits from New York and my predecessor, Emanuel Celler. We didn't know what to make of the man's charges.

Several months later, the immigration commissioner came before our subcommittee as part of a relatively routine hearing. I realized that here was an opportunity to ask about the INS official's allegations. The man's claims had reverberated when I read a newspaper article about Valerian Trifa, a bishop in the Romanian Orthodox church living in Michigan. The article described Trifa as a leader of the Romanian fascist student group, and stated that he had once instigated a pogrom against Jews in Bucharest. The immigration commissioner could set the record straight, I thought.

"Does the Immigration and Naturalization Service have a list of alleged Nazi war criminals living in the United States?" I asked.

The commissioner, a former marine colonel, answered crisply, without hesitation. "Yes," he said.

I had not expected that. Trying to suppress my surprise, I continued. "How many names are on the list?"

"Fifty-three," he said.

I knew right then that I had to get as much information as possible. "What is the Immigration Service doing about the fifty-three alleged Nazi war criminals on the list?"

The commissioner perhaps recognized he had begun something he didn't want to finish. He switched to jargon, throwing an impenetrable blanket of words over the hearing room. Rather than engage in a fruitless duel, I asked if I could see the files themselves. I didn't really know if I had the authority to make this request, but no member of the subcommittee objected, and the commissioner agreed to let me do so.

These files were located in Manhattan. I went to look at them the next weekend when I traveled home. I sat down at a metal table with a stack of folders that someone had neatly prepared for me. Each folder bore the name of an alleged Nazi war criminal. I opened the first file. It contained information from several sources, each claiming that the person had been a Nazi police officer in Latvia and had killed many Jews. The Immigration Service, in response, merely visited the man and inquired about his health. No effort had been made to determine the truth of the allegations or to request documents from the Berlin Document Center, the major repository of information about Nazi war criminals, or from the Soviet Union, which controlled the Baltic countries at the time.

The second file contained similar allegations and similar absurd responses. So did the rest of the stack of files. Even though the charges involved mass murder, the Immigration Service had not seriously investigated any of the cases. No one had bothered to determine if the allegations were true or to take steps to deport the criminals, as would happen if an immigrant had been suspected of even a single murder. Instead, it seemed as if the U.S. government quietly and deliberately gave sanctuary to these killers.

For the United States to give Nazi war criminals refuge showed contempt for Jews, for basic human rights, for democracy, for the sacrifice made by hundreds of thousands of Americans who fought the Nazis. Seeing the abuses of Watergate and now this, I longed for affirmation of decency in our government. It certainly wasn't here.

Public interest in the Holocaust was not widespread at the time. The Simon Weisenthal Center didn't exist. Survivor groups had little political involvement, although the Jewish war veterans sometimes spoke out. And obviously the U.S. government made almost no effort to take action against the Nazis.

As I pushed away the stack of files, I felt nauseous. Hadn't atrocities of the Holocaust occurred because so many people stood by idly and did nothing? Would I be like them?

I promised myself to bring Nazis hiding in America to justice, and with that I launched on a path that took me through years and years of involvement in fighting Nazis — getting this information out to the public for the first time; pushing the bureaucracy to take action; passing new legislation making Nazis deportable; setting up a Nazi-hunting unit. Over the years I undertook investigative forays into the covert world of Nazi collaborators, secret government documents, and foreign countries ranging from Germany and Israel to the Soviet Union and Paraguay. I met extraordinary people. Simon Weisenthal loomed as a hero to me, keeping up the search for Nazis almost single-handedly when few seemed to care. I got to know the Klarsfelds of Paris — Serge was a child survivor of Auschwitz, and Beatte was a non-Jew born in Germany. In uncovering Klaus Barbie's whereabouts, they forced the French to confront the Vichy government's collaboration with the Holocaust. In America Rabbi Silton was tenacious in keeping up efforts against the Nazis here. And the heads of the Nazi-hunting units — Martin Mendelsohn, Alan Ryan, Neil Sher, and Eli Rosenbaum — each tried in a decent and honorable way to write the last chapter on World War II.

Ultimately, information developed showing that as many as 10,000 Nazi war criminals lived in the United States, including the interior minister of the Nazi puppet regime in Croatia who had issued the orders that sent Jews to death camps; a key administrator of the Nordhausen slave labor camp; concentration camp guards from Auschwitz, Treblinka, and virtually every camp in Europe; vicious local police officers who had killed Jews. How they came to be in the United States was a mystery to unravel. In some instances, I learned, the CIA and its functionaries were secretly involved.

Karl Linnas was only one of many Nazi war criminals living in the United States; I became quite familiar with his case. In Congress, I worked for years to get the government to hunt down and deport Nazis living in the United States, insisting that a special anti-Nazi unit be created. The Immigration Service didn't have the people or expertise to handle these extremely complex cases. Proof might be in other countries or in documents written in foreign languages. Historians, translators, investigators, and lawyers were required.

In 1979, after I became chair of the immigration subcommittee, I finally succeeded in forcing the government to create an effective Nazi-fighting unit. The Office of Special Investigations (OSI), placed in the Criminal Division of the Justice Department, could, at last, do its work properly. In the following years it won worldwide acclaim. Hundreds of investigations were conducted, and a hundred Nazi war criminals were expelled from the United States.

I had also won passage of legislation, with the aid of Senator Ted Kennedy, to close a gap in immigration laws that had allowed some Nazis to enter the country after 1953. The new law, which was called the Holtzman amendment, meant that anyone who had committed Nazi war crimes could be deported, regardless of the year of entry. Evidence was amassed to expel dozens of Nazi war criminals, including Bishop Trifa, the Croatian minister, and the Nordhausen camp administrator.

Still, the Linnas case showed how strange Nazi expulsion cases could be and how far the U.S. government would go to protect Nazis. Linnas had been an administrator of a concentration camp in Estonia. He had been tried in absentia in the Soviet Union and sentenced to death. Our Nazi-hunting unit found Linnas in the United States and brought a deportation case against him. The U.S. courts upheld the charge and found that Linnas personally shot

Jews to death. They removed his citizenship and ordered him deported. Linnas was slated to be sent to the Soviet Union. But
Ronald Reagan took office as president, and behind the scenes the
Justice Department began to stage a different scenario to sneak Linnas out of the country to a safe haven.

No one knew about the secret plan of the Justice Department
on Passover in 1987. I was district attorney of Brooklyn at the time
and had taken the day off to observe Passover. But having forgot-
ten some documents, I decided to stop by the office early in the
morning. As I was collecting the papers, the phone rang. When I
answered, Neil Sher, head of the Nazi-hunting unit, blurted out,
"The Justice Department is planning to send Linnas to Panama today. They've worked out an arrangement for the Panamanian government to take him." Clearly, the Justice Department had planned
this for Passover, knowing that the offices of most Jewish organizations would be closed for the holiday.

I strongly opposed sending Linnas to Panama. Panama would
never prosecute Linnas for his crimes; instead he would live his life
out peacefully, resting on a beach under palm trees. Why was our
government helping him escape punishment? He had to account
for the murders he had committed. What to do at this late date?
And on Passover?

A top aide of mine, Ed O'Malley, was in the office and understood my sense of urgency. Ed should call the Panamanian ambassador, we decided, and ask for an immediate meeting. He would
say that Jewish groups were incensed that Panama would accept
Linnas. Of course, the Jewish groups consisted of only one person,
me. I needed some allies. I decided to try Menachem Rosensaft, a
brilliant lawyer who headed an organization of children of Holocaust survivors. Luckily, Menachem was in his office and agreed to
help.

Ed, Menachem, Eli, and I worked out a plan. Menachem called
the press and told them that Panama was going to give Linnas
sanctuary and that Jewish groups would be furious. Ed called the
Panamanian embassy in Washington, expressing indignation and
asking for a meeting. Menachem followed up with another call to
the Panamanian embassy. The strategy worked. With Ed, Menachem, Eli, and the press calling, the Panamanians believed that

the whole Jewish community had mobilized. The Panamanian ambassador in Washington agreed to a meeting at three o'clock that
afternoon. Menachem, Ed, and I caught the one o'clock shuttle. By
the time we landed in Washington, the embassy had released an
announcement: Panama had reversed its decision and denied Linnas refuge. Our hasty plan had succeeded, and Linnas was soon
deported. The Soviets jailed him in Estonia at once; he died of a
heart attack before the proceedings against him were completed.

Through the years, I and others kept asking, How did these Nazis
get to the United States? And why did the U.S. government allow
them to stay? I believed that the U.S. government's failure to act on
Nazi cases could not be attributed to mere benign neglect. I saw a
direct link to the U.S. government's cold war policy. Nazis were
anti-Communists, and despite the depravity of their acts, the
United States willingly used them in its war against the Soviets and
the "Communist menace."

The policy rested on the premise that when it came to fighting
communism, the ends justified the means. The use of Nazi war
criminals against the Russians marked the beginning of a policy
that persisted throughout the cold war. The U.S. support of anti-
Communist dictators across the globe was another, later manifesta-
tion of this ideology. Expressions of that mindset cropped up
particularly during the Iran-Contra scandal, where laws were
flouted and crimes committed by the executive branch to fight the
leftists in Nicaragua. The use of Nazi war criminals, as it turned
out, was a secret policy, hidden from the Congress and the American people. It was, therefore, deeply antidemocratic.

The General Accounting Office (GAO) had tried to investigate
how the Nazi war criminals got into America. Its efforts to see the
actual files in the Central Intelligence Agency or the Federal Bureau
of Investigation were blocked. Nonetheless, the GAO ascertained
that U.S. government agencies had brought some Nazi war criminals into America, and in some cases had actually lied to other
agencies — and possibly President Truman — to get them here.
The GAO found that U.S. government agencies, including the FBI
and State Department, employed some Nazi war criminals here.

The U.S. government employed Nazis abroad as well. Klaus Barbie, for example, an SS officer and a major Nazi war criminal known as the Butcher of Lyons, worked for the U.S. Army's counterintelligence corps in France. Another similar case involved a Belgian SS officer. There must have been dozens, possibly hundreds, of such cases.

Even as late as 1980 the government, including the CIA, was still working to protect Nazi war criminals. Congress had carved out a special immigration provision for the CIA, allowing it to bring 100 persons every year into our country without regard to the immigration laws. Nazi war criminals were among them.

Despite the fact that fifty years have elapsed since the end of World War II, the whole history of U.S. involvement with Nazi war criminals remains to be revealed. I called for the creation of a commission to investigate the facts. Why should the evidence — which in some instances involves the commission of crimes by American government officials — be kept secret from the American people?

Our government was working hand-in-hand with mass murderers, both here and abroad. The government brought them to our shores, protected them while here, and concealed its policy. From a whistle-blower inside the INS I learned the sad and ugly truth — that the government cannot be trusted to do the moral thing. People must be continually willing to question government policy and change it.

Fighting Nazi war criminals brought me face to face with evil and indifference to evil, sometimes frightening in their scope. But I also encountered goodness. On one occasion in the 1980s, a group of Hungarian Jews arranged for me to meet and honor a Hungarian man who had saved their lives. He was a poor farmer who had hidden more than twenty people from the Nazis in his farmhouse.

When the man arrived, he scarcely looked like a hero. Short, with a grizzled beard, he wore a brown suit that was much too big for him and in which he seemed extremely uncomfortable. His hands were rough and worn with labor, but he tenderly held a tiny Bible in them.

The man spoke no English, and others had to translate. I expressed admiration for his bravery and thanked him for saving so many lives. He replied simply, "I did what God told me to do." He gave a clear message: no one could be thanked for doing his or her moral duty.

Meeting this man reminded me of what I had learned from the civil rights movement. His courage came from an unshakable moral conviction, a refusal to conform to bigotry or hatred. Bravery, I saw, had many faces, and this Hungarian farmer's was one.

# 6

## Making Government Work

$P$EOPLE'S CYNICISM ABOUT GOVERNMENT THESE DAYS is a predictable result of the incessant attacks by conservatives, ranging from Ronald Reagan to Newt Gingrich. This corrosive raillery is furthered by a scandalmongering conservative press that fails to tell the positive news about what government can do. Government programs seem wasteful, bloated, unsuccessful, unnecessary, bureaucratic. Many elected officials, even those unleashing their barrages on government programs, take no steps to make the programs efficient and well managed. Such efforts are tedious and unglamorous. Why bother? What practical or political benefits accrue from doing so?

I went into office with an interest in reforming government. My sentiments, I soon learned, were not necessarily shared by my colleagues.

Even under difficult circumstances, I found that positive reforms could be made in many programs, with one exception. Nothing could be budged in the colossal preserve of the military, as if the military's right to spend were surrounded with a hypercharged electric fence that, demonically, could expand at will but did not contract.

When the Vietnam War ended, many of us looked forward to the "peace dividend." At last the money poured into war making could be spent on important domestic needs — schools, affordable housing, better social services. I wanted a program of conversion to help war industries switch to useful nonmilitary production.

The peace dividend never came. No matter who occupied the White House, no matter how swollen the defense budget, spending on the military never declined. America's defense establishment used two tactics to keep stoking the Pentagon's budget: the cold war and jobs.

Even after America stopped fighting in Vietnam, the cold war was blowing hot. The United States had overwhelming military strength — huge armies stationed in Western Europe, more than 10,000 nuclear warheads. Whatever we had, the government always seemed to need more.

Our government portrayed Russia as a mighty behemoth, which was true from a strictly military point of view. But the Soviet Union was a second-rate economic power. I first observed this when I accompanied my mother on a research trip to Russia in 1959. Again in 1976 I traveled to Russia, this time with a congressional delegation. The standard of living did not match that in any Western European country. Weaker economic capabilities affected Russia's military power, but this point was never discussed in U.S. military analyses. To question either the military budget or the Soviet Union's strength opened anyone in Congress to refrains of being "soft on the Soviet Union" or even "soft on communism," stifling most opposition.

The Pentagon enhanced its budget monopolization with the code word "jobs" and a mastery of congressional politics. Military facilities were located in as many congressional districts as possible, so that the economies of these districts became intertwined closely with the military budget. A bigger budget meant more contracts for military suppliers.

On every item, such as the B-1 bomber or the MX missile, military suppliers and contractors, labor unions, and local elected officials would get into the act and pressure the representative or senator for passage. Newspapers usually served as boosters for the local economy, too, since their survival depended on it.

This weaving of local economies and the military came back to haunt both the public and the Pentagon. Decisions about weapons depended on political clout (how many congressional districts would benefit, and how important the members were). The real considerations — merit of the product or need for the item — lost out. Even today, Congress is voting for military systems that the Pentagon doesn't want and can't use.

I was troubled by the constantly escalating military budgets, and representing an urban district, I knew how much the money was needed to fight real problems of poverty, crime, and transportation. I hoped to change our priorities. I had an opening to do so when Congress created the first budget committees in 1975.

The House Budget Committee was set up in response to Watergate. After President Nixon abused his authority by impounding money, Congress wanted to establish a counterweight to executive budgetary actions. I argued that a woman should be on the new committee. The leadership agreed, and named me as the woman.

Now on the inside track, I had to conquer the strange vocabulary of budgets and master concepts about econometric models used in economic forecasting. Having had some economics in college helped, although I found out that economists do about as well — or badly — at predicting the future as anyone else. (In fact, when the committee allowed us to hire professional staff, Butler Derrick of South Carolina and I joked about bringing a crystal-ball reader from Times Square to Washington.)

Committee discussions seemed surreal. We dealt primarily in billions. How should we split hundreds of billions among various categories — defense, environment, education, housing, transportation? Whatever had been spent in the previous year marked our starting point, and the question became how much more we should allocate to the category this year. We never knew exactly how the money would be spent on any specific program.

At that time I was serving on the board of overseers of Harvard University, not exactly an impoverished institution. Budgetary oversight at Harvard dealt with details, ways of squeezing out more revenues or containing expenses. Why shouldn't the taxpayer's dollars be handled with the same care? On the Budget Committee we acted largely as allocators — how to split up the pie of government money.

I could see clearly that the bigger the slice of the pie that we gave to the Pentagon, the smaller the slices would be for everything else. The Budget Committee showed me in black and white how budgets are tradeoffs. Increasing the Pentagon's slice continued year after year, even though the amounts seemed unnecessary. How much overkill did we need?

Then too, there was the waste, which was gargantuan. Stories emerged later about the military's purchases of $500 toilet seats and $1,000 automatic coffeemakers. But when looking at the spreadsheets, I saw that the waste went much deeper. Mismanagement was enormous. Three separate services built their own planes, radios, and other equipment. Although competitive bidding could lower prices, the Pentagon elbowed it aside.

Much of the equipment was totally unnecessary. In that category was the huge and growing stockpile of nuclear weapons, which included the MX missile. Another absurd idea involved putting missiles on trains and laying thousands of miles of track, so the missiles couldn't be targeted by the Russians. To my delight, newspaper humorist Art Buchwald mused that we'd save billions by putting the missiles on Amtrak and sending the Russians the schedule.

Much of the waste lay in cost overruns. Secretary of Defense James Schlesinger once told the House Budget Committee that our military budget needed to be increased because the Russian budget had been increased. This was standard fare. I asked him whether the Russian increases were due to cost overruns or were going to improve the quality of their weapons. How did we know the Russians weren't wasting their increases — and how did we know that the U.S. military wouldn't waste its increases? He didn't answer.

Several billions were spent on a massive — and preposterous — program named "C-cubed" or "c3." Its objective was to create a plan to save the president and top leadership in the event of nuclear attack on the capital. The mission proved truly tough: only eight minutes would pass from the time a Russian submarine launched a missile to the time it landed in downtown Washington. In that time the top echelon of the U.S. government had to make its getaway. Initially, the plan was to have a helicopter at the White

House whisk the government leaders to Andrews Air Force Base in Maryland. From there the leaders would get into larger planes.

But reality injected certain complications. First, how would the military get the nation's leaders to sprint at top speed to the helicopters? Tip O'Neill, the Speaker of the House, was third in line for the presidency. Tip was a hefty guy, and he didn't run a three- or even a four-minute mile. Others, including the president, weren't that speedy either. This problem was never solved.

And assuming everyone got into the planes that took off from Andrews, how could anyone know who among the leaders survived? Who then could give orders, and how would anyone know whom to obey? What would happen if the lowest cabinet member was the only one to survive — who would pay attention to orders from the secretary of education? This aspect grew tricky because no one knew what communications systems would outlast a nuclear blast over Washington and elsewhere in the United States.

The final problem (P-cubed) had to do with how long the planes could stay aloft and where they would land. This problem wasn't solved either. For this, though, the government spent the fortune of Ross Perot, cubed.

When President Jimmy Carter was elected over Gerald Ford in 1976, I saw a tiny window of hope. As a member of Congress I was invited to the presidential inauguration — my first. Carter took his oath of office in cold and biting weather, and most of my energy was spent trying to stop shivering while he delivered his address. I began to pay close attention when Carter made an earnest call for the abolition of nuclear weapons. Finally, after Nixon and Ford, there was someone in office with whom I shared at least some basic values.

Despite President Carter's pledge, he produced the biggest buildup of nuclear weapons in years. Instead of being cut, the defense budget rose again. And Carter added a bizarre new nuclear weapon: the neutron bomb. The genius of this bomb lay in its ability to annihilate people but leave buildings, factories, and other structures intact.

A defense bill vote was scheduled on the House floor, and the neutron bomb issue was going to come up. Wanting to know more about it, I asked for a classified briefing from the Pentagon. A young officer came to my office with charts and diagrams. He briefly explained the weapon's capability, the number of people it would kill, and its ease in use. The bomb was supposed to be launched on the ground, not far from the target. What would happen to our troops, I asked, if they launched the bomb and then the wind shifted and blew the radiation back in their direction? It couldn't happen, the officer kept saying, but he couldn't explain why. Didn't this antiperson bomb potentially pose as much of a danger to our own troops as to the enemy?

When I got to the House floor, two young, respected liberals, one from Long Island and one from Michigan, were engaged in the debate. As I tuned in, I realized that the two were arguing *for* the bomb.

I felt very sad; I wondered why they took the military industry side. Even they had to show support for at least one of the newfangled weapons systems that the Pentagon wanted, I concluded.

Something needed to be done about stopping the bleeding of our domestic funds by the Pentagon. And I decided to try. I came up with the idea of a transfer amendment: Congress could take money out of the military budget category and add it to various domestic needs.

While I knew I would lose, I nonetheless thought that starting the discussion was important. The amendment was modest in the amounts it dealt with, yet radical in its direction. Maybe support at the outset would be small. But as public understanding grew, we might prevail. That was how opinion had changed about the Vietnam War.

I didn't want to be laughed off the floor of the House. I had to be prepared to explain my proposed cuts in the military budget without being called irresponsible. I culled through the military budget carefully with the budget committee's defense expert. After this analysis, I proposed the transfer amendment, suggesting that a portion of the money allocated to the military be transferred to social programs. It lost.

Even though I never felt certain whether the voters in my district would understand my votes against military spending, I included them in my newsletter anyway. One day, a man came to visit me at one of my outreach programs in Brooklyn. He strongly disagreed with my position. Why, he asked, did I oppose the military budget? Was I a pacifist? I said no and explained my reasons. Although he wasn't sure that he agreed with me, at least he understood that I had a reasoned point of view.

There is no question that in other ways, my opposition to wasteful military spending hurt me politically. Once, during the Carter administration, an important liberal union leader was recruited to call me and get me to support the budget. I declined, explaining that it cut too many social programs and that voting against it was a matter of principle to me. The union leader scoffed, "Principle. Don't talk to me about principle."

When Ronald Reagan entered the presidency, he thought he was going to bankrupt the Russians by increasing our military spending and forcing them to increase theirs. Bankrupting the Russians worked. But our own deficit increased by three trillion dollars, making it impossible to fund improvements in life here at home.

Reagan, I believed, had more than bloating the military in mind. He and his budget director, David Stockman, who served in Congress with me, concocted a different plan. They were going to force Congress to undo the social programs of Franklin Delano Roosevelt and Lyndon Johnson. They would shift money in the budget pie to the military and at the same time lower taxes so that Congress would have to either cut social programs, as Reagan wanted them to, or amass a deficit, which he didn't think Congress would do. (Stockman once admitted this in a magazine article.) This was the transfer amendment turned on its head.

The Stockman scheme didn't work then; Congress didn't dismantle social programs. But the thrust of the scheme is working now, with the manical emphasis on a balanced budget. Everyone seems to support the concept, even though a zero deficit is unnecessary and an enforced zero deficit could be very harmful in difficult economic times. The cry to balance the budget after the Reagan deficit buildup is forcing major cutbacks in federal spending for social programs, unless the cuts are found elsewhere — in the military, for example. And the military is not being cut.

Even after the end of the cold war our nation can't kick its dependence on military spending. No new rationale has emerged. We are not going to be invaded by a foreign power in the foreseeable future. The nation's current military budget of $267 billion is more than the combined military budgets of every other nation in the world. This amount comprises 48 percent of the federal government's discretionary spending. Inertia keeps the system going, and the consequences for the rest of us are clear.

The irrational, inflexible support for military appropriations seemed to represent the worst of the Washington establishment, while in other ways, I was finding that a legislator could make a difference. At times I could fashion creative solutions to problems. I can't say that every effort worked, but there were many that did.

Orphan drugs were not something that I ever heard of before Sharon Dobkin called my Brooklyn district office. Sharon was not an orphan, and, as I came to learn, orphan drugs had nothing to do with parentless children. They were drugs that had been abandoned by pharmaceutical companies because the diseases they treated were rare and the companies determined that too few people would use the drugs.

Sharon actually called my district office about a clogged sewer. I didn't have any authority over the sewer system, which was strictly a local government affair. Nonetheless, a very enthusiastic volunteer by the name of Sydelle Berman took Sharon's call. In describing the sewer problem, Sharon eventually raised a second concern. She suffered from a rare neurological disease that had a degenerative effect on her nervous system, so much so that she was flat on her back and barely able to hold a pencil. One drug helped her. With it, she could function normally. But getting access to the drug was trying. Sharon's doctor had to make the medicine by hand, an extremely expensive process, and Medicaid refused to pay.

Sydelle persuaded Medicaid to pay for Sharon's treatments, but she was also an extremely persistent person and insisted that Sylvia Lerner, then the head of my Brooklyn office, raise the issue of the drug with me. I was mystified. Why would drug companies refuse to develop a drug? With Sharon's permission I met with her doctor, who worked at Mount Sinai Hospital in New York. No drug companies were motivated to manufacture the drug Sharon needed because there were too few people who had the same disease as Sharon. Unless 100,000 people suffered from a disease, a drug company found it didn't pay to develop the drug, and this left patients in the lurch. This was a problem that affected thousands of Americans with "rare" diseases, including Huntington's chorea, Tourette's syndrome, dwarfism, and other medical conditions, the doctor said.

This was truly a matter of life and death. Drug companies were pushing aside lifesaving treatments because the people affected by a disease did not hit some magical number. How could we get research completed on cures for these rare diseases? What kind of legislation could I introduce to change this situation? I got my staff together, and we brainstormed.

We came up with a couple of ideas to prompt drug companies to take on the research and manufacture of these rare drugs. Extending the patent life on the drugs would give the drug companies exclusive ownership for a longer time. Since they could recoup the costs, they would have an incentive to do the research and manufacture. And in addition, direct federal grants for research on rare diseases might spur companies to get started.

With these ideas drafted into an "orphan drug bill," I needed a strategy to get it passed. Since I wasn't on the subcommittee that had jurisdiction over the bill, I approached Congressman Henry Waxman, chair of the committee. Waxman supported the idea strongly and agreed to hold hearings promptly.

Next, we needed to build support for the orphan drug bill. John Jonas, a member of my Washington staff, took on the assignment. His first obstacle was the association of pharmaceutical companies. Amazingly, the association was suspicious of the legislation, even though the bill would have benefited its own members. The drugmakers weren't interested.

John turned his attention to patients, who welcomed the measure. They were willing to lobby not only Congress but the pharmaceutical association. Hearing of the legislation, people stepped forward to help. The widow of folksinger Woody Guthrie offered to testify. Guthrie had died of Huntington's chorea, one of the diseases that could be treated by an orphan drug. I was especially moved by his widow's interest. Woody Guthrie had lived for a while in Coney Island, near my high school. The way he had raised his voice for the poor and the needy had made him a particular hero of several high school classmates. Others offered to help. Jack Klugman, the actor on television's popular show *The Odd Couple*, also had a personal interest in an orphan drug and wanted to testify. *The Odd Couple* even ran a show that dealt with the orphan drug problem.

The hearings took place and were very touching. Ordinary people with rare diseases came to Washington to describe how a simple bill might change their lives. Their courage was extraordinary. Abby Meyers, the head of a Tourette's syndrome organization, spoke about the difficulties she faced as the mother of a child with Tourette's syndrome, the perplexing disease that makes people swear and sputter irrationally. And Sharon Dobkin, who had spoken up initially only because her sewer was backed up, came from New York to testify. The pharmaceutical companies began seeing the wisdom of the bill.

Unfortunately, after the hearings, time ran out in the legislative session to bring the bill to the floor, so the bill didn't pass the first year it was introduced. In 1980 I decided not to seek reelection for my House seat and to run for the Senate. I worried that without my presence the ball might be dropped. Fortunately, other legislators — Congressman Waxman and New York City's Ted Weiss — agreed to carry on.

Soon afterward the orphan drug bill passed. In the next twelve years, more than seventy new drugs were developed, giving life and hope to millions of Americans. One of the drugs developed under the orphan drug legislation was AZT, initially a key treatment for people with AIDS.

Throughout the years, I and members of my staff kept in touch with Sharon. She became a dear friend to the office. She got married, had children, and leads a normal life. The orphan drug act has helped thousands and thousands of others in similar ways.

Currently some issues have been raised about windfall profits by drug manufacturers, particularly related to a drug that prevents dwarfism in children. I still think that the value of encouraging the development of lifesaving drugs is worth it. Of course, legislation can always be fine-tuned. If price gouging truly is a problem, I would look for a slightly different formula to prevent excessive profits and still provide incentives for research and manufacture.

My most intense encounter with government waste came in the summer of 1976, with a federal program that should give ample warning to those conservatives who rave so effusively about privatization. Here was a stunning case study of how privatization can rip off taxpayers and fail completely to serve its purpose.

In this case the symptom was literally garbage. A call came into my district office in Brooklyn complaining about "federal garbage." The caller, Hazel Brooks from the Vandeveer Senior Citizen Center, told Sylvia Lerner on my staff that no one could walk in the neighborhood without stepping on trash — she mentioned bologna sandwiches — distributed by the federal government. Sylvia and I got into my car and drove to nearby Vandeveer Houses, a huge complex of high-rise brick apartment buildings covering at least one square city block.

We didn't need to be Sherlock Holmes and Watson. We followed a trail of food that included full milk containers, uneaten oranges, and untouched sandwiches. It led us to the porch of one of the apartment buildings. A man was handing out the food from cardboard cartons. We saw kids hanging around, eating while standing up or sitting on makeshift seats. There was no refrigerator and no tables or chairs for the kids to sit down and eat properly.

Something was terribly wrong. Why was so much uneaten food thrown away? Why was there no refrigerator to keep the food fresh on these hot summer days? Why was there no place for the kids to sit and eat?

When I got back to the office, I asked my staff to get whatever records they could. The program, we learned, was operated by the U.S. Department of Agriculture (USDA). The idea of the program was good: to provide nutritious meals to hungry children during the summer. An item on the application for the Vandeveer site caught my eye. A question asked for a description of recreational facilities near the site. The application said there was a tennis court across the street. As an avid, but not very good, tennis player, I knew all the tennis courts in the central part of Brooklyn. The nearest courts were at least a mile away. If someone lied about the tennis courts on the application, what else had been lied about?

We stepped up our inquiry, visiting other sites. The problems were the same or worse. One summer feeding program was located on a construction site: kids ate while sitting on concrete blocks, surrounded by debris. There was no refrigerator at any site. Ice cream melted immediately, so when kids got their lunches, they ate the ice cream right away, and threw away the other food.

At one summer feeding location in Crown Heights, the woman in charge told Sylvia that she had fifty children for lunch. But, Sylvia pointed out, 250 lunches were being delivered. The man who provided the lunches had told her that she had to take 250 or nothing at all, so she had to throw away the extra.

In some cases you couldn't blame the site operators for throwing away the food. Inside sandwiches we found green salami. And at other locations, we opened boxes of frozen knishes. The man who had delivered the knishes suggested thawing them in the sun. Since they looked a bit like frozen pops, my staff members jokingly dubbed them "knishicles."

When we scrutinized the program guidelines for the summer feeding program, we soon caught on to what was happening. Private companies bid to participate as vendors on the program. After the companies were selected for the summer feeding program, they were paid a fixed amount for each meal served — at the time, 80¾ cents per meal. The more meals served, the more reimbursement would come from the federal government. In order to collect as much as possible, the program sponsors doctored the numbers. They said they were feeding hundreds of kids, even if only ten or twenty showed up. No one ever came by to check, and the sponsors were confident that they could get away with this heist. The excess food was thrown on the streets or, in some cases, sold at big markups. In the most grotesque case, 16,000 sandwiches were dumped one night in a Brooklyn schoolyard. Poor kids were being used by greedy profiteers.

There was also another scam on the part of the private vendors. More money could be made if they reduced the quality of the food they served. They were paid the same amount, no matter what food they delivered. Using low-quality, second-grade food, they made profit margins zoom.

A monitoring agency — the State Education Department — was supposed to stop this kind of abuse, but it too was paid an administrative fee for each meal served. The supposed "watchdog" agency had no incentive to staunch the waste.

After we uncovered what was going on, I decided to make it public. Informing people about the scandal would, I hoped, bring corrective action. But even that, we learned, had its dangers. To provide firsthand proof, Sylvia Lerner drove out with a reporter and photographer from the *New York Post*. They turned onto a street strewn with food and parked in front of a house where they saw several boxes marked "USDA" stacked on the stoop. Sylvia and the reporter went inside and asked if they could get some food. A tall man handed them a case of milk, which the reporter carried back to the street. When the photographer jumped out of the car and began snapping pictures, the tall man ran out, cursing and shouting. Sylvia, the reporter, and the photographer all jumped into the car. "Sad to say," Sylvia wrote in a later report, "the car would not start, and a small crowd gathered around and began to shake it." They finally got the car going and escaped unharmed, and the photo appeared in the *Post*.

Once the news got out, my office was deluged with complaints from all parts of the city, well beyond my district. The problem, it turned out, was even bigger than we knew.

The groups that had received contracts under the summer feeding program immediately attacked me. One man called and screamed at the office staff, "Why is Holtzman the Great Liberal trying to close down a facility that feeds poor kids?" Those who were literally stealing from the mouths of kids were blaming me for calling attention to their boondoggles. My real goal — stopping abuse of the programs — was getting drowned.

Outside my district office, pickets arrived. They carried big signs that read, "Holtzman wants to starve poor children." I later learned that they had been sent as foils by the private vendors whose corruption I was exposing. Sylvia treated the picketers with extraordinary graciousness, offering them water, letting them use the office bathroom. All the while she gently explained that I was interested in seeing poor kids get good food — during the school year and the summer. The waste in the programs robbed poor kids of decent meals, and robbed taxpayers, as well, she would tell them. One of the lead picketers called us several weeks later to apologize. After that I took care to mention in all my public statements that of course I supported food for kids, but not the ripoffs.

More and more improprieties came to light. Who was behind this waste? Two excellent lawyers, Dan Feldman and Ibby Lang, switched from a food trail to a paper trail to find out about the operators of these programs. They discovered that one group of individuals had covertly created a number of companies to bid on the food sites. These companies gave the appearance of being different, even though they were all the same. The conspirators decided which company would provide the lowest bid at each site, subverting the very idea of competitive bidding.

All told, the crooks in the program were from every ethnic and religious group — Irish, Italians, Puerto Ricans, African-Americans, Hasidic Jews. They divided up the city in some way best known to them, and they got along well together, without any signs of ethnic friction. I felt slightly optimistic about this; if the crooks could organize a wholly integrated operation, why couldn't the rest of society?

I must admit, however, that the involvement of the Hasidic Jews created a special uneasiness for me. Especially when I discovered that the head of one of the most corrupt organizations was Leib Pinter, a rabbi. Rabbis, I had been taught, were spiritual people — holy in their ways. A rabbi had been a special mentor to my father as a young man. My father had met Rabbi Brown, an ardent art collector, while working on an extra night job at a newsstand near the rabbi's home. It was from him that my father developed a love for collecting original art that he had passed on to me. Nothing prepared me for the phenomenon of a crooked rabbi.

Rabbi Pinter's organization was one of those most extensively involved in fixing bids, not only in New York but in other states as well. As the summer wore on, we actually got calls from Florida, Los Angeles, and St. Louis asking about Pinter's multiple organizations. His outfits were among the most flagrant abusers: inflating the number of recipients, providing bad food, and colluding to destroy the bidding process.

Pinter understood the nature of politics well, handing out awards to various politicians with substantial monetary honoraria attached. He even gave Gerald Ford the Silver Mezzuzah Award and an honorarium.

In some cases others pretending to be "rabbis" defrauded people. I remember a woman who called our office to complain that she had ordered kosher food for the summer feeding program (even though the kids who were going to eat it were mostly nonkosher African-Americans). When bologna-and-cheese sandwiches arrived, she called the "rabbi" to complain, since under Jewish law, meat and milk products cannot be eaten together. The "rabbi" told her that kosher cheese and kosher salami made a kosher sandwich — by no means a strictly kosher statement. The swindle actually had no religious preference; another sponsor pretended to be a church in order to qualify.

The activities we were uncovering amounted to criminal behavior. We first turned over the information to the Brooklyn district attorney's office. It refused to do anything. I went to see the U.S. attorney for Brooklyn. He and his top aide met with me but were less than enthusiastic. I finally went across the river to the U.S. attorney for Manhattan, Robert Fiske, whom I had never met before. We had a simple, professional meeting at which I turned over the material that my staff and I had gathered. He agreed to investigate and did. Politics was not an issue with him, an attitude that I respected enormously.

The abuses, it turned out, extended beyond Brooklyn to programs in many states. Fiske's investigation led to a member of Congress, Daniel Flood of Pennsylvania. Flood cut an unusual figure: tall and rail-thin, he sported a meticulously waxed handlebar mustache. As head of an appropriations subcommittee, he was accused of accepting a bribe from one of the food vendors. Ultimately he resigned from office and pleaded guilty to conspiracy to accept bribes. Rabbi Pinter went to prison, although his time was reduced from fifteen years to two for testifying against Flood. In the end, Fiske — the epitome of an incorruptible and fair prosecutor —

convicted nineteen people of fraud against the federal government.

Aside from prosecuting the crooks, my concern was to make the program work properly. How could the food be refrigerated and handled and served in decent, clean surroundings with chairs and tables? The answer suddenly came to me: the public schools. It seemed so obvious. Schools served lunches and breakfasts during the school year. They had refrigerators, tables, experience, and practice. We reorganized the entire program, using the schools as the distribution program for summer meals.

By the next summer, schools were serving food. I toured several of them. It gave me great pleasure to see kids receiving healthful meals — no more green meat, no frozen knishes. And something refreshing and special happened — mothers accompanied their children. Thanks to the presence of larger numbers of adults, there was great decorum. On the practical and financial side, by deprivatizing the program and placing it under the aegis of the schools, the government was able to save $40 million a year.

Some people in the Hasidic community never forgave me for the criminal investigations and convictions. I paid a political price in the loss of support.

I have reflected often on the subject of the summer feeding program. Conservatives have become fond of attacking programs aimed at ameliorating the problems of poverty. "Look at the money spent on fighting poverty," they say, "but there is still poverty." Too often poverty programs have been so badly structured that they inevitably become riddled with corruption and disarray. When this happens, the people the programs are intended to help become victims, along with the taxpayers.

Poor management has often been the cause of faulty programs. Many poverty programs have also been treated as opportunities for political patronage, putting friends of politicians to work. The actual programmatic objective has been at best secondary. Reforms that affect who gets to give out the jobs inevitably meet extreme political resistance. If the country needs jobs programs — and we desperately do — we should call them by their real name and design them as jobs programs, instead of disguising them and distorting other programs to achieve the jobs objective.

When poverty programs fail, racism or a deep prejudice against poor people may be at work. Some think that as long as the programs are intended to serve "them," why bother to strive for the best? Social services are vital, and the emphasis in and out of government should be on finding methods to ensure they succeed.

# 7

## Justice and Its System

*I*N 1981 I HAD LUNCH with longtime Brooklyn district attorney
Eugene Gold. Gold was retiring, and I had been elected as his successor. I wanted to hear his advice in a face-to-face meeting. In the
middle of our pleasant small talk, he lowered his voice. As DA, he
whispered, do not go to just any judge in the courthouse to get a
wiretap order signed. You can trust only one or two judges, he said.
The top prosecutors in the office know their names.

I listened calmly, but Gold's comment startled me. From the
experience of twelve years as DA, Gold was telling me that the
majority of judges sitting on criminal cases in Brooklyn could not
be relied upon to keep a wiretap order confidential. Obviously,
wiretaps had to be secret — if the subjects of a wiretap knew their
phones were being tapped, they would never reveal what was
really happening. And you couldn't avoid going to judges about
wiretaps. The law required judges to approve wiretaps because
they were so invasive of privacy.

My spirits sank. How could I function amid such corruption?
Had I made the wrong decision, after all, in running for this
position?

I should not have been surprised. I knew that machine politicians wielded enormous influence on government in New York
City, including the criminal justice system. They controlled, for example, some of the people who were hired as prosecutors. I vowed

Bucuresti Romania March 25, 1921

Safe in Bucharest after a mass escape from the Soviet Union organized by Liz's grandfather (extreme left), Liz's great grandparents (to the right of her grandfather), mother (front row left, with black ribbon), and fifty-four others prepare to come to America in 1921. The father of Zev Yaroslavsky, a supervisor of Los Angeles County, is also in the group (front left, with girl in his lap).

Posing with twin brother Robert at the age of four.

Getting involved: in Georgia as a civil rights activist in the summer of 1963 with fellow law clerk Dennis Roberts and noted civil rights lawyer C. B. King.

1972 campaign flier for the primary race against Congressman Emanuel Celler. Celler, an incumbent of almost fifty years, compared the likelihood of Liz's winning to "a toothpick's chance of toppling the Washington Monument."
*(Photo © 1972 by Diana Mara Henry.)*

WE NEED LIZ HOLTZMAN IN CONGRESS

DEMOCRATIC PRIMARY
JUNE 20, 1972
POLLS OPEN 3-10 PM
LIZ HOLTZMAN FOR CONGRESS
1508 FLATBUSH AVENUE
ULster 9-8221

Discussing strategy during the race.
*(Photo by Judith S. Ames.)*

Storefront campaign headquarters
on Flatbush Avenue in Brooklyn.

Thanking voters at a
Brooklyn subway stop
after victory over Celler.
*(Photo © 1972 by
Diana Mara Henry.)*

Deliberating with the House Judiciary Committee during impeachment proceedings against President Richard Nixon. *(Photo courtesy of U.S. House of Representatives.)*

Conferring with Judiciary Chair Rep. Peter Rodino and Congressman John Conyers during the Nixon impeachment proceedings. *(Photo courtesy of U.S. House of Representatives.)*

With Barbara Jordan, the only other woman on the House Judiciary Committee. *(Photo courtesy of U.S. House of Representatives.)*

At the House Judiciary Committee's hearings on President Gerald Ford's pardon of Nixon in 1974. Liz was the only committee member to ask Ford if the pardon was part of a deal. *(UPI/Bettmann.)*

*The day of the hearing arrived. Most of the subcommittee members spent their five minutes congratulating the president....My turn came. I hesitated. I really didn't want the confrontation. I thought about the advice I had solicited, about the piles of letters that ordinary people had sent to me. I looked around and realized if I didn't ask the questions, no one would.*

*By then I had the questions virtually memorized. I said that the resolutions that prompted the hearing resulted from dark suspicions that had been created in the public's mind, brought about by the circumstances, the secrecy, and the implausible reasons given for the pardon, which caused people to question whether there was a deal.*

*The president sat silently until I said the word "deal."*

With Ford at the hearing. *(Photo courtesy of U.S. House of Representatives.)*

Cartoon satirizing
the hearing.
*(Larry E. Barton,
The Sentinel,
Winston-Salem,
N.C.)*

President Carter signs the resolution extending the deadline for ratifying the Equal Rights Amendment (ERA). Looking on are (right to left) Rosalynn Carter, Rep. Martha Griffiths, Liz, Eleanor Smeal, Sarah Weddington, Rep. Bella Abzug, Rep. Gladys Spellman, Senator Don Riegle. *(Photo courtesy of U.S. House of Representatives.)*

Washington march in support of the ERA. Liz, whose bill won more time for ratifying the amendment, joins with (right to left) Peggy Heckler, Barbara Mikulski, and Betty Friedan.

Congressional hearing on Liz's bill to encourage the development of drugs for rare diseases. Sharon Dobkin, a Brooklyn constituent whose illness prompted the bill, testifies along with Liz. *(Photo courtesy of U.S. House of Representatives.)*

As chair of House Immigration Subcommittee, meeting with orphaned children in the Thai refugee camps (1979). *(Photo courtesy of the Schlesinger Library, Radcliffe College.)*

Speaking on efforts to pursue Nazi war criminals in the U.S. with Simon Wiesenthal (left) and Martin Mendelsohn. *(Photo courtesy of the Schlesinger Library, Radcliffe College.)*

Meeting in Israel with former prime minister Golda Meier. *(Photo by Judith S. Ames.)*

Meeting with Israeli Prime Minister Menachem Begin and House Speaker Tip O'Neill.
*(Photo courtesy of U.S. House of Representatives.)*

In Egypt, Liz visits with
President Anwar el-
Sadat shortly after he
makes his historic first
visit to Jerusalem
*(Photo courtesy of the
Schlesinger Library,
Radcliffe College.)*

Winning the Democratic primary for U.S. Senate in 1980, with (right to left) father Sidney, David Dinkins, Gloria Steinem, brother Robert, Andrew Stein, sister-in-law Pamela. *(Photo © 1980 by Diana Mara Henry.)*

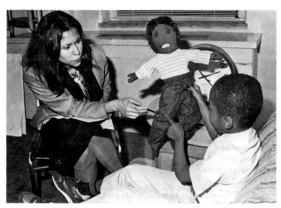

An assistant district attorney demonstrates how anatomically correct dolls and videotaping in comfortable surroundings can lessen the trauma for children of testifying in sex abuse cases. *(Photo by Matthew Barcia.)*

As Brooklyn District Attorney, Liz appears in court with Homicide Bureau Chief Dale Campbell (left) and Assistant District Attorney Bruce McIntyre to prosecute the racial murder of Yusef Hawkins in Bensonhurst.

Governor Mario Cuomo signs Liz's bill providing stronger protections for crime victims and witnesses.

Announcing prosecutions for major thefts from parking meters with Mayor Ed Koch, Kenneth Conboy, and Transportation Commissioner Ross Sandler.

A punishment to fit the crime: petty offenders are sentenced to scrub graffiti off subway cars. *(Photo by Deborah Gardner.)*

New York City Council members announce support for Liz's proposed bill to ensure access to abortion clinics (1993): Ronnie Eldridge, Charles Millard, Kathryn Freed, Stanley Michaels, and Ken Fisher are joined by Planned Parenthood's Alex Sanger and NARAL's Kelli Conlin. *(Photo by Lynda Downey.)*

With Brooklyn children who are protesting against the major expansion of a nearby garbage incinerator (1993). *(Photo by Lynda Downey.)*

# "FORGET ABOUT HER, SHE'S TOO HONEST!"

—What the mob said about D.A. Liz Holtzman on a phone call wiretapped by the FBI.

This tribute to Liz Holtzman's integrity comes as no surprise to New Yorkers. For nearly two decades, Liz Holtzman has provided honest, caring and better government. She has provided innovative and effective leadership as a member of the U.S. Congress and as Brooklyn District Attorney.

## HERE'S WHAT SHE'S DONE:

### ESTABLISHED TOUGH NEW MEASURES TO FIGHT DRUGS
- Established a special program to evict drug dealers from apartments and commercial locations.
- Created joint DA/police task forces that dismantled and prosecuted two killer drug gangs.
- Set up Major Narcotics Bureau to investigate and prosecute big-time drug sellers.
- Formed special crack unit to get tougher sentences in misdemeanor crack cases.
- Fought for new laws to toughen penalties for drug sales near schools and to stiffen fines on drug dealers to pay for drug treatment programs.

### DRAMATICALLY IMPROVED THE TREATMENT OF SEXUALLY ABUSED CHILDREN AND VICTIMS OF RAPE AND OTHER CRIMES
- Eased the trauma of sexually abused children by securing new laws enabling them to testify via videotape before the grand jury and via closed circuit television at trial.
- Led reform of state rape laws that demeaned women and hindered prosecution.
- Successfully fought for elimination of marital rape exemption.
- Created comprehensive in-house counseling unit for crime victims and their families.
- Got courts to order more than $1.5 million in restitution from defendants for crime victims.
- Gave victims a voice at sentencing through the use of victim impact statements.
- Initiated state's first court-ordered counseling program for incest victims, their families and offenders.
- Led successful fight for the nation's first statewide witness protection program.
- Urged city hospitals to develop procedures for recognizing and reporting elder abuse.

### FOUGHT RACISM AND BIGOTRY OF EVERY KIND
- Only prosecutor in the nation to urge the U.S. Supreme Court to end jury discrimination in criminal cases.
- Only local prosecutor in the U.S. to file a friend of the court brief in Webster urging the Supreme Court to uphold a woman's right to an abortion.
- Established bias unit to investigate crimes motivated by race, religion, ethnic origin, gender or sexual orientation.
- Created only bureau in New York to investigate allegations of misuse of force by law enforcement officials.
- Developed training program for prosecutors in handling cases involving anti-lesbian/gay violence.
- Helped draft and fought for proposed state legislation increasing penalties for bias-related crimes.
- First prosecutor to call for state task force to explore sex discrimination in judicial system.

### CREATED INNOVATIVE PROGRAMS
- More than 12,000 defendants were sentenced to clean subway cars, paint stations, repair park benches and do other community service work in a unique program for low level offenders who previously received little or no punishment for their crimes.
- Started pilot program that cut police arrest processing time in half by using two-way video technology.
- Led effort to urge New York State to develop computerized finger-print identification system.
- Created first Environmental Crimes/Worksite Safety unit in a local prosecutor's office; led efforts to strengthen criminal laws on infectious medical waste.

### HERE'S WHAT SHE'LL DO:
Liz Holtzman has a lifelong commitment to make government work for people. As comptroller, she'll be your watchdog at City Hall, making sure that taxpayers' money is being spent honestly and efficiently, and reaching the neediest, not the greediest. Her integrity and effectiveness – which have served Brooklyn so well – can now serve all New Yorkers.

## HOLTZMAN FOR COMPTROLLER
### New solutions for a new New York

Campaign ad for 1989 New York City Comptroller race. Liz becomes the first woman to win that post.

With parents after 1989 campaign victory. *(Photo by G. Paul Burnett/NYT Pictures.)*

Joining Mayor David Dinkins and others at a rally for health benefits for domestic partners. *(Photo by Lynda Downey.)*

With President Bill Clinton in New York (1995). *(Photo by Todd Maisel.)*

during my campaign to eliminate machine influence in the Brooklyn DA's office. Meade Esposito, Brooklyn's cocky boss, laughed. "I control only three positions", he said, "so what's the fuss all about?" I never determined whether there were three or more than three, but when I became DA, I took strong measures to weed out any machine-appointed prosecutors I could identify. One, I believed, headed a bureau that was privy to information about organized crime investigations.

The machine also controlled the selection of many judges. Although most judges were elected, the machine nonetheless dominated the process. In some cases, the machine even handpicked the judges' law secretaries.

The court system represented a rich lodestone of opportunity for the machine. For example, the justice system had hundreds of jobs that the machine could fill with loyal workers or their families. The district attorney's office alone had close to a thousand positions, many outside the civil service laws. These people were selected on the sole say-so of the district attorney.

Picking the judges and the prosecutors gave the machine the chance to influence the outcome of cases. That could be very useful to litigants and targets of a criminal investigation. In one case Meade Esposito personally asked a judge to postpone a court decision as a favor to him. The judge complied and later lied about his actions to the FBI; he was ultimately removed from the bench.

Not surprisingly, then, when I decided to run for district attorney in 1981, Meade Esposito and the entire Brooklyn machine put up a terrific fight. They sponsored an obscure prosecutor in the office to run against me and backed him vigorously and lavishly. One single campaign check to my opponent was for $50,000, an astonishing amount for a district attorney campaign. When the press asked about the contribution, my opponent shrugged and said the donor must have had a tremendous interest in criminal justice.

So did a couple of organized crime figures who were taped by the FBI discussing my campaign. "Holtzman elected as DA?" they worried. "That's bad news." Crooks understood a key precept — what was done with the job depended on its holder. Harvard Law School had never taught this. There we studied the law in its abstract embodiment. The curriculum didn't acknowledge the reality of boss-selected judges or patronage-filled prosecutor's jobs, much less the impact of corruption on the fair administration of the law. Being DA would teach me about a whole new world.

My decision in 1981 to enter this milieu began with a lunch with my former campaign manager and a *Village Voice* reporter. The year before, I had given up my seat in the House of Representatives to run for the U.S. Senate, losing by less than 1 percent of the votes. When the DA position came up, I was teaching at New York University in the law school and graduate school.

My lunch companions urged me to run for the office of DA. At first I thought they were kidding. At the time, I didn't hold prosecutors and police in particularly high regard. As a civil rights worker, I knew that they had acted as violent enforcers of segregation. I watched police beat demonstrators and prosecutors charge those engaged in peaceful protest with capital crimes. During the Vietnam War I watched again, indignant, as law enforcement attacked peace marchers to stifle protest. And in the Watergate era the abuses of Nixon's Justice Department had sickened me. The law could inflict harsh injustices and act viciously against those who opposed the status quo. Still, I promised to consider more closely the possibility of being DA.

As I thought about the job, the prospect of serving as DA started to intrigue me. Crime ravaged the lives of urban Americans. I remembered as a twelve-year-old going alone to Manhattan from Brooklyn by subway to take music lessons every Saturday morning. Twenty-eight years later, parents would not let children of that age travel alone.

Crime was no abstraction to me. My parents' home in Brooklyn had been burglarized several times. Once, when I was young, my father came home to find the house empty, except for a burglar. The thief held a gun to my father and forced him to lie on the floor while he filled up a bowling bag with our personal property. The police caught the man shortly afterward, walking in the neighborhood with the bowling bag. I remember that his last name was "Grace" and my brother and I made a joking song about the man's "fall from grace." My father was not amused.

I was reminded of his experience in 1995 when two young men robbed me at gunpoint — the gun had the longest barrel I have ever seen — at a midtown Manhattan bank ATM. The men asked for my ATM card, my PIN number, the cash in my wallet, my necklace. Although I succeeded in foiling their attempt to get everything except about $80, doing so entailed a genuine risk to my life. The gun, as it turned out, was loaded with four bullets. Luckily, I escaped unharmed. So did the firefighters who gave the robbers chase and the police officer who apprehended one of them.

In the position of DA I would have the chance to work on crime at close range. Instead of looking at the world through a telescope, as I did in Congress, I would look at a tiny piece of it under a microscope — social reformer as microbiologist. But could close analysis of a social disease, scrutinizing its cell structure, viruses, and immune system, help in finding cures? Could I better understand the causes of crime from the perspective of the Brooklyn district attorney's office? Would I have the chance to fashion better solutions to reduce crime?

Ever since the 1970s conservatives have dominated the debate about crime. Conservatives have tried to separate crime from the rank soil in which it grows. They want to ignore poverty, educational deficiency, joblessness, drug use, and the rampant availability of handguns. Just get tough on the criminal and crime will wither, they say. Build more prisons, bring back the death penalty, add more police, and crime will go down. Don't bother with the social problems. In the face of this ideological onslaught, liberal political figures have retreated, switching their position on the death penalty and supporting new programs like "three strikes and you're out," concepts that I believe amount to no more than slogans and wishful thinking.

As a liberal, my ideas ran in a different direction. I had a viscerally negative reaction to the fact that as a society we spent as much to house a prisoner in jail as to send a person to college. I opposed the death penalty for humanitarian reasons. On a sheer practical level, I knew that it could not be applied to most of the 90,000 criminal cases prosecuted every year in Brooklyn — the death penalty, under law, can be invoked only in murder cases.

As DA, I thought, I could begin to explore more deeply the connection between crime and the social environment. Was there really an alternative to the conservative law-and-order agenda?

Was there a liberal take on law enforcement? Crime fighting, to me, meant more than tracking down and punishing criminals: there were victims to be considered as well — women, children, elderly people. What could be done to ameliorate their plight? What, too, could be done to fight the corruption that perverted the ideal of the law's fairness and equity?

After I was elected DA, my fascination gave way to apprehension. I found myself in new territory — heading one of the largest prosecutor's offices in America, dealing with 30,000 robberies, 2,000 rapes, 300 homicides, and tens of thousands of other crimes every year. The office employed over 400 lawyers (known as assistant district attorneys or ADAs), who were organized into ten or more bureaus. Each bureau dealt with a major crime category, such as homicide, rackets, sex crimes. In order to facilitate a transition effort, I called on my good friend Bernie Nussbaum. Bernie and I had gotten to know each other at Wachtell, Lipton, and later our friendship was renewed when he served on the staff of the House Judiciary Committee during Watergate. I asked him to help pick a team of top people who could make the district attorney's office one of the best in the country. Bernie, a public-spirited person, gathered a prominent group to assist him.

Walking into the office on the first day in January 1982, I confronted enormous legal and practical issues. On the organizational level, things were a mess. Even though crime went on twenty-four hours a day, no one answered the office phones after 5:00 P.M. Computerization was nil. Even desks for the assistant district attorneys were in short supply.

And the old ways of Brooklyn politics had left their historical markers on the DA's personal office. When I first entered, I discovered two doors a foot apart from each other; both opened into exactly the same room. One bore a sign that read "Private"; the other was blank. The two doors served no functional purpose. Then I recalled Celler's double-door law practice. In the past DAs had a private law practice. They saw clients in their public office. How to separate the inseparable? Like Celler, they had two doors. The private clients went through the door marked "Private"; everyone else went through the other door. The two doors ostensibly separated the private from the public. I had the doors painted over.

Together my staff and I gathered to formulate our mission: developing methods to ensure that cases were fairly and effectively prosecuted; helping crime victims; creating ways to reduce crime; upgrading, modernizing, and professionalizing the office. Beginning something fresh energized us. We took a broad approach. We welcomed women and minorities into the top ranks to assure that all voices were heard and considered. We pulled in outside organizations like the Kennedy School of Government to keep us focused on a big-picture strategy. And we tapped into a public-private consortium to get management assistance.

We had a team, a sense of excitement, and common goals. Often several of us would venture across the Brooklyn Bridge to Chinatown, just on the other side of the river. There we would enjoy a dim sum lunch at the Silver Palace or another bustling establishment. (Investigators warned me to stay away from some of the best Brooklyn eateries because organized crime figures hung out at them.) Sitting at a big round table in Chinatown, my staff and I pulled dish after dish from the rotating servers, all the while talking intensely, probing the law, bandying about new approaches, and brainstorming. I felt buoyed and encouraged by my colleagues. Sacrificing high-paying jobs, they dedicated themselves to the public interest.

But the criminal justice system that I encountered as DA was entrenched. When systems are set, they get really uncomfortable with people who come in and shake them up. And, I found out, this is especially true when that person is a liberal, an activist, and a woman.

# 8

## Frontlines on Race

*L*ESS THAN SIX MONTHS AFTER I TOOK OFFICE as district attorney, a violent episode in Brooklyn exposed the ugliness of racial animosity in our society, prompting me to take action on problems of lingering racism in the courts.

On June 21, 1982, Willie Turks, a black transit worker, completed his shift at midnight and drove with two other black transit workers to a nearby bagel shop on Avenue X in Gravesend to get a bite to eat before heading home. Gravesend is a white, largely Italian, working-class section of Brooklyn. As the three transit workers left the shop, a mob of fifteen or twenty young white men started harassing them for no reason. The white youths shouted, threw bottles, yelled racial epithets. The workers rushed into their car, but the car stalled. The white mob then surged around the car, smashing the windows with bottles and rods. Two workers, Dennis Dixon and Donald Cooper, fled from the rioters, running in opposite directions. Willie Turks could not escape. Pulled out of the car by the white youths, the thirty-four-year-old Turks was dragged across the street, kicked, punched, and bashed over the head with a club. Left bleeding and unconscious, Turks died in the hospital that night of massive head injuries.

How could this be? This wasn't the South; it was Brooklyn. A person beaten to death because of race? A peaceable man's life snuffed out by mindless racial rage? The murder was shocking, and a failure to prosecute vigorously and speedily could create an intolerable impression of indifference. I pressed the DA's staff to work closely with the police to make arrests. Four white youths were identified. I made sure that the best trial lawyer in the homicide bureau handled the case.

My efforts to make sure that the Turks case had special attention were aided by Zachary Carter, who had joined my staff earlier in the year. When I began in the DA's office, there had been no top-level African-American attorneys. I found it unacceptable that one of the office's major crime bureaus did not have a single minority lawyer. I had resolved early on to remedy this and searched for a high-level African-American prosecutor who had an understanding of the black community. I was fortunate to find Zachary, a talented, warm, and fair-minded man. Previously he had worked on federal civil rights enforcement, and he was later named as the first African-American U.S. attorney in New York State.

New York City could have faced rioting after the Turks case, and Zach's input made a tremendous difference. Tension was high. A single incident in Gravesend or in one of Brooklyn's black communities could have set off a furious reaction. Zach knew how to deal with sensitive situations. When members of a national organization of African-American motorcyclists decided to demonstrate on Avenue X in front of the bagel shop where Turks was killed, Zach was able to prevent a violent altercation. He met with the top police brass, and together they came up with a plan. Zach persuaded the motorcyclists to accept a route near, but not through, the neighborhood where the murder had occurred. Actually, the route was one that would take them right back out of Brooklyn without going through local streets. As a result, when the motorcyclists conducted their demonstration, no incidents occurred.

The first defendant on the Willie Turks case came to trial in 1983. I was now faced with a problem of racism inside the courts, specifically in the selection of the jurors. The issue would command my attention for years to follow.

Sixteen African-Americans were in the jury pool on the Turks case. The prosecution discharged one African-American juror based on a reason not related to race. Then the defense attorney removed the fifteen remaining African-Americans. I could not believe that this kind of blatant racism still persisted twenty years after I had worked on cases challenging racially biased jury selection in the South. I thought the matter had been settled; but apparently not so in Brooklyn — nor around the nation, as I soon learned.

With my prodding, the prosecutor handling the Turks case in court objected to the removal of the African-American jurors. But the judge ruled against us and allowed the jurors to be dismissed. As a result, not one African-American person sat on the Turks jury. An all-white jury heard the case of a white youth charged with the brutal, racially motivated, unprovoked lynching of a black man. Although a conviction resulted, the white youth had been charged with murder and was convicted only of the lesser crime of manslaughter.

Would the verdict have been different had African-Americans been on the jury? What did the spectacle of removing all the African-American jurors from the jury do to the image of justice in the community? Was justice served if no blacks were permitted to sit on a case of racial violence?

I understood the effect of racial exclusion. When people feel that the decks are stacked against them, that the system isn't responding, or that the result is engineered by keeping a group of people off the jury — because of race or religion or gender or national origin — the results can be volatile. In Los Angeles, the acquittal by an all-white jury of white police officers charged with beating Rodney King brought days of outrage. In Miami a deadly riot erupted when Hispanic police officers were acquitted of alleged brutality against blacks. Again, the jury had no African-Americans. The only way justice itself can survive is by opening the system to everyone.

The use of an all-white jury in the Turks case was not an isolated matter. I had received a letter from a black man who had been called to jury duty in Brooklyn. The letter writer was indignant because he had taken time from work to serve but had been summarily rejected, along with the other African-Americans, by the lawyers on the case. "Why are we being called down and treated like children?" he wanted to know.

The man knew that he had been dismissed because he was

African-American, and felt humiliated because of his race. And, he pointed out, had he refused to show up, he could have been subjected to a fine. He was so mad he had to write somebody. If it wasn't my job to handle such a problem, he said, could I forward his letter to someone who could do something about it?

Like him, I burned at the notion that people were rejected merely on the basis of race. Was it my responsibility to act? It didn't really fit into my job description as DA. Control of the jury system was part of the court administration, not the district attorney's office. On the other hand, if I acted, I might be able to have an impact. I decided to do everything I could to change the system.

The practice of excluding black jurors resulted, I knew, from hundreds of years of history and a web of legal interpretations. I soon became more familiar with this subject than I could imagine.

In the 1960s in the South, African-Americans were not even called for jury service. That had been corrected in the twenty years since I worked in Georgia. But just because African-Americans were in the jury pool did not ensure that they would serve. That's because jurors in the pool were screened by the attorneys on a case through the process of voir dire. Jurors could be removed at an attorney's request in two different ways — "for cause" or by peremptory challenges.

Race had been eliminated as a for cause exclusion. So the real problem was wrapped up with the peremptory challenges, an ancient trial procedure. Under the system of peremptory challenges, lawyers could discharge a certain number of prospective jurors without stating any reason whatsoever. No one could question the lawyer's choices for peremptory challenge. Some attorneys — prosecution and defense — used peremptories to remove African-American jurors, or Latinos, or women, or Jews, or gays. The practice was a commonly accepted feature of trials throughout the country. But nobody, it seemed to me, had given much thought to the excluded jurors and how they might feel, or to what this practice did to the system of justice.

Very early in my tenure, I discovered that the biased use of peremptory challenges had come up in the Brooklyn DA's office before. The prior district attorney's view was starkly opposed to mine. He asserted that prosecutors had the right to use racial peremptory challenges. This view was not without support. In 1965 the U.S. Supreme Court had ruled in *Swain v. Alabama* that peremptory challenges could be used to remove black jurors. The only exception was if the defendant could prove that black jurors were removed on a systemwide basis, a standard virtually impossible to prove without an enormous wealth of resources to study and document jury selection.

A New York appellate court had just ruled against the former Brooklyn DA when I first came into office. The court said that prosecutors could not eliminate African-American jurors by using peremptory challenges. Prosecutors, like other lawyers, hate to lose appeals. Having lost, the prosecutor's office was in the process of appealing to the state's highest court. One of the staff attorneys came to me. What did we want him to do with the appeal?

There are few issues on which I will immediately and firmly decide. Usually, I listen to a wide variety of views and consider a problem from many different angles. On this issue, I knew exactly what I wanted to do.

But to make sure my instincts were right, I asked my top staff members, each of whom had excellent credentials, to consider the subject. In a relatively short time, they came back with their opinions. Each one believed that a prosecutor should not use race as a basis to remove jurors. There are more important values than gaining a tactical advantage in a case, and not engaging in racial discrimination is one of them. As I listened, my spirits soared with the recognition that we shared these basic values.

I announced my decision: the office would withdraw the appeal. At the same time I issued a policy statement prohibiting any prosecutor in the office from using peremptory challenges to remove a potential juror on the basis of race — or religion, gender, or national origin. Unfortunately, this policy applied only to prosecutors, not to defense attorneys. But I wasn't going to stop there. I wanted to stop *all* use of racial peremptory challenges. I didn't know how yet; in an exciting way, that was the challenge that lay before us.

I knew I was going to meet significant resistance from defense attorneys. Since defense attorneys, unlike prosecutors, are not government agents, the legal analysis was more complicated. Some people believed that defense lawyers should have free rein to do anything to get their clients off — even discriminate. I sympathized with defendant's rights, but defense lawyers worked within other judicial and ethical limits. Above all the system had to be fair.

Aside from intellectual and moral considerations, there were practical problems to consider if the idea of nondiscrimination were to be adopted completely. If an African-American juror were dismissed on an attorney's challenge, how could you ever really know why? What if it were based on a reason unrelated to race? Shouldn't that be allowed?

Barbara Underwood, head of the appeals bureau, developed a sensible solution. If it appeared that peremptory challenges were being used on a racial basis, the lawyer would be required to explain the reason for the peremptory challenge. The reason could be anything — except race. As Barbara argued, once the principle was established that racially motivated peremptories could not be used, most lawyers would comply. The procedure probably would not stop the single use of a racially motivated peremptory challenge. But it could be very effective in stopping blanket exclusions based on race in a particular case, like the Willie Turks trial.

Changing the system would not be simple, or quick. We nevertheless decided to move forward to challenge racial discrimination in jury selection on all fronts — in the courts, in the legislature, in the arena of public opinion. We introduced a bill in the legislature to end the discriminatory use of peremptories, but it went nowhere. Neither did a long conversation I had with Governor Mario Cuomo. I explained the problem and asked for his support. He told me to send him the legal papers, which I did. That was the last I heard from him on the subject.

On the judicial side, there was an even bigger problem. To abolish the discriminatory use of peremptories required that the U.S. Supreme Court overrule the precedent it had established in the *Swain* case. The Supreme Court did not reverse itself often, but twenty years had shown that *Swain* wasn't working, and that intentional racial discrimination against jurors was still going on.

On appeal from Brooklyn was a robbery case in which an African-American defendant, McCray, was accused of a street mugging of a white art student. McCray, who had no prior record, had been standing on a street corner three weeks after the mugging when the art student was driven around by the police to look for the mugger. The victim identified McCray as one of his robbers. McCray had two trials, both of which occurred before I started as DA. In the first trial, he had a jury of nine whites and three African-Americans. The trial ended in a hung jury. McCray was tried again. This time the prosecutor used peremptory challenges to remove all seven African-Americans and one Latino. McCray's attorney argued that this was discrimination. The court said that attorneys had the right to use peremptory challenges however they saw fit. McCray was tried by an all-white jury, and this time he was convicted. His lawyer appealed.

Barbara Underwood thought that this was the right case in which to make a constitutional challenge to *Swain.* The defense attorney attacked the constitutionality of racial peremptory challenges, claiming the prosecution had used them in McCray's case. We could agree that the discrimination was unconstitutional and should be outlawed, while denying that it had occurred at McCray's trial. This case wound its way through several appeals, state and federal. New York's highest court found that racially based peremptory challenges were constitutional. This was an utter surprise to me. Two dissenters said racially based peremptory challenges were unacceptable, but those based on gender would be absolutely proper. If that was the "friendly" point of view, I thought justice was in real trouble.

McCray's case next went to the U.S. Supreme Court. Even if the Supreme Court didn't take the case, we felt it was important to raise the issue and the reasons that *Swain* should be overturned. The Supreme Court decided not to hear the case. At the same time, in an unusual step, a majority of justices indicated that they were not content with the *Swain* decision. Some invited lower courts to consider the issue. Barbara thought this was a good sign: maybe our efforts would pay off.

McCray's case continued on a long journey, going next to a lower federal court in Brooklyn. The case was assigned to Eugene Nickerson, a patrician Democrat who used to be county executive on Long Island. Acting on the Supreme Court's invitation to reconsider *Swain,* Nickerson decided that the Supreme Court had wrongly decided that case, and in essence, he overruled it. Racially based peremptories should be eliminated, he said. For a lower court judge to take this step was virtually unprecedented. Still, the Supreme Court itself would have the last word.

Around this time, I was speaking in Cambridge, Massachusetts, where I ran into Laurence Tribe, the noted professor of constitutional law at Harvard. We had been in college together, and I admired his unabashed liberalism and vast intelligence. I took the opportunity to ask his advice. The Supreme Court wasn't really interested in the issue, he said, and our position would never win anyhow. This was probably the only time he was wrong. The Supreme Court did decide to hear a similar case from Kentucky that raised the same issue, *Batson v. Kentucky.* Our office filed an amicus, or "friend of the court," brief, describing how we had worked out the practical aspects of banning racial peremptory challenges, and that it produced no particular hardship.

I thought it would be a good idea to get other prosecutors to join with us. We called prosecutors around the country, focusing on those who had a liberal reputation, such as Janet Reno in Miami and John Van de Kamp, the attorney general in California. Not a single prosecutor's office would join with us. In fact, the National District Attorneys' Association argued on the other side. We filed our friend of the court brief alone.

Barbara Underwood and her staff prepared an excellent brief. Before sending it, I remembered the African-American juror who had written to me and asked me to forward his letter to someone who could do something about the situation. Who better than the Supreme Court? I thought. Despite grammar and spelling flaws, his letter spoke eloquently about the harm to racially excluded jurors. We attached the letter to our Supreme Court brief, and waited.

Our efforts paid off. In 1986 the Supreme Court reversed the old ruling of *Swain* and banned prosecutors across the nation from using peremptory challenges to remove blacks from the jury in its ruling on *Batson.* The court accepted the argument about the harm to jurors, and in a footnote Justice John Paul Stevens referred to the work of our office in helping to bring about this result.

There was real exultation at our offices on Joralemon Street. I bought a few bottles of champagne and went up to the appeals bureau, where we all toasted the decision. To achieve a real victory

against bias, to fight successfully against discrimination as a prosecutor — these were no small matters. I felt really proud of the extraordinary work that had been done by Barbara and the appeals
bureau.

Over the next nine years the Supreme Court expanded the
*Batson* decision further. Defense attorneys in criminal cases and attorneys in civil cases were required to follow *Batson*. A 1994 decision held that lawyers couldn't exclude jurors on the basis of
gender. But as we celebrated the demise of discrimination in jury
selection, my enthusiasm was dampened by one small detail. The
man who wrote me the letter didn't sign his name. I was never able
to let him know how his experience may have helped to influence
the U.S. Supreme Court and protect jurors against bias.

In my opinion, New York City never took the Willie Turks case seriously enough. The case was considered merely an anomaly, an
aberration. When we tried to get city or community officials, including the priest in the relevant parish, to take steps to address the
underlying racial tension, no one responded. Possibly because the
Willie Turks case was quickly and rather successfully prosecuted,
everyone could forget about it — and did.

After the Willie Turks case, a similar incident took place nearby.
As in the Turks case, several African-American hospital workers
stopped to buy a pack of cigarettes on their way home from work.
A white gang attacked them. This time the police showed up before
anyone was murdered.

We even had another racial murder, although the police didn't
classify it as such. In 1988, a twenty-year-old African-American
supermarket clerk, Samuel Spencer, rode his bicycle home along
Surf Avenue. A group of young white men armed with baseball
bats followed him in a car. They knocked him off his bicycle,
cornered him, and, screaming racial slurs, clubbed him. One of
the attackers pulled out a knife and stabbed Spencer, leaving him
to die. The four attackers were convicted. In another incident in
1988, a group of young white men in Greenpoint attacked a
twenty-four-year-old Latino man, Richard Ocana, who was sleeping on a bench. Yelling anti-Latino epithets, the white gang beat up
Ocana with boards, a brick, and a tire jack. Ocana died. Three at-

tackers were arrested, and all were found guilty of first-degree manslaughter.

These incidents reflected intense racial animosities in New York. Then the Howard Beach incident in Queens occurred; a group of white youths violently assaulted three black men. One man, trying to escape, was struck and killed by a car. The Howard Beach attack suggested racial hostility so severe that it could jump out at any time.

Some Brooklyn communities always seemed to be on edge. Another troubled section was Crown Heights. Here Hasidic Jews lived in close proximity to the African-American community, which included many people from the Caribbean. Part of the district had lovely homes; part was poor. The Hasidim had put down their roots. So had the African-Americans.

Unfortunately there were few points of communication. The Hasidim created a crime patrol made up of their adherents; African-Americans perceived this as vigilantism out of control. African-Americans, troubled by crime as well, were incensed that there was a twenty-four-hour police guard stationed in front of the religious headquarters of the Hasidim while there were no such guards in front of African-American churches. Crown Heights, during my eight years as district attorney, was always potential dynamite, ready to ignite at any moment. And several years later, after I left office, it did erupt.

We did manage to stave off an explosion for eight years. I believe it had a lot to do with the fact that my office established credibility with both the black and white communities. Zach Carter had the trust of the black community, and Ed O'Malley, a gregarious, outgoing Irishman, was particularly well liked by the Hasidim. Time after time, as tension rose to the near-breaking point, we were able to work with the police and community leaders and eventually calm things down.

Later, when Zach was appointed to a judgeship in Queens, I appointed Harry Dodds, a former deputy police commissioner and African-American, to a top position in my office. Harry was very bright, experienced, and mature. He too, like his predecessor, came to play an important role in the office, particularly when the Bensonhurst case arose.

One August evening in 1989 a young African-American teen-ager named Yusef Hawkins, answering a newspaper ad for a used car, went with three friends to Bensonhurst. Hawkins, sixteen and coming from the other end of Brooklyn, had no idea what Benson-hurst was like. A tightly knit working-class community like Graves-end, it had a large proportion of Italian residents and suffered from typical urban problems, like a substantial school dropout rate. No African-Americans lived in Bensonhurst, and it's safe to say that few ventured there on their own.

Hawkins walked into an ambush without any warning. Local toughs were riled up because a neighborhood girl of Italian descent was dating an African-American youth. The locals were waiting for the date to show up. They didn't know what he looked like, but they had baseball bats and were standing in the local school yard. When Hawkins walked down the street, the gang of white men went after him with the bats, trapping him in a circle. One of the white attackers had a gun and shot Hawkins, killing him.

Unlike the Willie Turks case, the death of Yusef Hawkins at-tracted intense publicity from the outset. Our office went into high gear. I knew that it was critical for the police to apprehend every-one involved and to do so quickly. Our concern needed to be trans-lated into concrete action. In the hot final days of summer, any sign of inaction could mean riots and bloodshed. The stakes were very high.

From the beginning, we worked very closely with the police to ensure that no leads were ignored and that any legal questions about the investigation were promptly and properly handled. Or-dinarily in a homicide case assistant district attorneys from the in-vestigations bureau immediately go to the precinct to help the police. I directed the bureau chiefs of investigations and homicide to be there as well. I went to the local precinct also, to talk with the police and assure myself that my office was doing everything it could to help. We received information about the shooter's identity, and the police apprehended him. Seven other young white men were also arrested.

The case presented unique challenges. One dealt with the teen-age girl, whose romance had so agitated the white teens. She was, if you will, the Helen of this tragedy. She also had been looking out the window and was able to identify the youths who encircled Hawkins. It was imperative that she be kept in protective custody, but she was a particularly irrepressible adolescent with many problems. How to keep her voluntarily secluded was a constant headache.

At the outset, some African-American leaders called for a special prosecutor. The term suggested special treatment, which is what they wanted for this case. I agreed with the need for special treatment but thought my office was best equipped to provide it. We had a seasoned team of attorneys who had already handled several racial murder cases, with convictions in every one.

Only the governor had the power to name a special prosecutor. I caught up with Governor Mario Cuomo as he was visiting a downtown Brooklyn facility. We sat down together, and I explained our expertise and that we had the case well in hand. He agreed that no outside prosecutor was necessary.

Traditionally in New York the district attorney did not appear in court. Instead, ADAs or bureau chiefs represented the DA's office. But given the level of cynicism about the criminal justice system, I felt that my presence would assure the public that this case was getting the top-level attention it deserved. I appeared in court with the homicide prosecutors at the arraignments of the defendants who were arrested.

The criminal court building was ringed with television cameras. We asked that no bail be granted. I glanced at one point at the youths we had charged. They seemed so slight, so young, to have caused such horrendous damage.

Although the defendants were arrested for murder, under New York law they couldn't be tried unless a grand jury indicted them. The prosecutor was the legal advisor to the grand jury. In this instance, there was a tricky legal question. Could the entire group of youths be charged with murder? Or were they responsible — legally — for only a lesser charge?

There was no crystal-clear conclusion. For the shooter, murder was clearly the correct charge. But what about the others who encircled Hawkins, making it impossible for him to flee? If they knew that the shooter had a gun, then murder charges would have been undeniable. But did they know he was carrying a gun? And even if they didn't, wasn't it enough for a murder charge that a number of the circlers had bats, which were in and of themselves capable of causing death?

I convened just about all the top prosecutors in the district attorney's office who had anything to do with the case. I encouraged everyone to be absolutely frank. To charge murder or not?

The group split into two. The homicide bureau chief, Dale Campbell, a careful, experienced prosecutor, was opposed to murder charges. He believed that it would be difficult to sustain the charges at trial. Harry Dodds argued just as vigorously for presenting the murder charge, as did Bruce McIntyre, a young African-American prosecutor from Yale. Barbara Underwood and her research staff believed that the law permitted going forward with the most serious charges.

I found myself in the position of Solomon. Which side was right? I knew that the popular thing to do was to present the murder charges to the grand jury, but that wasn't enough. What did the law require, and what was the just thing to do? After the group left, I singled out the relevant cases and piled the books high on my desk. I read all night. Barbara was correct. The facts did warrant murder charges.

Before making my final decision, I met again with the prosecutors and bureau chiefs. After regular office hours, the team crammed back into my office. We debated again. Barbara, Harry, and Bruce strongly argued to present the murder charges. Dale continued to be firmly against. These meetings illustrated to me government at its finest — dedicated, experienced professionals tussling with issues of the highest moment and doing so in a thoughtful, intelligent, fair way.

I finally came to the conclusion that we would present the murder charges. If the law permitted a grand jury to indict on these grounds, we should go ahead, despite the difficulty of proof or the possibility that we might lose at trial. The grand jury promptly issued the indictments for murder. From a tactical point of view, perhaps we were wrong to present the murder charges, and the homicide bureau chief was right. I had left the DA's office when the trials took place. Except for the gunman, all the others were acquitted of murder charges (most were convicted on lesser charges).

Since I no longer served as district attorney, I couldn't second-guess the reasons for the acquittals.

Were we right or wrong to charge murder? In retrospect, it occurs to me that being wrong and being fair are two different concepts. We cannot ask for more from government than that it honestly, intelligently, and fairly consider all sides. We can make mistakes; we are all human. I still believe that we made the right decision, and just as important, we did it in the right way.

Our problems with the Hawkins murder were not merely legal. Al Sharpton, a minister, activist, and aggressive, mostly self-appointed spokesperson for the African-American community, had become involved in the case. He had an uncanny ability to insinuate himself in provocative ways into high-visibility racial issues. During the infamous Tawana Brawley case, he accused the attorney general of New York, who was Jewish, of being like Hitler. Things seemed to be going fine in our case when Sharpton announced he was coming to see me with Yusef Hawkins's mother.

I was very interested in talking to the mother of the slain boy about the case. But Sharpton's involvement made me nervous. I envisioned the worst. If I said no, it might create an enormous, tangential issue. If I said yes, and Sharpton came, who could predict what would happen? Reluctantly, I agreed to a meeting with Sharpton, members of the family, top prosecutors familiar with the case, and Sylvia Lerner, the head of our Citizen Action Center. The event was quiet and polite. The prosecutors explained the status of the case. The family asked a few questions, which we answered. We described our desire to maintain open channels of communication, something we tried to do with the family of any victim of homicide or serious crime. To my relief, the family — and Sharpton — seemed reassured.

The mood of the city was tense following the murder. The prospect of riots hung in the air like the summer humidity. Outraged by the murder of Hawkins, demonstrators, many African-American, sponsored several marches in Bensonhurst. They were met by crowds of whites, some yelling racial epithets and holding up derogatory signs.

The issues raised by the Hawkins case were difficult enough

for any hot summer. But it was also the year of a city election. Ed Koch, New York's mayor, made an intemperate comment chastising the demonstrators who protested Hawkins's murder. At the same time he expressed sympathy for the white Bensonhurst community, claiming that it was being unfairly condemned. People generally admired Koch for his outspokenness, but this time they realized that there could be a price to pay for unconsidered comments.

Koch faced a ballot contest with David Dinkins, the Manhattan borough president, whose quieter manner seemed to be the right style to bring calm to the city. Dinkins, if elected, would become the first African-American mayor of New York. The Hawkins case set the tone and tenor for the election, and black voters came together in record numbers to support Dinkins. That fall Koch was rejected in favor of Dinkins.

At the same time, against the backdrop of this terrible racial murder, I was running for comptroller of New York City. I was anxious. Aside from other consequences, I knew that any misstep in the case would come crashing down on me. As it happened, I was aided by the perception that the Hawkins case was proceeding with steady competence and professionalism. And the high turnout of African-American voters worked in my favor — in my electoral bid for city comptroller that fall, they voted for me in overwhelming numbers.

Another issue acted like oil on a fire in New York's African-American and Latino communities when I served as DA: police brutality.

Over the years the police misuse of force — and the unwillingness of city officials to punish brutal police officers — left undeniable scars on the minority communities. I saw the depth of feelings on the subject again and again when I gave speeches around the city.

By 1982, when I entered the DA's office, the issue of police brutality was simmering. Having seen police brutality in the South, I vowed never to allow the issue to be pushed under the rug.

In the DA's office we dealt with police officers every day. The majority were hardworking and dedicated and did not beat up citizens. Working day in, day out with the officers, and especially getting to know the detectives assigned to protect me, I gained tremendous respect for the judgment and decency of most officers. There were, I knew, many great cops.

But there were not-so-great officers, too. Police brutality cases are extremely sensitive. When the public views these cases as not being handled properly, the response can be explosive. Police unions, on the other hand, waged intense fights to stop controls on the police.

When I began as DA, I called upon Zach Carter to oversee the cases of police misuse of force. As an assistant U.S. attorney, he had been assigned the case of a man who had died when arresting police officers had grabbed him in a special hold. After a thorough investigation, Zachary concluded that the police were not guilty of criminal conduct, despite great pressure to prosecute the officers. I knew he wouldn't succumb to demands from any side and would handle cases carefully and fairly.

The office had a variety of police brutality cases. One of the early cases in my office involved a rookie police officer, the son of a hero detective. The victim was a young African-American man. As he waited at a bus stop, the rookie cop asked him for marijuana. When the man said he had none, the officer hit him and called him names. A Transit Authority police officer, standing nearby, stopped the beating. The rookie was ultimately convicted of assault and removed from the force. Other cases, however, were not prosecuted so successfully. One officer who attacked his girlfriend and a restaurant owner who had tried to intervene in the fight was convicted, but the conviction was overturned.

After examining how the office handled police brutality cases for about a year, Zachary came to me saying that the existing system had many flaws. He felt he could not adequately monitor the escalating number of cases. Assigned to prosecutors throughout the office, cases could suffer from breaches of security. For example, Zach mentioned that in one instance a prosecutor was investigating a case against a police officer while at the same time the prosecutor's officemate was working with the officer to fight crime. I suggested that Zach find out how other district attorneys' offices handled these cases and that he make recommendations for change.

Several months later Zach reported back. He recommended creating a special unit for all the police brutality cases. We could monitor the work more efficiently and assure fair and professional processing. Conflicts could be avoided. Manhattan district attorney Robert Morgenthau apparently assigned police brutality cases to his Rackets Bureau. That was another option, but we were already trying to upgrade the Rackets Bureau to fight organized crime. I agreed to accept Zach's proposal: we would set up a special unit, the law enforcement investigations unit. It would have a bureau chief, and Zach would be responsible for supervising it. My top staff reviewed the proposal and fully concurred.

The creation of the bureau — which we had designed as a better system of handling our existing caseload — broke loose a form of hell. The head of the police union, Phil Caruso, promptly denounced me, saying that I was out to "get the cops." The police union accused me of trying to handle cases that I had no right to handle.

Caruso called for a police demonstration against me. On the appointed day, about 5,000 police officers snaked their way around the municipal building in Brooklyn, where my office was located. At first, I wasn't even sure I wanted to go to my office that day. I refused to be intimidated. Seven floors up, I could hear the chants. Although I couldn't make out the individual words, I was assured by others that they were hateful. I could see the line of blue.

Surprisingly, I felt very calm. A kind of eerie quietness persisted, despite the shouting below. I knew I was right; I did not have one doubt or second thought. The police were trying to scare off prosecution of police misconduct. Previously, police had picketed the Bronx DA after a grand jury indicted police officers in the notorious Eleanor Bumpers case. There, officers were trying to evict an elderly African-American woman when one officer decided that she was going to stab him with a knife. He shot and killed her.

The long day of picketing ended. I felt alone. No political figure called to support me except Bella Abzug. I appreciated her phone call. The police left, and the unit stayed, but I paid a very big price for standing up. The union tried to paint me as anticop, a charge that I couldn't shake for a long time.

I had not anticipated that a purely internal management decision would blow up in this way. Maybe if I had given the press release a softer tone by using "police misuse of force" instead of "police brutality," my decision wouldn't have seemed so provocative. On the other hand, given the police attitude, nothing short of nixing the idea of a special bureau could have made a difference.

The unit functioned very well. Its head was a talented African-American woman, Edna Wells Handy, who previously had clerked for a federal judge. Robert H. Straus, a very experienced prosecutor who later became a criminal court judge, served as her deputy. Cases were more carefully supervised and more effectively prosecuted. The bureau brought professional, well-prepared cases when issues of police violence arose. But after I left the office, the unit was dismantled by my successor.

In the interim, nevertheless, we had seen a very interesting result — one that probably would bear serious study. The number of police brutality cases had begun to diminish. This was also happening in other boroughs. I believed that the reduction in serious police brutality cases resulted directly from the fact that prosecutors appeared determined to take action against it without hesitation.

Aggressive and effective prosecution of police officers who misuse their power helps the policeforce do its job in the community. Citizens feel assured that rogue cops are being reined in, and the work of the good cops who follow the rules and don't abuse their positions is enhanced. Law enforcement as a whole gains in the process.

# 9

# Gender and Justice

## GENDER ANNALS

$B$EFORE RUNNING FOR DISTRICT ATTORNEY IN 1981, I hadn't given much thought to gender as a central factor in the election. I should have. My opponent ran a simple radio commercial featuring a woman with a distinctive Brooklyn accent. The voice said, "My name is Goldie Abramson. Liz Holtzman is a very nice girl. I'd even like her for my daughter. But not for DA."

A "girl" couldn't do a man's job. The message was clear. No woman had ever held the job of DA before in New York City. Even women assistant DAs were largely invisible in the days before *Law and Order* and Marcia Clark. Crime was a matter for men to handle. Surprisingly, voters began to parrot the sentiment of the radio ad. People approached me while I campaigned with comments just like Goldie's. "I voted for you for Congress and the Senate, but this is not a job for a woman," one person said to me on the street. Others came up to me asking, "Liz, what will it be like having men work for you?" Or, "Won't the pressures be too great?"

I didn't understand why the ad had provoked such concern about whether, as a woman, I had the mettle to do this job. How did Congress, where I had served for eight years, differ from the office of the district attorney? Perhaps the public saw a congressperson as someone who talks — women are, according to the stereotype, certainly capable of that. A district attorney was a "real" job. Could a woman do that? Later I realized the questions were not necessarily hostile. People were seriously confused as to what a woman could or could not do. So few women managed any big organizations. In the campaign I wasn't running against a flesh-and-blood opponent; I was running against the idea of what a district attorney looked like. And the district attorney didn't look like me. He was distinctly "he," and he looked like Perry Mason or his prosecutorial opponent.

When I ran again four years later, I was reelected by a great margin. But those hidden biases against women expressed during the first campaign were just under the surface. I couldn't shake the feeling that, like camouflaged traps, they might pop up at any moment with the smallest wrong step.

As soon as I entered office, I began to see that the Goldie Abramson commercials were right, after a fashion. Gender did make a difference, but not in the way that the ads projected.

I discovered that prejudice existed against women employed within the DA's office. More than 30 percent of the prosecutors were women, but no woman headed any of the twelve bureaus. Some women had served for ten or more years and were top-performing prosecutors. They had been passed over repeatedly for promotion. The same held true for African-American prosecutors and other minorities — anyone who didn't fit into the Perry Mason mold.

What, I kept musing to myself, was wrong with the employment discrimination laws? Why weren't they being enforced against government agencies when there was such clear racism and sexism? Was it that elected officials didn't want to apply the same standards to themselves as they did to others?

I picked up quickly on one nice thing about being boss of an agency that doesn't have civil service constraints. I could crack that glass ceiling just about as quickly and simply as snapping my fingers. As far as I was concerned, only professionalism counted, not race or gender. Rather quickly, with the help of the transition team, I placed talented minority and women prosecutors in key positions.

Barbara Underwood, for example, was one of the most brilliant people I had ever met and a person who wanted to see the system of justice used to do justice. When I named her special counsel and head of the appeals bureau, she became the first woman bureau chief in a prosecutor's office in New York City. Subsequently I promoted two women to bureau chiefs and hired a woman prosecutor from the Manhattan DA's office as a deputy. At one point, roughly 50 percent of the bureau chiefs were women.

Gender played a part in other subtle ways. Sometimes they were insidious, other times almost silly. For example, the standard forms used for legal motions began with the caption "Sirs," as if no attorneys were women. When wiretap requests were first handed to me, I discovered the forms referred to the district attorney — me — as "he." I found myself inserting the letter s. A new style sheet was quickly prepared.

And then there was the squad of detectives assigned to the district attorney's office. About fifty worked in the office, including the bodyguards assigned to me. The squad contained some women, but curiously, no women detectives were assigned as bodyguards. I spoke to the captain in charge about my concerns. He assured me that women would be assigned to the bodyguard detail. A woman did come for one day and then disappeared. She was said to be on vacation. Her "vacation" continued for some time. I soon learned that the day she came to the office was also the day preceding her retirement; she wasn't even on the force anymore. I spoke to the captain again. He looked at me rather paternalistically, expressing some impatience at my slowness. "You don't really want a woman detective," he said. "After all, this is a matter of life and death." I looked him straight in the eye. "Since it's *my* life, I'll take the risk," I said. He finally assigned a woman.

Through the years I continued to hear many stories of gender bias that women prosecutors in my office faced. A judge, angry at one woman prosecutor, said he would take her over his knee and spank her. Once, a defense attorney called a prosecutor a "bitch" in front of the jury; the judge refused to admonish the attorney. A woman prosecutor overheard a judge and his law clerk snickering;

she later found out they had been crudely joking that because her breasts were large, she might "tip over."

Each time I heard a story about the poor treatment of the women prosecutors in the office, I blanched. (One judge told the press that I had never gotten over being a woman, as if being a woman were something you had to "get over.") After a commission in New Jersey reported on widespread bias against women in their courts, I called the then–chief judge in New York State, Lawrence Cooke, and suggested that a similar study be done in New York. He became testy: how could anyone even raise the subject of possible gender bias in New York courts? He said New York didn't need a commission. "No one," he said, "has done more for women in New York State than I have." His bragging suggested just the opposite to me, particularly given the reality of what women faced as attorneys and as witnesses and victims. I wrote to him, making the suggestion again. I got others to write, too. Reluctantly, Cooke finally appointed a task force. Of course he named a man as its head, and a majority of men as its members. Fortunately, that didn't stop the truth. The task force held hearings and found pervasive and systematic discrimination against women in the courts. In addition, women judges were scarce, a mere 10 percent of the total. When a block of judges was named in 1986, only three of twenty-two were women. The problem persisted. In June 1995 New York's Republican governor George Pataki named a half-dozen new judges, none women. Not a rumble of protest was heard.

As a woman district attorney, I discovered my view of cases sometimes differed from that of many male DAs. The case of the two sleazy doctors who committed medical fraud and took advantage of women was just one example.

My attention was drawn to the medical issue in 1984 by a small mention in a report from the Citizen Action Center, a department Sylvia Lerner had started. The center helped people who had problems with the prosecutor's office or the criminal justice system generally. The report described a woman who complained about a Brooklyn medical clinic run by a husband-and-wife team. The clinic ran ads: "Free Pregnancy Test. Confidential. Full Gynecological Services." The woman, fearing that she might be pregnant, went to the clinic to have the test done. The receptionist took some information, had her provide a urine sample, and told her to wait. In a short while one of the doctors came out. He told the woman the test results. She was in fact pregnant — six weeks pregnant — the doctor said. He urged her to have an abortion and said he would perform it right away. The woman was puzzled. If she were pregnant, she knew the conception had not occurred six weeks earlier. She grew suspicious and refused the proposed abortion. The woman then went to her own doctor, who tested her and found she was not pregnant. Angered by her experience with the clinic, the woman undertook an experiment. She had a cousin — who was infertile — go to the clinic. The doctor told the infertile woman she, too, was pregnant and suggested an immediate abortion. Together, the cousins came to the Citizen Action Center and told their stories to Sylvia Lerner. Sylvia understood the problem at once. After initial verification, she thought the case important enough to forward it to one of the prosecutorial bureaus.

But the report that I saw indicated that there had been no follow-up by any prosecutors. I immediately sensed a medical scam, and a serious one — telling women they were pregnant when they were not and performing medical procedures on them. With the come-on of free pregnancy tests, women were being duped and conned. Not only were their pocketbooks at risk, but if they went for the phony abortion, they put their bodies on the line as well.

I got on the phone with the prosecutors and described the urgency of the matter. An investigation should begin, I told them. We needed a woman investigator to go in and pose as a patient. On staff were detective investigators whose usual jobs involved locating witnesses. Pretending to need an abortion was not their idea of fun, especially the part that took them to the surgical table. We explained that if they were offered the abortion, they had to go through only as much of the procedure as presented no risk to them. Finally a woman investigator volunteered to pose as a patient. She went to a real hospital first, and doctors certified that she wasn't pregnant. Then we sent her, "wired," to the clinic. Exactly as the women had reported to Sylvia, the receptionist at the clinic asked for the urine sample. The investigator complied. Shortly after, a doctor appeared and told our investigator she was pregnant and urged her to have an abortion immediately. The investigator agreed. The doctor asked no questions about her medical history or experiences with anesthesia. She went to a medical examination room, undressed, and arranged herself on the surgical table in preparation for the procedure. The doctors entered, ready to give her an injection of anesthesia. A moment before the injection, the investigator announced that she had changed her mind. She got dressed, and the doctors — Judith Cameau-Samuels and Maxen Samuels — were arrested.

The scam was as bad as I had anticipated. The receptionist confessed: the clinic never performed pregnancy tests; the doctors simply told the women they tested positive for pregnancy whether it was true or not. As a result, women who were not pregnant were duped or frightened into an "abortion." No medical history was taken. If women agreed to the abortion, they were slapped into the procedure and given anesthesia. The doctors totally disregarded medical standards and created a risk to patients' lives. And hundreds and hundreds of women walked out of the clinic believing that they had had an abortion, sometimes wondering and worrying if they had done the right thing. Even though they might not have been pregnant at all, guilt or doubt or the huge range of feelings that pregnancy and termination can provoke would have remained with them for life. The doctors performed not just a physical assault on the women, but a mental assault as well.

Upon announcing the arrest, I urged other women to contact our office. Hundreds did. Several had suffered medical complications. Others described their feelings of confusion. Because of the clinic's shoddy record-keeping, the women could never really know for certain if they had been pregnant or not. We seized all the assets of the clinic, and the doctors were convicted.

We persisted, pressuring the state's Office of Medical Responsibility to review the doctors' right to practice medicine. Their licenses were finally revoked. Despite all the evidence, New York State would not take steps to prevent other women from being victimized at such so-called clinics. We urged the state health department to inspect all clinics, but it refused to undertake the effort to protect women from other sleazy operators.

## RAPE

Thousands of cases of violence against women came to the DA's office: rape, battering, incest. (Although incest sometimes involved boys as victims, the vast majority of cases involved an adult man preying upon a young girl; all cases were awful.)

I was already familiar with the subject of sexual violence. In the 1960s and 1970s the women's movement had begun to expose the terrible treatment of rape victims. Susan Brownmiller's book *Against Our Will* made a deep impression on me. I started reading it one night while I was in Congress and couldn't put it down. I stayed up all night, transfixed by the disturbing picture of how women are demeaned by rape and again by their treatment at the hands of the criminal justice system. When I finished the book, I vowed to do something about rape.

Of course, sexual violence was not something I learned about only from books — like most women, I had my own ordeals. While I was never a victim of rape, I had encountered frightening situations that made me realize how vulnerable I could be as a woman. As a young lawyer with an apartment on the Upper West Side of Manhattan, I often left work late in the evening, as young lawyers in New York so often do. One night I had no money for a cab — in those pre-ATM days, I had barely enough change to catch the subway. I usually didn't worry because my apartment was only a block from the subway stop. That night, I walked the block from the subway and went into my building. A man followed me in. I tried not to worry. I stepped into the elevator, which was one of those old types that had two doors, one facing the hallway, which opened automatically, and another one inside the elevator, which had to be shoved open from the inside. The man came into the elevator as well. After I pushed the button for my floor and the elevator began moving, the man stepped in front of me. He demanded my money, which was at this point hardly enough to clink in one hand. I gave him what I had — only 33¢. Then, abruptly, the man pushed all of the buttons on the elevator panel. I panicked. He stood in front of me, blocking the inner door. I had to do something. When the elevator stopped at the next floor, I slammed past him, threw myself against the inner elevator door, and began screaming. I ran into the hall, berserk. The man fled. I knew that I had survived a close call.

I never forgot the incident. While serving in Congress, I wanted to change the federal evidence rules to protect the privacy of rape victims. Women who took the stand in rape cases often faced questions about every sexual encounter they had ever had. This stemmed from the absurd notion that only a "chaste" woman could be raped — that there was no harm in raping a woman who had already been sexually active. There was an unspoken, but firmly implanted, view that a woman who had sex outside of marriage was "bad" and could not be believed. The theory held that if a woman ever said yes, she could or would never say no.

This attempt to shift the blame to the victim did not occur in other areas of the law. There was, for example, no inquiry into how robbery victims handled their bank accounts or whether they had been swindled or robbed before. Some defense attorneys had become so zealous in attacking the rape victims that women sometimes felt that they were being raped twice — once by the physical incident, another time in court.

This practice was atrocious. I couldn't help seeing the subject in personal terms. What if I were the rape victim? What would I have to go through on the stand? Why should I, or any woman, have to tolerate this humiliation, this exposure, this pawing in public by strangers at the most private of relations? No one had any business inquiring into a rape victim's prior sexual life. As a member of the House Judiciary Committee, I wrote a law to stop defense lawyers from humiliating raped women in court. This would become the federal rape shield law.

I thought I had a certain understanding about the nature of rape before becoming DA. But holding that office brought me up against a much darker reality. I began to grasp — with growing horror — the extraordinary scope of the violence confronting women in this country.

Every morning, as DA, I would be handed the "scratch sheets" as I walked into the office. These were the reports of all the sex crimes and murders that had taken place in Brooklyn in the prior twenty-four hours. A daunting spectrum of human violence and greed opened up to me for the first time. I learned more about these subjects than I ever wanted to know. The murders were grisly. But usually I had already heard about them from television news and or the tabloid papers, and was mentally prepared to deal with them.

Nothing prepared me for the staggering and ugly number of incidents of rape and incest. There were reports of rape after rape after rape; on rooftops, in cellars, in empty lots, at parties, in cars; of six-year-old girls, pregnant women, grandmothers. The crime was reported with almost a mechanical quality, as though it were fated to happen.

The statistics alone shocked me: a woman raped every six minutes, according to the Justice Department. Later statistics doubled the previous numbers. The numbers of incidents of battering were even worse — a woman battered every thirty seconds in America. And then there was incest, the least reported crime of all.

All the statistics and theory could not prepare me for the real reports, the details of the actual victims or their suffering. The cases never ceased to disturb me.

One reported case involved a Brooklyn man who, just before Christmas in 1982, offered to give his fifteen-year-old neighbor a ride to the grocery store. Instead he drove her to an abandoned school, dragged her up three flights of stairs, raped and sodomized her, and then threw her out a window. Landing on a pile of debris, she survived the fall, although she had broken bones and bruises all over her body. The man found her and raped her again, leaving her for dead. In another case a man went to a woman's apartment after he had broken her skylight, claiming that the superintendent had sent him to make repairs. He tied her up with electrical wire, raped her, and stole her money.

The cases went on and on. Shortly after taking office, a case came up about a man who had broken into the home of an elderly woman in the Coney Island section of Brooklyn and raped her. A top prosecutor in the sex crimes bureau called me to describe a problem with the case. The rape might not legally qualify as a rape, and we might not be able to prosecute the crime as rape. The reason, the prosecutor told me, was that the woman did not fight back. Unless the woman fought back, the law did not consider it a rape.

With this case, the whole mythology of rape and its treatment in the law began to unfold for me in a three-dimensional way. No longer was this intellectual or remote, a matter of changing the rules of evidence in a committee room on Capitol Hill. This was an elderly woman, in real life. She lived not far from where I grew up. The episode epitomized how strenuously the law protected rapists.

Women weren't treated as credible when it came to rape. Historically a woman's word that she was raped was not enough for a conviction. The law required corroboration as evidence. For every other crime, a woman's word was adequate. If a man shot at a woman and she lived to tell of it, her word alone, without any witnesses or any other corroboration, could be enough to convict him. But if he raped her, she would need witnesses or other supportive evidence. Unspoken behind the law was the presumption that women did not mind being raped, that they even "wanted" it. Or that women used the claim of rape to cover up illicit sex. The premises behind the law humiliated women.

By 1982, when I took office as DA, the requirement of corroboration had been repealed in New York and many states. "Earnest resistance," or fighting back, was one of the barriers that remained. I thought the term "earnest resistance" itself was a quaint Victorian way of sugarcoating the seriousness of the rape. To prove she had fought back, the woman had to show scratches, bruises, some signs of struggle. The law assumed that unless a woman fought back, she had consented. But what if the rapist had a weapon, such as a gun or a knife? What if he threatened to kill her or her children if she resisted? What if she had been grabbed unaware, or had been sleeping when the attack began? Why should a woman risk her life or additional bodily injury just to prove to the legal system that she did not consent to the rape? An assault victim didn't have to fight back. A robbery victim didn't have to fight back. Common wisdom in cities like New York held that if you were mugged, you should not fight back but give the mugger what he wanted, to prevent serious injury.

The law had to be changed. Efforts had already begun in the

state legislature, and I joined them, urging that "earnest resistance" be earnestly abolished. To my surprise, the lawmakers in New York State, who were overwhelmingly male, could not bring themselves to abolish the provision and came up with a compromise substitute. They would drop "earnest resistance" only if a new obstacle could replace it; a woman would have to prove that she feared permanent bodily injury or immediate death. This new provision was known as the specific fear clause. Some of the advocates of rape law reform were so anxious to get rid of the old law that they accepted this new version.

But for me, it was not acceptable. The new provision had the same innate flaws. Behind the facade stood the concept that a woman's word about rape was untrustworthy. The results, I thought, could be tragic. Sadly, I was right. The law passed, but soon enough its problems loomed. A woman in the Bronx — which was not in my office's jurisdiction — was raped by a gang of four youths. The young men were convicted at trial, but the appellate court overturned the conviction. The reason? The woman was asked at the trial whether she feared being killed or permanently injured. She said only that she was so terrified that she didn't know what they would do to her if she resisted. The appellate court let the rapists go, saying that the victim didn't fear immediate death or permanent bodily injury.

I was determined to go back to the legislature and get this law changed again as soon as possible. Women's advocates now stood up to it also. This time I drew upon my Washington experience. One of my first lessons in Washington had come from an early adviser, Marilyn Shapiro, whose golden rule held that "the first person with a piece of paper wins." What she meant was that a proposal on the table could shape the debate.

In 1983 my office drafted new language that would eliminate the so-called specific fear clause from the law. We circulated the draft among the small number of women in the state legislature and got promises of support. Since male legislators seemed to have enormous misunderstandings about this issue, we decided to approach them in a different way — from their own backyards. We sent letters to women's groups around the state and began to educate them so that they could lobby their lawmakers. The effort worked. The legislature deleted the specific fear provision, and New York finally joined the ranks of other states in eliminating some of the most sexist provisions of rape laws.

Aside from changing outdated laws, it was clear to me that we had to infuse the system with more compassion for rape victims. I made this a personal priority in Brooklyn.

Rape was a largely underreported crime because many women feared coming forward, believing that the police and prosecutors would sneer, or humiliate them in the courtroom. Although the women's movement had forced the reform of rape laws and the treatment of rape victims, it was hard to persuade the press to publicize these changes. Women themselves didn't always know that progress had been made.

Every official in the justice system, and even in medical institutions, who came in contact with a rape victim could have an impact on the victim and on the future case against the rapist. With the chiefs of the sex crimes bureau, I went step-by-step through the system, searching for ways to make it more responsive, more humane and caring. We drew up a list and began to implement each item on it.

The police had an important role. Officers dealt with the victims early in the process, in most cases being the first official presence. The police needed to see the victim as a victim—to question her sensitively and to provide concerned and professional assistance. We conducted seminars to teach police officers how better to handle rape cases.

Rape victims had to see doctors early on, but generally doctors have no special legal training in rape cases. Some, through their carelessness or perhaps indifference, harmed cases against rapists. For example, doctors in hospital emergency rooms had to know that a rape could take place without leaving physical bruises or other signs of violence. Bruises weren't the only evidence of rape — semen or the victim's statement, for example, were valid evidence as well. But by writing on the patient's chart that there was "no evidence of rape" because there were no bruises, the doctor could create enormous problems when the case was prosecuted. Doctors needed to note only the patient's condition, not make legal conclusions, and they had to understand the difference. We decided to provide training for doctors who treated rape victims in emergency rooms.

Collection of medical evidence in rape cases was often haphazard. We wanted to get all the hospitals in Brooklyn to use special rape evidence collection kits, named Vitullo kits after the forward-thinking former detective who designed them. These small cardboard boxes contained all the basic tools for collecting evidence in a rape case. There were small orange sticks for scraping under the victim's fingernails. The woman may have scratched the rapist's skin or pulled off pieces of his clothing or hair. The doctor could then deposit the material into a container, also provided by the kit. Remnants of a rapist's pubic hair could be entangled in that of the victim's. The kit had a small comb to be used on the pubic hair. There was a checklist of the kinds of evidence that a doctor might notice. Some hospitals were already using the kits at the time I took office; others — mostly private hospitals — flatly refused. We started a campaign to convince all of them to join our effort, and ultimately all did.

The psychological distress to rape victims also concerned me. Many cases showed that the victim felt an acute, overwhelming sense of personal violation. The suffering could be intense and long-lasting. Rape is not simply a sex act but essentially a crime of violence in which the rapist aims to degrade and humiliate the victim. Absorbing the cues from society that blames the victim, too many women ended up blaming themselves. Some are in fact so severely traumatized that they cannot have sexual relations for some time after the rape. Other victims find that their husbands or lovers become hostile to them afterward. I remember one women in her early twenties who refused to leave her apartment after a violent rape. The young woman, along with her mother, required intense counseling. And some women were irreparably damaged, never able to resume a normal life.

I was constantly inspired by the prosecutors and social workers in our sex crimes bureau who were especially trained to work sympathetically with the victims of rape. I watched them time and again put their hearts and souls into trying to make a difference for crime victims.

Our rethinking on victims prompted the establishment of a new crime victims unit. Our office hired a trained psychologist who could provide counseling to rape and other crime victims. The humanitarian aspect of helping victims appealed to me, but it was also practical from a legal point of view. Victims who are helped by the criminal justice system are more willing to testify in court.

The importance of moral support to the victims was underscored in one rape case in our office that involved two sisters from Philadelphia. While they were visiting relatives in Brooklyn in 1983, the sisters were forced into a dark alley by a former felon. The man raped and sexually abused one sister, threatening to murder her if the other sister fled. The rapist then forced the two sisters into the basement of a building, where he tied them both up and raped and sodomized them. A man was arrested and identified by both sisters in a lineup. The sisters came back to Brooklyn for the trial in 1984. When it came to testifying, however, the viciousness of the crime came rushing back to the sisters, overwhelming them. One sister repeatedly broke down on the stand, to the point of physical collapse. The trial judge allowed a recess, and the psychologist from the Crime Victims Bureau counseled the sisters. The sisters found renewed emotional strength and went back to testify. Unfortunately, despite their valiant efforts, the case ended with a hung jury. But because the young women were grateful for the emotional support and knew they could rely on it again, they agreed to come back and testify at a second trial. This time there was a conviction.

But of course we knew that our office could provide only immediate or emergency counseling for victims. The problems suffered by rape victims could be long-lasting. They needed places to get help on a prolonged basis; and there I found a stunning void. Although rape crisis centers existed in almost every state, there were was no comprehensive rape counseling center in all of Brooklyn, with its two and a half million people.

I set up a meeting with the Board of Family and Children's Services of the Federation of Jewish Philanthropies, which had an excellent professional reputation. After explaining the problem to the director, I asked whether the agency would consider establishing a comprehensive rape crisis center. The director agreed without hesitation. The board set up a comprehensive rape counseling program that made services available on a nonsectarian basis to every woman who cooperated in the prosecution of a case in Brooklyn. The program was so successful that five satellite offices were set up around the borough.

Another troublesome area on the subject of rape had to do with judges. Too often their consciousness about rape was frustratingly limited. Weren't judges supposed to be alert to making the system fair and to rooting out bias? In too many cases, though, judges were insensitive.

One Brooklyn judge asked a twelve-year-old rape victim to describe her dreams about sex. An upstate judge imposed a very lenient sentence on a man who had broken into a woman's home with a mask on his face and raped her. The judge explained that while the rape may have started out with force, "she probably wound up enjoying it." In Wisconsin there was a judge who gave a lenient sentence to a rapist after he claimed that the victim wore provocative clothing and therefore brought the rape upon herself. The clothing in that case, it turned out, consisted of a bulky sweater and jeans. U.S. Supreme Court justice David H. Souter, when serving on the Supreme Court of New Hampshire, wrote an opinion about a rape case. He suggested that the woman might have provoked the attack by acting flirtatiously in a bar earlier that night. In another case in upstate New York in 1993, a rape victim was attacked in a bar by a group of four men while she was unconscious. The men carried her to a booth, undressed her, and raped her. They confessed. The prosecutor let them plead guilty to a misdemeanor, and the men were set free by a justice of the peace, who fined them $750 and $90 in court costs. So little had changed over the years. But in this case women protested, marching and demanding further action, finally forcing the state attorney general to try to reopen the case.

It was also a rape case that led to one of my most tumultuous moments as DA, when I publicly challenged the actions of a judge and was subsequently reprimanded for it.

My struggles against the mistreatment of women and against

corrupt institutions converged for a brief explosive moment. In undertaking what I saw as a major battle to combat the demeaning treatment of women, the tables turned on me — I became the one accused of misconduct. It was one of the most trying events in my career.

The whole matter began when the chief of the sex crimes bureau, Barbara Newman, informed me about a courtroom incident that had occurred in a rape case. Barbara, an excellent bureau chief, had also served in my predecessor's office and subsequently became a criminal court judge. I often relied on her judgment, and with good reason.

Characteristically, Barbara was calm as she related what happened. She was always calm about difficult matters. I became increasingly upset as she described a misdemeanor rape case tried before a Brooklyn judge. During the trial, the judge — hearing the case without a jury — moved the proceedings into a small adjoining robing room. There the rape victim, a black woman, had to get on the floor on her hands and knees in a doglike position to demonstrate how she had been raped.

Barbara's account raised the whole problem of judicial mistreatment of rape victims. No rape victim should ever have to personally reenact the sexual abuse. Demonstrating the crime can be accomplished at trial with drawings, models, or, if a reenactment is absolutely necessary, by having someone else take the part of a victim. A demonstration of the rape by the victim was precisely the type of courtroom behavior I had been fighting for years.

The judge involved in this matter was Irving Levine, who had been a figure in Brooklyn machine politics for as long as I could remember. In his years on the bench, Levine's crude, vulgar comments had become legendary. He derisively referred to the Sex Crimes Bureau as the "Pussy Patrol." In another sexual misconduct case that Barbara described to me at the same time, the judge had publicly belittled an African-American witness by mocking her religion. Later Judge Levine was removed from the bench after an FBI wiretap picked up information about a meeting between Brooklyn's political boss, Meade Esposito, and him. Levine agreed to postpone a particular case at Esposito's request, although the judge lied about the conversation when questioned by the FBI. Levine was then found "not fit to hold judicial office," but at the time Barbara came to me he was very much a fixture in the Brooklyn courts.

The case in which the rape demonstration took place had been handled by a young prosecutor, Gary Farrell. Barbara and I discussed how he should have objected and stopped the rape demonstration. I asked Barbara to talk to him.

As for how to deal with the demeaning courtroom treatment of rape victims, I met with Bill Donnino, my chief assistant, and asked for his advice. Bill and I decided that I should make a formal complaint to the judicial disciplinary committee, which reviews judges' behavior. Even so, the judicial disciplinary committee had the power to take action only against the individual judge. I wanted to see this treatment of rape victims ended — in his courtroom and others. I decided I would also report it to the Task Force on the Status of Women in the Courts, which could recommend new guidelines or training programs for judges.

In order to proceed, my office decided to get a copy of the transcript of the proceeding at once, and in this my first obstacle arose. No transcript of the proceedings had been typed. Since Judge Levine had found the defendant not guilty, to obtain a copy of the transcript we had to file a motion, including with it a sworn statement from Gary describing what had occurred. The court granted our motion. We waited for the transcript.

In the meantime, the chief judge of the Brooklyn criminal court, Judge William Miller, had been informed of the rape demonstration in the courtroom. Judge Miller, I later learned, had received another complaint about Judge Levine. Some jurors had gone to Judge Miller when Judge Levine had belittled the African-American witness in court. Judge Miller had told the jurors to take their complaints back to Judge Levine, and when they did, Levine told them to withdraw from the case if they were so upset. After hearing about the rape demonstration in Gary's case, Judge Miller informed Bill Donnino that Judge Levine was going to take a short vacation and, upon return, he would be transferred to civil cases. This would resolve the problem, Judge Miller thought.

I didn't agree. I thought the matter was being shunted aside. As the elected district attorney, I felt a special responsibility to do something about it. Much stronger action was needed to send a message to the entire court system and the public about respecting the dignity of rape victims.

Getting the typed transcript, which had to be prepared by the court reporter in Judge Levine's courtroom, was stalled entirely. We not only couldn't get the transcript but couldn't get a date by which we could get it. I felt the matter needed immediate attention and sent off my letters to the judicial disciplinary commission and the task force, releasing the second letter publicly. Little did I know that releasing the letter would be one of the worst miscalculations I ever made. I later wished I had listened more closely to members of my top staff who thought it would be better to have the transcript in hand first. But when my special counsel, Barbara Underwood, told me that her research found no legal or ethical prohibition against the release, I went ahead, anticipating no problem.

The press initially reported on my complaint about the rape reenactment. Headlines bannered the judge's actions, and it seemed as though the attention focused on the mistreatment of rape victims might force some positive reform in the courts.

Suddenly, the sand began to shift beneath my feet. The defense lawyer in Gary's case held a press conference denying that any demonstration took place and that the judge had anything to do with it. He was joined by a union representative for one (but not all) of the court officers. They accused me of fabricating the incident, although no one attacked Gary, who first reported it. The onslaught against me simmered with nastiness. Questions about the mistreatment of rape victims were soon tossed to the background and barely mentioned again.

I checked my reading of the situation. Had Gary Farrell lied to Barbara? And lied in his sworn statement? If so, an injustice had been done to Judge Levine that needed to be corrected.

What, I wondered, had happened to the victim? Her description of the events could confirm whether Gary was telling the truth. Investigators went to her apartment and asked if she would come to the office, and she agreed. I asked Barbara Newman to question the woman and make the process as gentle as possible. I knew that I could rely on Barbara's sensitivity and personal commitment to victims. The victim took an oath, swearing that she would tell the truth, and, on videotape, Barbara discussed the incident with her.

Right from the start, the victim said she felt comfortable with Barbara and stated that she was not coerced into making a statement. The victim then described the event in the court robing room. She recalled being very upset about it. "I was crying," she said. "I was kind of tense, and I demonstrated from the very beginning to the end, I felt very dirty. I felt disgusted."

Afterward my top staff and I looked at the tape together. The victim's answers were simple, direct, and credible. After seeing the tape, we all relaxed: Gary had not lied. To reassure the public, we released the audio contents of the tape, withholding the video portion to protect the victim's confidentiality.

Within days, in a press conference, the victim appeared with a lawyer, who denounced me and my office. The taping was coerced, the lawyer said. The victim reaffirmed that she had been asked to do a demonstration but said that it had been ordered by the defense attorney, not the judge.

The tangle was becoming more twisted. Was politics behind this? How did this lawyer come to represent the victim — who had little money — so quickly? The lawyer, it was known, had close ties to the political machine in Queens. Every possibility ran through my mind. Meanwhile, the forces against me mounted.

The courts invoked a clause, rarely if ever used before, by which they could conduct an administrative investigation. Now the transcript was typed up, but I was refused a copy. The administrative proceeding was assigned to Judge Robert Keating, a former aide to my predecessor. In an unusual procedure, Judge Keating showed a part — but not all — of the transcript to the witnesses and then asked them to tell what happened. I wondered how Watergate would have turned out if we had done that. Gary described the courtroom events as he had before.

Portions of the original transcript were leaked to the press. It showed that the trial had been moved to the robing room, as Gary said. The witness clearly had been on her hands and knees there, as Gary had also said. The transcript showed Judge Levine saying "hold it." And here entered the next sharp swivel of the case. Judge Keating interpreted this "hold it" as meaning that the woman had voluntarily left the witness stand, moved to the small room with the judge and attorneys, and started to get down on the floor of the robing room like a dog to demonstrate the rape, and that the judge said "hold it" to stop her. I believed that "hold it" meant something quite different — that the judge, like a photographer, was asking her to "hold" the pose so that he could get a good look. Still, there was no denying that — one way or another — a rape victim suddenly ended up conducting a physical demonstration of her rape in front of the judge.

I didn't actually get to see the transcript for another year. And when I did, I discovered another portion in which the prosecutor, in his summation at the original trial, referred to the victim's rape demonstration, saying "she demonstrated for Your Honor." This statement further underscored Judge Levine's involvement in the rape demonstration.

Since Judge Keating declared that Judge Levine's "hold it" proved he had done nothing wrong, it appeared that no action would be taken against Levine. This was discouraging. Worse, before I knew it, I was accused of wrongdoing as an attorney by the attorney grievance committee of courts. A disciplinary action was initiated against me for criticizing the judge. I was now faced with yet another issue to fight.

In the meantime, the special prosecutor for the state — Charles Hynes — was asked to consider criminal charges against members of the district attorney's office. But the report came back clearing everyone. There was no basis for any charge of perjury or witness tampering against Gary or anyone in the DA's office, said the special prosecutor. And I felt slightly buoyed when a Brooklyn juror made a public statement criticizing Judge Levine for inappropriate remarks.

I next had to face the attorney grievance committee. Fellow lawyers tried to warn me that the judiciary would do what was necessary to protect itself. The matter was referred to the committee in Nassau County, a notoriously Republican county on Long Island with Alfonse D'Amato at its political helm.

The formal complaint stipulated that: I had falsely charged the judge with conducting a demonstration; I had mistreated the victim upon questioning her about the incident (this was later dropped); and I had slandered the judiciary by mentioning Judge Levine's other misconduct (this was also dropped).

At the grievance hearing, Gary testified again that the judge had directed the demonstration. Barbara Newman and other supervisors testified to Gary's credibility. Witnesses disclosed other offensive conduct by Judge Levine. The transcript, with its "hold it" comment by the judge, was presented. All the evidence showed that the demonstration had taken place. Judge Levine was never called by the grievance attorney, nor were the court officers, the court stenographer, or the defense counsel.

When the decision came out, the committee held against me. Its ruling was subsequently upheld. I had supporters on appeal: the Committee on Professional Responsibility of the City Bar Association and the New York Civil Liberties Union filed briefs on my behalf. They argued that the First Amendment protected me. A prior New York case upheld a lawyer's right to free speech even though he had called judges "whores who had become madams" in *Life* magazine.

My crime had been to publicly criticize a judge without being "certain." I had of course been certain. As I later followed the Clarence Thomas hearings, it clicked. When a woman accuses a male judge — as Anita Hill had and as I had — there could be hell to pay.

Harvard law professor Alan M. Dershowitz took up my cause, stating that we needed more criticisms of judges, not less. "The issue of how rape victims are treated in our courts is an extraordinarily important and controversial one. We need public debate about the issue," Dershowitz wrote.

The ruling of the grievance committee still stands. Criticism of judges by lawyers in New York State is virtually nonexistent now, even though it is lawyers who should be blowing the whistle on courtroom misbehavior. Perhaps a courageous state legislature or the courts themselves will someday act to overturn the ruling and open the courts to public scrutiny.

Lost in the accusations against me was the central issue to which I was trying to draw attention: the profoundly demeaning treatment of rape victims. But problems persisted with the mistreatment of women. In 1995, nearly a decade later, a New York

City judge required a teenage rape victim, testifying on the stand, to touch her breasts and demonstrate how the defendant had molested her. The papers reported the incident. The outraged mother of the victim made some noise, and the judge apologized. But no remedial response from the courts seemed likely. Nothing, it seemed, had been learned from the Levine incident.

Deep-seated biases make the problem of rape almost intractable. Ingrained attitudes especially affect rape cases when the parties are married, friends, or acquainted. Even ancient attitudes of property ownership enter into it. If a husband is considered to be the "master" of his wife, if a man considers a woman his "property," then woman are accorded no autonomy. In this view, if a husband wants sex with his wife (even when they are separated, in some cases), she has no right to say no; her body is his, and if she resists he has an absolute right to use necessary force to overcome her resistance. Many psychologists find that the emotional harm of rape by husbands or partners is even more severe than in stranger rapes, because the physical violation is compounded by an intimate personal betrayal.

When I came into the district attorney's office, it was still legal in New York for a husband to rape his wife. My office filed a brief to urge the abolition of the concept that husbands were free to rape their wives. No other prosecutors would join us. Finally, in a landmark decision, New York's court agreed with us that the marital rape exemption was unconstitutional. Not every state has followed that step.

Date rape (my office called this "acquaintance rape") also implies an ownership interest. One study of teenagers in Rhode Island showed that 50 percent of the boys believed that if a man spent $15 on his date, he could legitimately force sex upon her. The latest statistics show that about half of all rapes are committed by a friend or acquaintance of the victim, although these rapes are far less frequently reported than those by strangers.

Juries consistently put a special burden on victims of acquaintance rape. Every action of the woman is questioned; she should have known better, she should not have entered the man's car or apartment, she should have done this or that. Jury members carry trunks full of societal baggage about rape into the jury room, and this makes cases extremely difficult to win. One Brooklyn case involved a couple that had separated. As the woman went to pick up her possessions from her former boyfriend, he proceeded to tie her up and rape her. The jury convicted the boyfriend of tying the woman up but refused to convict him of rape, giving him in essence the right to force sex upon her. Overcoming the prejudices of jurors, which merely mirror those of society as a whole, continues to be one of the greatest challenges to prosecuting rape. If social attitudes are so dismissive of a woman's right to refuse to have sex, how then can the courts, or the police, or a district attorney's office change them?

Battering cases represent a similar problem. As prosecutors we were at the last stop, trying to undo years — even centuries — of social inculcation and intimidation of women. Rape reveals the negative attitudes of society toward women; battering shows how much those attitudes could be internalized by women.

When I became DA, the criminal justice system did not take battering cases seriously. Its view again mirrored social attitudes, which for years had accepted a husband's right to use force against his wife. In the 1980s standard police practice was to tell the husband to take a walk around the block and calm down. Prosecutors refused to prosecute, and judges would not sentence.

Worst of all was how the victims viewed their situation. After filing the complaint that launched the case, many hesitated to go forward with the prosecution, aware that society blamed the women for their predicament and repeatedly accused them of not extricating themselves from the violent marriage or relationship. At first I did too. As DA, I soon came to see that the situations of battered women were far more complicated than people imagined and not so easily resolved.

Many battered women had come to believe that battering was their fate, the price of a relationship that they could not live without. Some were reluctant to leave the relationship when children were involved or if they had no independent means of financial support. The battered women's syndrome, which accounts for a woman's remaining in a battering relationship, was finally acknowledged in psychology and in court.

On a more day-to-day basis prosecutors found it very difficult to convince battered women to let them proceed with their cases. We tried many solutions. In the 2,000 cases that came into the office each year our efforts were aimed at encouraging arrest and prosecution. We worked with the police, hired a domestic violence counselor, and helped victims move back to their homes after they had had to flee. With the Victims' Services Agency, we also established a program of court-ordered counseling for the abusing partner, called "Alternatives to Violence," to be used when the woman could not bring herself to prosecute. Through this program, we addressed some of the violence faced by battered women who remained in their relationships.

Ultimately, prosecutors could only offer half-measures. I don't think that society will ever overcome the problems of rape and battering until we can challenge the cultural images that reduce women to sex objects and that make men believe that the only way to legitimate themselves is through violence. We have a long way to go.

## CHILD VICTIMS

Nothing in my years as DA could chill me physically as much as the reports of incest and sexual abuse of children. Seeing the reports over and over again, at least one every day, I realized that they reflected something horrible in human nature. If adults could behave in such cruel ways to little children, then any evil was possible. (Wasn't this Fyodor Dostoyevsky's point in *Brothers Karamazov*?) As I reflected on the pervasive violence against children, I came to see how Auschwitz could happen.

The cases we saw involved fathers, live-in boyfriends, uncles, brothers, cousins, babysitters, teachers, day-care personnel, even psychologists. With rare exceptions, the abusers were men. In the vast majority of cases — but not always — the victims were girls. Child sexual abuse cut across racial, ethnic, and economic lines.

One case involved a twenty-seven-year-old man who was babysitting his two nieces, eight and four, in May 1983. He called the eight-year-old into the room and shooed away the younger child.

He then attacked and raped the eight-year-old, who struggled to get away. Another relative found him in the midst of the assault, stopped it, and called the police. Another case involved four men who, after breaking into an apartment to commit burglary, found a seven-year-old girl and her thirteen-year-old brother. The men sexually abused both children and then killed them. In a different case a foster couple took in two young children and then sexually abused them, using the children as objects in their own sexual relations. Another young girl survived nearly a dozen years of sexual abuse from her stepfather, resulting in a pregnancy and subsequent abortion.

The sexual exploitation of children profoundly concerned me throughout my career. In 1978 I drafted the first law passed by Congress to fight the producers of child pornography or the parents who allowed their children to appear in such pornography. This law enabled federal prosecutors to take vigorous steps, but as with rape legislation, my congressional work was distant and intellectual compared to the actual cases of children in Brooklyn who were abused, raped, and misused.

As DA, I met regularly with the sex crimes bureau. The prosecutors in the bureau cared for the children: they were the ones who saw them in person, heard their stories firsthand, knew their pain. How could we improve the ways that the criminal justice system handled the cases of abused children? I asked them.

I was searching for creative, practical ideas. Too often prosecutors, like other government officials — and indeed like so many of us — accept the status quo as inevitable.

Since I knew how to get laws passed, I worked with my staff to suggest legal reforms. We understood how frightening it was for a child to appear before the grand jury — nearly two dozen strangers — and describe the intimate and painful experience of sexual abuse. But there was no way to prosecute the child molester on a felony charge otherwise. Children were terrified, even though every effort was made to ease them into the grand jury process — showing them the room, letting them sit in the witness chair in advance. What if the children could be exempted from appearing in person before the grand jury? There was no doubt in my mind that children could be spared trauma if they were questioned in a comfortable setting with a psychologist and prosecutor present. The session could be videotaped and then shown to the grand jury. We drafted a bill and presented the idea to legislators and community groups. New York State passed it into law.

We applied the law as soon as we could. And it worked. The children had a much easier time, and the grand jury readily accepted the videotape of the child in place of live testimony. How well it worked was obvious when, in two separate cases, children said that they wanted to make their statements in person. Each marched bravely to the grand jury room. As the door opened to the room filled with unknown adults, in both cases, the child froze, unable to enter.

For victimized children, the trial could be another frightening experience. Children testified only a few feet from their assailant, which could be emotionally traumatizing. Our effort to help them in this situation was not easy. Under the Constitution, defendants have a right to confront their accusers. The solution we used for grand jury testimony wouldn't work at trial. Richard Laskey, a thoughtful, experienced prosecutor, began developing ideas based on programs in other states that had tried to protect child victims at trial.

We settled on a solution to serve the needs of the child and the Constitution: two-way video. The child would testify from a separate room. The defendant could see the child while the child was testifying via a television monitor. The child could also see the defendant on a monitor.

Richard acted as our lobbyist in Albany. If you wanted a bill passed, someone needed to go to the Capitol to cajole, plead, persuade, and make legislation happen. Richard was able to win the respect of the state legislators, even its prodefendant members. Richard was very effective. The two-way video proposal passed, and the U.S. Supreme Court later upheld our idea as constitutional.

I was very proud of the sex crimes prosecutors and the serious, compassionate, and reflective way they had worked on this proposal. The public rarely knows about the hard work, thought, and care that go into some — unfortunately, not all — government work. Our efforts, I knew, would make a difference in the lives of children.

With this encouraging start, the sex crimes bureau initiated in-house changes, too. A children's room was created in the office, with child-size furniture and kids' drawings on the walls. Anatomically correct dolls were brought in, and our staff got judges to agree not to wear their intimidating black robes in these cases. Microphones were installed in courtrooms so that the children wouldn't be constantly upbraided for speaking so softly. Our prosecutors also observed that children could testify better if their feet could touch the ground, instead of waving uncertainly in the air, so they arranged for a smaller witness chair.

There remained one very uncomfortable problem in child sexual abuse cases. In many situations the child would be reluctant to cooperate, or the mother might be dependent on the molester — often a boyfriend to the woman or stepfather to the child — and would pressure the child not to prosecute. In some cases the child would be frightened at the thought of having the relative or family friend jailed. And we knew that without the child's cooperation, we could not prosecute.

A strategy was needed for those situations. Lucy Friedman of the Victims' Services Agency, probably one of the finest organizations in New York, and I would meet from time to time to brainstorm. We agreed that a counseling program for the adult offender might be possible. We had already set up a program in Brooklyn to deal with cases in which battered victims declined to prosecute.

Our plan was that when the child would not testify because of concerns about jailing the abuser, we would seek to have the offender participate in a treatment program. If the abuser did not attend, the case could go back to court. The mother and the victim would also be offered treatment to begin recovery from the serious emotional damage. Lucy got special funding for a program from New York State.

As I puzzled over these cases of sexual abuse of children, I spoke to experts in an effort to understand them better. Statistics were hard to come by. Child sexual abuse must be one of the most underreported crimes. More cases were being reported, but it was difficult to know if child sexual abuse was on the increase or not. If abuse had grown, what accounted for it? Did changes in the structure of family and social life add to child sexual abuse? So many cases involved stepfathers or boyfriends of the mother. I could find no excuse, no real answer, nothing that would assuage the pain of these cases.

Lamentably, children in this country suffer other kinds of abuse as well: beating, battering, burning, whipping, every kind and degree of assault and violence. Unlike child sexual abuse, which is committed mostly by men against girls, in child beating the abusers are both women and men, and the children are both boys and girls. While drugs or alcohol or poverty often play a part in the lives of child abusers, gender is not a distinguishing factor.

We had cases that were unbearable — a drug-addicted woman who withheld food from her months-old son, starving him until he died; a mother who scalded and permanently disfigured her two-and-a-half-year-old daughter; a man who killed and dismembered a three-year-old while the mother stood by (she later reported it); a man who, angered at hearing his girlfriend's child cry, whipped the child to death.

One of the most difficult cases I had to deal with as district attorney involved an appalling case of child abuse. Even seasoned investigators called it one of the worst they had ever seen. Police were called to an apartment by neighbors who had heard screaming. Neighbors described children's screams, previous violent incidents, a mother and her boyfriend. At the apartment the police found a small girl, Jessica Cortez. Bruises covered her entire body, face, and head, and she had a broken arm and a fractured skull. Scars indicated that she had suffered severe beatings for months, and later medical examination showed extensive internal injuries. She had also been sexually abused. Shortly after police rushed her to the hospital, Jessica died. It was one week after Jessica's fifth birthday.

The boyfriend was arrested and charged with murder, and the police questioned the mother. Where was her son? He, the mother told investigators, was in Puerto Rico. My office began to look at the case against the mother. She said that she had beaten her daughter and was present during the fatal assault. Could she have intervened to save her daughter's life? Did her failure to do so mean she was responsible criminally for the child's death?

Relatives told stories about having reported abuse before, but getting no help from welfare officials. Neighbors too complained that they had called police often. Her abuse of yet a third child came to light. The authorities had removed the custody of her three-and-a-half-year-old son after she had taken his battered body to the hospital and abandoned him there. He had bruises on his face, arms, and legs, a broken rib, and cigarette burns on his face. The mother had been living with a different man at the time. There was also evidence that the mother had been hit and threatened by her current companion. We were still in the midst of resolving the complicated legal and moral questions about how to charge the mother when a new report came in.

A police officer had gone back to the apartment to search for other evidence twenty hours after Jessica had been removed. He opened a closet door. And there he found something that staggered even him: a nine-year-old boy. Cowering under a blanket, the boy was malnourished and traumatized; his legs had been broken, and he couldn't walk. He had been left to die, and the mother had lied about his whereabouts. We now charged her with murder just as we had her boyfriend. At this stage of the proceedings, we couldn't make public all the facts about the mother's history and the boy who had been left to die.

The facts were stark, and brutal. But the highly publicized trial in Manhattan, another jurisdiction, for the beating death of young Lisa Steinberg had an unexpected impact on the response to our Brooklyn case. Some women's groups badly misinterpreted and mischaracterized our case, demanding to know why the mother in Brooklyn was being charged with murder. In the Steinberg case the father had been charged with murder, but the mother, who had finally called the police and was severely battered herself, had not. The women's groups leapt to conclusions, claiming that our actions were anti-Latina and antiwoman.

Why were these groups responding so loudly and with so much misinformation? It eluded me.

Eventually the mother pleaded guilty in open court. All of the facts about the boy in the closet came out. The horrifying truth is that some women do harm to their children. My office had acted with justification. The groups that criticized me were well-intentioned, but they had failed to recognize that not everyone in government is the enemy.

As a society, we sometimes speak the words of concern but stop there. Are we in mass denial? Do we wish away the abuse of children by pretending that it is not as horrible as it is? Having seen up close the ugliness of incest and child sexual abuse, I could never turn away from such matters.

Later, as comptroller of New York City, I moved to stop sexually explicit programming or advertising on cable TV during hours when children were likely to watch. There were advertisements for a phone line that promoted sexual encounters with "daddy's little girl," making young girls into sexual objects for adult partners.

Since I was in the midst of signing off on a city cable franchise contract, I negotiated with the cable operators to keep sexually explicit materials from being broadcast during daytime or early evening hours. Protest arose, this time from a segment of the gay community. My support for gay and lesbian issues was hardly in doubt. I had the highest ratings from human rights groups on gay and lesbian issues, and I was one of the first signers on a federal gay civil rights bill. I had provided special training in the prosecutors' office for handling cases of violence against gays and lesbians, I had lobbied for antibias legislation, and I was the first public official in New York City to support domestic partnership legislation. The removal of sexually explicit ads would jeopardize the funding of their prime-time shows, complained a small number of gay activists. For me, the protection of children was more important. The matter eventually died quietly.

Later, when running for the Senate in New York in 1992, I raised a question about an opponent and child pornography. This time a real fury arose, not over the child pornography but over the fact that I had raised the issue. In a television advertisement I questioned why my opponent had failed to keep an earlier promise to evict a child pornographer — actually the biggest child pornographer in America — from commercially leased space in a building that my opponent's family rented out. The opponent was Gerry Ferraro. Before I knew it, I was under attack for raising this subject, especially against a woman.

To me, child pornography was not a free speech issue, and it was not simply a matter of a few dirty pictures or videos that people could look at in the privacy of their homes. Child pornography used little children, hurting their bodies. I was so thoroughly rebuked for bringing up the issue that my chances for election were killed, and the bad taste lingered long enough to rip apart my political career. And the plight of child victims got lost.

Rape, battering, child abuse, and incest represent an enormous challenge for our society. We must seriously address the way that we shape fundamental values about not only the behavior of women but that of men as well.

A comprehensive strategy must be developed to fight sexual violence, including sex-offender programs inside prisons and ongoing treatment for ex-offenders who have reentered society. But ultimately we will not end the violence against women unless the attitudes that demean women end, and ones that present a more humane notion of what defines a man emerge as well.

## CODA ON CRIME

In eight years as district attorney, I learned that upgrading law enforcement can reduce crime. New technologies make better use of police officers' time. Greater sensitivity to victims, such as women in rape cases, produces more convictions. Curbing police brutality and corruption pays off.

Improving law enforcement alone cannot ensure a crime-free society. We need to address other issues as well.

Jobs are at the top of the list. I saw this in an innovative program set up by my office. Offenders who had scrawled graffiti on subways were sentenced to the job of scrubbing the cars clean — hard and grimy work. About 7,000 young people were sentenced over the years. After finishing their sentences, more than half of the offenders asked for paying jobs cleaning up subway cars.

For me the lesson was clear — and poignant. Scrubbing subway cars was the first real work experience for many of these offenders. Although it was a court-imposed sentence and a menial task, the work gave them a sense of accomplishment otherwise absent in their lives. Once they experienced the feeling of personal worth, they wanted more of it. Without work, the young people had no goals, no expectations, little self-esteem — and got into trouble.

I tried to find permanent jobs for these youngsters, but with no success. The city government refused to do anything. As a society, we cannot write off young people. There must be jobs for them if we want to reduce the levels of crime.

If we want to reduce the deadliness of crime, we must ban the manufacture and distribution of handguns, except to police and military personnel. As DA I watched the urban landscape transformed by guns. Merely accidentally cutting off another car could get one shot. Teens blast away at one another on playgrounds; infants die in their cribs, hit by ricocheting bullets. Parts of our cities have become war zones.

Although the liberal-conservative debate seems to be over who is softer on the criminal, the debate should really be over who is softer on guns. There is something deep and troubling about America's romance with guns. From the militiaman facing reduced opportunity and status to the inner-city minority male, guns offer a sense of control and empowerment.

In most Western countries and Japan, almost no one carries a gun. But in this country, thanks to the overwhelming power of the National Rifle Association, guns are rampant, threatening police, government agents, everyone.

As New York City comptroller I proposed making gun manufacturers pay when innocent people were injured by illegal handguns. Gun manufacturers sell vast arsenals of handguns, aware that criminals will buy them and use them, and these arms makers are getting rich. If gun manufacturers had to pay for injuries arising from illegal gun use, they would no doubt take strenuous steps to ensure that the guns did not fall into the hands of criminals. The idea seems simple enough. Newspaper editorials and citizen groups have endorsed it. But the proposal still languishes, even as the toll from handgun violence continues to climb.

If we hope to reduce crime, we will also have to change the mindset that adulates physical violence. Crime in America flourishes because we have deeply ambivalent attitudes toward the criminal, who appeals to anarchic, outlaw-as-hero strains in our culture. Look at how the Mafia is glamorized, even though it kills and steals. We also must curb the media's advocacy of violence.

More prisons, police, and law enforcement alone will not solve the problem of crime. My years as DA have taught me that to be truly safe, we must instill values of respect for others in all of our people.

# 10

## Money

*I*N 1992, ABOUT HALFWAY INTO MY TERM as comptroller of New York City, the son-in-law of Mafia chieftain John Gotti, Carmine Agnello, reportedly threatened to kill me. Little did I know that becoming comptroller would put me in direct confrontation with the Mafia, the *New York Times*, the pollution lobby, and deep-seated ideas of gender propriety.

On the surface the position of district attorney would seem far more life-threatening than that of comptroller. But when I ran for the citywide position of comptroller after eight years of prosecuting criminals because I wanted to work on broader-based issues, I was soon confronting a different kind of cutthroat. When I was DA, most of the criminal defendants were poor; if convicted, they were sentenced to prison, parole, or a fine. The people I challenged as comptroller had lucrative city contracts, financial resources, connections, and apparently something more precious at stake — their wallets and bank accounts.

Agnello was furious when I objected to the city's awarding him contracts for towing illegally parked cars. Since he was paid for every car that he towed, the contracts were worth tens of thousands of dollars, possibly as much as $1 million. The comptroller's power to object stood as the sole check on the handing out of contracts by city agencies. Agnello had an interesting history, which made the decision to challenge his right to get city business fairly routine. In addition to lying to the city on multiple applications, he had fake driver's licenses, prior convictions for auto theft, and convictions for running an illegal chop shop. With that record, why should he have a city contract to tow cars? It was a clear and easy call. His lawyer grabbed headlines at Christmastime by telling the press I was a "scrooge." Workers for the tow company made a spectacle of it by circling the Municipal Building in Lower Manhattan in their trucks with big signs exclaiming how terrible I was to them. I thought I was impervious to charges from someone like the son-in-law of John Gotti, but I didn't appreciate the name calling — even from him. (Later, Agnello was arrested again when he allegedly ran over a police motorcycle after the police officer began ticketing vehicles around his shop.)

As comptroller I entered the world of city business with an eye for reform. But the city preferred business as usual, and it didn't really want to be reformed. Fighting corruption was a centerpiece of my campaign and one of my major goals as comptroller. In a way, it evolved from my years as district attorney and some of my work in Congress.

From my experience with the summer feeding program, I knew that corruption robbed the taxpayers as well as the people who were supposed to get services from the government programs. Every dollar stolen from the city by a crook was a dollar taken from a needy person.

My promise to fight corruption was well received by the voters. Interestingly, our polling showed that standing up against corruption especially struck home with African-Americans. Oddly, my campaign pledge against corruption drew the ire of a *New York Times* editorial writer, who opined that fighting corruption was for prosecutors, not the comptroller. Shouldn't every responsible elected official fight corruption? I wondered. Especially one of the officials most accountable for city finances and contracts?

The editorial writer must have been unaware that the new city charter placed anticorruption responsibilities in the hands of the comptroller. The mandate to the comptroller was to object to contracts if there was possible corruption in the "letting of the contract" or if the proposed contractor was "involved in corrupt activity."

I won many important victories, some that surprised even me.

Yet attempting to reform the system of government in New York City would ultimately lead to a disastrous political loss.

I had decided to run for comptroller because I longed to be more involved in the future of New York City. I thrived on New York's intellectual pull, the intense collection of artists, writers, and political commentators. New York's opera, theater, museums, and music inspired me. I had settled into a Civil War–era brownstone in downtown Brooklyn, with my own garden and a wonderful mix of Latino and yuppie neighbors. The area had no pretensions, which I liked. Yet it was close to a bookstore that stayed open late at night, a movie theater, and Middle Eastern food shops with enticing culinary selections. And of course New York was home to my family — my parents, Robbie and his three children, our many relatives — and other friends and colleagues.

Comptroller would be a different challenge, I thought, connecting financial policies and social policies, government budgets and individual human needs. Budget balancing tends to be associated with conservative ideologies. But numbers, I realized more and more, are at the heart of government. Pythagoras is in charge.

After winning the election in November 1989 at the same time as Mayor David Dinkins, I worked with a transition team to select a group of highly respected top managers for the comptroller's office. The office itself had nearly 1,000 employees in sixteen bureaus. Unfortunately, as an elected official, you rarely get credit for excellence in hiring. And more often than not, many politicians find it easier to employ "yes-sayers" or to put political cronies on the payroll than to seek out the exceptional.

The comptroller served as an independent watchdog on the sprawling operations of city government, with its 250,000 employees and responsibilities for police, schools, public hospitals, welfare, and more in all five boroughs. I was in a position to make policy recommendations on a vast canvas of issues that concerned me — women's rights, human rights, a cleaner environment, employment, programs to help the needy. The job reached way beyond mere number crunching; behind every government number was a human face.

But unlike the mayor's office, the comptroller had almost no ability to implement change. Much of the comptroller's job meant acting as a critic. How could I act creatively, get things done, in the midst of a stony bureaucratic system?

My first glimpses into the building where I was to spend the next four years were not heartening. In Washington, even though many of the government buildings were old, they were freshly maintained and spotless, with marble that shone. Even the Brooklyn Municipal Building, although more modest, was relatively clean.

But the central headquarters for city operations, the Municipal Building in Lower Manhattan, was a Taj Mahal of squalor. The rooms used by our transition team hadn't been painted in twenty years. The floors were covered with brown cracked linoleum or carpeting so dirty, ripped, and smelly that nothing could clean it — that is, if anyone had tried. You couldn't use the bathroom without recoiling at the filth and worrying about security. The women's bathroom always had a line, especially since at least one of the facilities was perennially out of commission.

Assessing the offices gave me a sinking feeling about the city government's ability to manage. And in fact the building was a kind of paradigm of what I was later to encounter. Thousands of city employees worked in the Municipal Building. If the city couldn't clean up its own house, how could it sustain suitable conditions for the rest of the people in the city? What did this mean about the city unions? How could they let city employees work in such awful conditions? I never discovered the answer, although I did raise the issue of the working conditions with a prominent labor leader, to no apparent effect.

I soon detected a typical attitude inside city government. It went like this. Change — any change — is bad. From a bureaucratic point of view, doing something new takes courage. For example, at one point we received a complaint in the Citizen Action Center — an office I had established — about frustrating delays in getting photo identification cards from the welfare department. The caller described the chaos at the welfare office, how unkempt and unhealthy the facilities were. People stood in line for hours, some sick, others with children in tow. I visited the photo ID office. The caller was right. I found a system so antique that it could have been turned over to the historical society. Applicants for welfare crammed the facility. Applications were filled out in an interview with a case worker. If the applicant didn't speak English, as was true in many cases, a translator had to be summoned. More time was lost. The case workers made individual decisions about eligibility, and decisions were inconsistent. Staff members were still hand-typing welfare checks. Here again, the waits were unbelievable.

Computerization was an obvious solution. Errors would be reduced, and processing would gallop. Beneficiaries would be helped, and the city could save money on the administrative side. The applicant could input answers to standard questions, which would appear as prompts like those on an automatic teller machine. Information could be processed in multiple languages. The computer could do most of the calculation to determine eligibility. For example, persons could not qualify for welfare if they owned a car above a certain value. Welfare case workers were constantly looking up the value of used cars in blue books, a slow process that was prone to error. The computer could take care of it. We found a system in use in one California city that had great potential. Case workers could spend their time counseling the applicants and helping them become independent, instead of pushing paper.

The city's welfare department remained indifferent to our proposal. The department wanted to stick with the old bureaucratic system. Despite the nightmarish system, officials opposed computerization. They didn't want to make it too easy for people to get on welfare. Compassion for those in need was utterly lacking. I couldn't get the welfare department to see the benefits of a streamlined system with a reduced error rate. Their disdain for the applicants made everybody pay, taxpayers and beneficiaries alike, and worked to no one's advantage. If people were in need and entitled to welfare, why should the city sadistically make the process burdensome? If the city could save money by streamlining, why set up obstacles and moats like a fortress of times gone by?

It was the same old story: change was a threat, and any reason, no matter how irrational or inappropriate, would be used to stave it off. Agencies and people preferred to dig in their heels rather than take a step forward, or even wiggle their toes. Change required a strong manager with lots of backbone. Over and over, I confronted this problem as I tried to find my way through the confounding swamp of stasis in the city bureaucracy. What was the prevailing mindset in city government that had allowed this to fester? At times I discovered that the explanations lay in wasteful self-interest, corruption, or criminality of some kind. Other times the explanation was one of simple arrogance — a refusal to admit a mistake, a refusal to go along with an idea because it was someone else's, a refusal to budge.

The comptroller's job was singular — it dealt with money. But it was also completely ubiquitous; money affected every single aspect of government operations.

Money was given out when the city let contracts for goods and services. Money was estimated in budgets that we reviewed. Money affected whether children had immunizations, whether schools had books, whether X-ray machines in the city were inspected — all subjects analyzed in our audit and policy management review units. Money was invested by the city pension funds in over 2,000 corporations and other assets. Money was borrowed from investors when the city sold bonds.

Money could be saved; money could be invested; money could be multiplied. Or money could be wasted and stolen. My goal was to save money and put it to use for socially beneficial programs.

The city borrowed billions every year to repair roads, build new schools, and replace water and sewer pipes. New York City was the largest municipal issuer of bonds in the country — about $4 billion worth each year — and sometimes even eclipsed California, the largest state issuer of bonds. The city was suffering a serious budget crunch, and Darcy Bradbury, whom I had hired to oversee the city's bond operations, quickly persuaded me that city money could be saved by cutting interest costs on the bonds. The city's borrowing did not involve a liberal or conservative "take." Only professionalism and creativity counted.

We had the opportunity to innovate because there was no

bond bureaucracy, no group of civil servants with a stake in the old ways of doing things. We let people know we were interested in new approaches.

The ideas started rolling in one by one. What would make New York City bonds more attractive? How could we expand the base of buyers? Swiftly, we recognized that more varieties of bonds would help, such as variable-rate bonds and zero coupon bonds. Zero coupon bonds, for example, are a good deal for people saving up for a big future expense such as college education for their kids because the bonds can be purchased relatively inexpensively, and the interest accrues over the years. City officials had talked about these varieties of bonds for ages, but new state legislation was needed. Here was my specialty. We drafted legislation and got it passed. By March 1991 we had issued the first variable rate bonds, selling $50 million worth and saving the city $2.3 million in interest costs.

We tried almost any new idea that held promise, even selling city bonds to the Japanese payable in yen, making New York the first municipality in the country to make a public bond offering in Japan. The plan to sell Japanese bonds produced great excitement in Japan. Pitches to Japanese banks and insurance companies were scheduled. To show the city's backing, I was asked to go along with Darcy and one of her top assistants. The Japanese perhaps did not expect us, nor were we quite prepared for Japan. We made presentations in front of the business groups. The inevitably all-male audiences stared in seeming wonder at three women discussing bonds. One queasy night, each of us was stricken with the George Bush syndrome of stomach trouble. As the boss, I had to visit the Finance Ministry. Overcoming the obvious hazards, I managed to persevere without humiliating myself in public. The city sold $200 million of Japanese bonds, saving the city $3.8 million over the life of the bonds.

In total, we wound up saving the city about $1 billion through these innovative efforts. While this isn't the kind of work that gets a lot of public attention, I knew that saving money on bonds could mean saving other essential city programs — funding a senior citizens' center or buying hospital equipment. Toward the end of my term we generated millions of dollars of savings by redesigning a bond deal. I used the opportunity to persuade city hall to spend a portion of the savings on a health project.

Saving money also meant trying to staunch waste, and there the city was far more intractable. Bureaucrats threw government money away, even though the city faced extensive budget cutbacks and jobs were on the line. The Board of Education warehouse spent hundreds of thousands of dollars to install an alarm system that it never turned on. Anyone could simply drive away with supplies — and many undoubtedly did. The Human Resource Administration warehouse had the identical problem. It simply couldn't keep track of inventory. Attempts to identify and call for corrections of these practices got nowhere.

Vested interests also reached into the city's pocket and grabbed its wallet. School bus contracts — which added up to an expense of $500 million a year — had not been competitively bid for over ten years. The whole purpose of competitive bidding by government was to keep costs down. Our office estimated that, done correctly, the city could save $100 million a year if the monopolies were broken.

When the issue of the school bus contracts first arose, I was already familiar with some of the school bus companies, which I had encountered as DA. We had prosecuted several companies for bribing inspectors to overlook safety problems, an act of incredible indifference to the lives of our schoolkids.

No public officials really wanted to touch the school bus contracts. Despite the huge need for up-to-date textbooks (we found that some textbooks predated World War II) or computers, the bus contracts remained sacred. The ABCs were beyond me. Was it fear of labor violence? Fifteen years before, when the Board of Education had tried to institute competitive bidding, strikes and work stoppages erupted. The Board of Ed didn't want to face this again. Was it the fear of political fallout? The emotional nerve was undeniable and had been manipulated readily in the 1970s strike. One needed little imagination to envision the TV footage of schoolchildren standing at their corner, waiting for a bus that never came. Or was it that the lobbyist for the bus companies played tennis regularly with the mayor?

Whatever the reason, the school bus companies didn't take kindly to my driving their lucrative private deals out into the open air. With the aid of state legislation, we at least forced a formal study of the contracts, although I would have preferred a simple requirement of competitive bidding. When I ran for reelection, school bus companies mobilized, raising tens of thousands of dollars for my opponent. The move backfired slightly. Newly elected mayor Rudolph Giuliani engaged in a political struggle with the bus companies. The mayor got the companies to pare down their costs, although the system of noncompetitive bidding was left intact.

Wasteful spending did not depend on whether a project was run directly by the city or turned over to the "private" sector. Shortly after I took office, a massive water main break flooded the streets of Manhattan, flushing water into people's homes and destroying their property. I learned that nearly 600 water mains break in New York each year, some causing worse damage than others. I asked our engineers to go out and take a look. The city had an ongoing billion-dollar program to replace its hundred-year-old water pipe system. Instead of doing the work itself, the city had contracted it out to private companies. The pipes were being laid by a private company, and the monitoring was done by another private company. In the course of their investigation, our engineers discovered that the entire program was a disaster. The pipes were badly installed. Because the pipes were not laid on a uniform surface, they would settle over time. The effect of this neglect posed double danger for city residents. It created potholes on the road surface, perilous to every car that passed. And it created tremendous stress in the pipes' metal, which meant that they could readily break.

Here was a billion-dollar program literally going down the drain. If jobs were to be shifted to the private sector, the city had to have knowledgeable professionals develop specifications, monitor the project, and reject shoddy work. That wasn't happening. Our engineers prepared a report on the water main breaks, but the city ignored it. I was out of office in 1995, when subways had to be closed for two days because of another major water main break. I didn't have to think hard about what had happened. New York City government, I discovered, was extremely difficult to reform.

Nowhere did this become more apparent than in trying to put an end to the corrupt, wasteful, fraudulent, and outmoded system of contracting. New York City spent about $7 billion on contracts with private businesses for services and goods each year. There were 9,858 contracts in 1992.

Fighting corruption, however, meant taking an active stance — like saying no to John Gotti's son-in-law. In the natural world, vacuums are abhorred; in politics and government, vacuums are welcomed. The boat-rockers, the defiers, the challengers, and the shakers of the system may suddenly find the welcome mat missing from their doorstep.

I was no doubt naive in failing to understand how attacking corruption could turn me into a lightning rod. Or else I was simply oblivious, relying on my previous experiences as DA and in Congress, in which I had attacked corruption and survived without too much difficulty.

I wanted to find a coherent, systematic way to address corruption in New York City, so I asked Rhea Dignam to help formulate a plan. A superb lawyer with excellent analytical skills, Rhea could work longer hours than almost anyone I've ever known. The staff joked that she was known to take a fax machine with her when she went on vacation. I had total confidence in her.

Reforming the system of contracting in New York City was not a simple one-shot assignment, since contracting involved many technicalities and details. We wanted to professionalize and streamline the process. Many good companies shied away from doing business with the city because of the red tape, delays in payment, and the aura of corruption.

For me formally to object to corrupt contracts, the companies needed to be scrutinized with a knowing eye. Obviously, contractors seeking millions of dollars of business did not voluntarily proclaim that they gave bribes or offered kickbacks or were involved with organized crime or had a record of crimes and violations. While I never doubted that fighting corruption in city contracting served the public interest, I quickly found that doing so can boomerang.

As Rhea and I studied the question of corrupt contracts, we realized that in order to make conscientious objections, we needed solid information. Rhea created a special unit for investigations, a first. The unit would concentrate on uncovering and gathering information on troublesome contractors. We named the unit SPIN (Special Investigations).

The SPIN unit was unique. Like detectives, trained investigators went to work, trying to rip the lid off corruption and fraud. A hotline was set up so that people could call in with their tips. Hundreds of tips came in, from both people who worked for the city and the general public. SPIN investigators went out into the field, hustling through court files and scanning computer databases to track down the people who were stealing money from taxpayers.

All manner of nefarious activities were found. The variety and quantity of crooks, thieves, and con persons constantly amazed me. One business seeking a contract to sell the city asphalt actually owed the city $800,000 in back taxes. Another company looking for a contract to dispose of recyclable paper had been indicted in New Jersey for unlawful disposal of solid waste. The applicant for a $257 million contract to dispose of sludge (the residue of sewage treatment plants) had major problems in other states with its production process. Pressured by our questions, the company withdrew the contract.

After uncovering each of these problems, SPIN would painstakingly prepare a complete analysis. Rhea would review it and make suggestions to me. Should I object to the registration of the contract? SPIN's findings enabled me to object to a quarter of a billion dollars' worth of contracts. And we were only getting started.

Unfortunately, a major flaw existed in the design of the new city charter. Although I had the responsibility of objecting to corrupt contracts, the mayor had the power to overrule me. This was one of the many mistakes the charter revisers had made. Even though on the state level the New York State comptroller had unilateral power to overturn contracts, historically there had been too much distrust of the city comptroller's office to vest the same power in it. The drafters believed — at least, this is what they told me — that a mayor would face political consequences for overruling a comptroller's decision on a contract, and this would discourage a mayor from doing so lightly. But they were wrong. Unless the press makes a major ruckus about it and informs the public, there are no political consequences at all.

Frustratingly, Mayor Dinkins refused to uphold three-quarters of the objections I made to bad contracts, and the contracts were given out anyhow. In some ways I understood the mayor's reluctance. The contracts came to the comptroller only after being solicited and agreed upon by city agencies — essentially, the mayor's own subordinates. The political pressures on the mayor to approve contracts was great. And the price for objecting to key contracts could be severe. I learned that the hard way.

One of the contracts to which I objected — and here the mayor's office agreed with me — involved a request by the city Corrections Department for $270 million on an emergency basis to build 2,900 jail beds. Emergency contracts did not have the same rigorous bidding rules as regular contracts. Because emergency contracts could be abused, the city charter required that all of them be approved by my office. The city had given the Corrections Department an emergency contract the preceding year for jail beds. I asked David Eichenthal, an attorney dedicated to good government who had a tremendous grasp of the intricate web of government spending and policy, to find out what was going on. David's report showed that the Corrections Department had exaggerated; the so-called emergency was not so urgent. I rejected the emergency request. That, of course, resulted in the head of Corrections charging in the newspaper that I was setting free 4,000 inmates (somehow 1,100 more than the beds they claimed they needed.) Eventually, the Corrections Department reduced its request to a more reasonable 800 jail beds, and I approved that.

In the course of trying to understand the need for the emergency jail beds, David learned that the Department of General Services (DGS) was thinking of contracting with a major construction company (I'll just call it "Company A") to build them. When the contract came through, naming Company A, David, a no-stones-unturned researcher, had already checked it out.

Company A had connections to two of the major organized crime families in New York City — the Gambino and Genovese families. Fat Tony Salerno of the Genovese crime family and the

Genovese family's head had been owners in a concrete company with the owner of Company A. Organized crime was reaching into my life again. While I was DA, my office had prosecuted, together with the U.S. Justice Department, the so-called Commission case. The biggest anti-Mafia case ever brought to that point, it involved high-ranking members of New York's "five families" and charges of murder, extortion, bribery, racketeering, and loan-sharking. In organized crime cases, the landscape can be tricky. Organized crime leaders are especially good at "deniability" — trying to hide their involvement in illegal activities. Trials involving them usually have wall-size charts tracing the connections of one company to another.

Allegations of bid rigging surrounded the concrete industry in general. Later Company A's owner took on a different partner in a new concrete firm, this time a son-in-law of Paul Castellano, head of the Gambino family and the head of the Mafia in New York.

Rhea believed that this contract deserved an objection. I knew all about Castellano, of course, because he had been part of the Commission case. From Rhea's previous work in the U.S. attorney's office in New York, where most of the organized crime cases landed, she knew that the connections between the mob and business were difficult to prove in a criminal proceeding. The "beyond a reasonable doubt" standard was hard to meet. But this was a case, she said, that showed the connections. And involved here was a civil standard, not a criminal one. After listening, I agreed to her recommendation.

Devastating information about Company A continued to find its way into our office. Paul Castellano's personal interest in the concrete company that had been owned by Company A was underscored by the fact that Castellano had been taped by the FBI discussing it. Rhea believed that the wiretap conversation was particularly strong evidence. And since Company A's owner had denied any link in testimony, a question of veracity arose.

More information developed. The owner of Company A decided he would ease any worries by submitting to New York City a copy of a letter from the office of the New Jersey attorney general. The letter was meant to show us that New Jersey had cleared Company A of any organized crime connections. In it an extensive history of troubling concerns with Company A was laid out, but it ended with the line that the "investigation of Company A failed to show any negative information."

Company A had not counted on David to be so thorough. David was puzzled by the letter and called the office of the New Jersey attorney general. Given all these problems with Company A, David asked, why did you say that there was no negative information? The lawyer at the AG's office stated that the letter had not said that at all, and forwarded his office copy to David. That's when we learned that the letter had been altered. The "no negative information" comment referred to someone else altogether. The someone else had been whited out, and the name of Company A typed in. At once Company A's owner denied altering the letter, claiming that his lawyer had done it. Rhea believed that the false statement, even if made by the lawyer, could be attributed to Company A.

On this occasion the mayor's office agreed with my objection to giving city business to Company A. After an independent review, he ordered that the contract not be granted. Company A's owner immediately sued, throwing the matter into court. Instead of my staff, which was so familiar with the issues, the city was represented by the city's lawyers, the Corporation Counsel. Unfamiliar with the corruption provisions in the new charter and the tangled tentacles of organized crime, they floundered. My staff was nervous.

When the matter was heard in court, my staff reported back that the judge seemed as confused as the Corporation Counsel. This did not bode well. The judge's ruling was worse. She ruled against the city, not only a bad decision but a frustrating one as well.

Most upsetting to me was a gratuitous comment that the judge included in the opinion, singling me out and assailing me personally. As the head of an agency, I expected to take the flak. But the judge had declared that the decision to reject the contract was, in her opinion, anti-Italian, and she specifically accused me of being anti-Italian. My staff had worked so diligently to protect the people of the city; I was distressed that the judge cavalierly dismissed their efforts. Fortunately, other judges have refused to follow her decision.

The contract that may have exacted a steep price, however, didn't faze me when the SPIN unit rejected it in February 1993. The SPIN unit objected to a $1.34 million contract for replacing a library roof, awarded to a construction company called NAB. The head of the company had previously operated under a different business name and as such was being investigated by other agencies for a trail of problems and debts. The claims included unpaid state taxes and unpaid subcontractors. The company had also failed to disclose occupational safety violations in its city application. And the company was part of a joint venture on a proposed $20 million city contract with a second firm that, on its own, raised a host of problems. SPIN had questions about the second firm's connections to organized crime because of allegations that the head of the second firm may have made payoffs to an organized crime family. Upon inquiries by my staff, the second company decided to withdraw from several city contracts worth tens of millions of dollars, including the one involving the joint venture with NAB.

There was so little question about the right course of action to take on NAB that the SPIN unit objected to the contract without sending it to me for review. The staff followed the "rule of the easy case": whenever a situation fell squarely within the unit's guidelines, it was not necessary to bring it to my attention.

The head of NAB was not happy. He was also, according to a later report in the *Village Voice,* the son-in-law of the publisher of the *New York Times*. Naturally, none of us knew this. But then it didn't matter: it was the right decision.

Although the mayor had allowed the library contract to go through, the head of NAB was reportedly angered by our objection. He went on to raise substantial sums of money for my opponent when I ran for reelection later in the year. Coincidentally, I was the subject of a rather strenuous attack by the *Times* during my reelection bid in 1993, a short time after my office's contract objection.

This incident brought home a central point about corruption

and government. What is to be gained by an elected official who stands up to corruption? Wouldn't every person having an interest in one of the contracts I had rejected be keenly focused on getting me out of office? Some of those whose contracts were rejected by my office, including the owner of Company A, did in fact raise large amounts of money for my opponent. They helped defeat me. If there is a specific political price for standing up to corruption, how many political figures will risk their careers to do so? After I left the comptroller's office, the SPIN unit was largely dismantled, and the comptroller's office has reportedly challenged few, if any, contracts.

Nonetheless, our strong efforts brought some results. Because of the seriousness with which we scrutinized contracts and sought better bidders, many city agencies have raised their own screening standards. But government is not being "reinvented," and it won't be until corrupt influences are yanked out and kept out.

# 11

## Unleashing Change

$B$EFORE BECOMING COMPTROLLER, I had only a slight notion that buried in the dull world of pension funds was a cache of rich potential for a liberal. The funds were important, since they represented the retirement security for over 500,000 former and current city employees, including my mother. As a retired Hunter College professor, she received her pension check from a New York City fund. I wasn't going to do anything that would jeopardize the checks to beneficiaries.

But pension funds, I came to realize, could unleash some of the most far-reaching change in America and even across the world. They presented enormous creative opportunities, but they were — and still are — obscure to too many who could harness their power.

As I entered office, I became increasingly focused on the opportunities to work for social justice and corporate responsibility. The funds had money — $36 billion. Where and how should that money be invested? Could those investments produce a solid return and also achieve valuable societal goals?

To understand the potential impact of pension funds, I only had to look to Nelson Mandela. When Mandela was released from prison in South Africa and came to the United States, New York City opened its arms. A parade was held on lower Broadway. It was the modern version of the old-fashioned ticker tape parade — since ticker tape was no longer used on Wall Street, people threw confetti made from shredded computer printouts. Huge crowds converged to see Mandela as he rode down the street in a bullet-proof bubble. People of every age, accent, and color lined the streets. African-American parents held their children aloft so that they could have a look at him. Teenagers put on black, green, and red T-shirts with the image of Mandela.

When I stood on the tarmac among the officials assembled to greet Mandela as his plane touched down in New York City, I had a special mission. I told him that as a protest against apartheid the city pension funds had divested more than $600 million of their stocks from companies doing business in South Africa. This effort started before I became comptroller. The groundbreaking divestiture work of New York City became one of the critical pressures that helped to dismantle apartheid, and Mandela's presence underscored that. The white South African leaders simply could not afford to live without foreign investment. New York City's leadership had extended across continents.

If this effort worked in South Africa, I wondered, why couldn't it work elsewhere? Not only internationally but right here in the United States? As comptroller I sat as a trustee on the boards of four of the five pension funds, and my office was responsible for managing the assets of all the funds. Money talked, and half of the pension fund money was invested in corporate stock. Why couldn't that money speak up against bigotry? Against dangerous products like cigarettes — especially when marketed to children?

And what about the money that was not invested in stocks? We could use it to create jobs, to spur development, to encourage people to build affordable housing or help them open businesses. There was no mistaking that my paramount responsibility was to protect beneficiaries and to see that the funds earned the most they could. Even my mother insisted on that. But couldn't still more be done? I believed it could; we just had to figure out how.

I began to think more about how pension funds could finance socially valuable programs, like building housing in impoverished neighborhoods, while still getting a good financial return. Not many public or private pension funds had ventured in this direction.

New York City pension funds had already made some investments in affordable housing — and they had worked. Housing got built, and the funds were protected by state insurance or federal guarantees. If a homeowner or developer defaulted on the loan, the pension money was insured and safe. The pension funds set aside money specifically to develop projects in New York City. The programs were called "targeted investments." I decided that we should jump in and do much more targeting.

There were no existing agencies putting together programs like this. These investment programs weren't coming to us pre-packaged and premade, so why couldn't we design our own? I hired Tom Bettridge, a former vice president of Chase Manhattan Bank who had worked for years with community housing programs, to head up the new Targeted Investments Unit.

Tom's job was both conceptual and hands-on. He would identify vital housing or small-business development projects that were languishing for lack of investment. Then, working his way through complex regulations, he would mix and match the necessary ingredients until we had a program with safety nets for the funds *and* a blueprint for social progress. The trustees of pension funds were receptive — they were New Yorkers who wanted to help their community. Once a fund agreed, Tom went out and put all the pieces in place to kick a program off. Things began to happen.

HOME happened. HOME was a program begun under my predecessor to build new townhouses for moderate-income families. We strengthened and expanded it, and 1,000 new townhouses were built with a $100 million commitment from a pension fund. Before I left office, families had actually moved into some of the homes in Queens. In another targeted investment program designed to make decent affordable rentals available, I had the privilege of giving out the keys to the 20,000th rehabilitated apartment to a young Latino couple with two children. Their delight was infectious.

Neighborhood development happened. Striver's Plaza, one program, planned to renovate an entire block in Harlem, including grand old apartments, a landmark jazz spot, and retail storefront slots. Housing, tourism, and business opportunities were all going to be jump-started.

Business growth happened. The police pension fund was the first to commit to loans for small businesses by investing $50 million, guaranteed by the federal Small Business Administration. Perhaps the police knew better than anyone that small businesses were the engine of New York neighborhoods. Soon three men got a start-up loan to open a tool rental store on Staten Island. It was a great idea — they rented high-quality building tools to homeowners for do-it-yourself projects. Other business enterprises popped up, from a beauty salon in Brooklyn and a meat packager in the Bronx to a software retailer in Manhattan. At a time when jobs were being lost in New York, the pension funds were putting opportunities and paychecks in people's hands, without risking a dime.

More and more programs opened up in every borough, with every pension fund participating. By the time I left office, New York pension funds had committed nearly $1 billion to targeted investments and a half-dozen innovative housing and business programs. This was 2 percent or less of the funds' total assets, but what a boost for community investment so decimated by the economy and federal neglect.

Today $3 trillion is held in U.S. pension funds, the biggest pool of capital in the country. There is more money in pension funds than in banks and insurance companies put together. Imagine what this money could do. With intelligence, prudence, and compassion, it could help rebuild the country.

Unlocking the potential of pension funds also meant recognizing a startling fact: the funds were one of the nation's largest owners of corporate America. New York City funds owned stock in over 2,000 companies, adding up to tens of billions of dollars of investments.

Few individuals would ever invest so much money in a business and then forget about it. Good investors usually keep a close watch on the companies in which they invest. After all, stockholders are the real owners of the company. The company's chief executive officer works for the shareowners, and the board of directors is elected by them.

In the United States some of the major owners of stock are pension funds, known generically as "institutional investors." Institutional investors might be church pension funds, state employee pension funds, corporate pension funds, and so on. Their emergence as major players in the stock market came fast and furious. In

1970 institutional investors in the United States owned only 9 percent of the publicly traded equities; by 1990 they owned 40 percent. Soon they will own over half of America's companies.

But pension funds have been largely silent investors, idly sitting by. Some haven't appreciated their role as major investors, with enormous stakes in the future of the corporations in which they invested. I believed they should. If corporate managers took shortcuts or didn't act responsibly, the shareowners needed to speak up and object. Whether pollution or racism or ignoring the safety of a product, irresponsible actions ultimately hurt the corporation's bottom line and its image, and could cause irreparable damage to individuals and the community as a whole. I believed that shareowners had a duty to communicate with corporations in which they were invested, and to help them find responsible solutions.

Exxon, for example, had big troubles when I first came into the comptroller's office in 1990. Not long before, people from around the world watched the stomach-turning television images of the *Exxon Valdez* spewing tons of oil into the clean waters off Alaska. Birds drowned in Exxon's oil; dead fish were washed up on the shore in waves of blackened water; people stood by aghast, their livelihoods in fishing and related industries destroyed.

A New York City pension fund owned a huge chunk of Exxon — 3.3 million shares, valued at $169 million in 1990. The oil spill had created not only an environmental catastrophe but a corporate disaster as well. The cleanup, restoration, and litigation cut the earnings of Exxon shareowners' by $1.68 billion in one year. The company's image was in disarray.

New York City's harbor had its own version of the *Valdez*. Another Exxon tanker dumped large quantities of oil in New York's Arthur Kill in 1990. The oil damaged fragile wetlands areas. Although newly elected, I immediately asked my staff to seek money from Exxon to restore the wetlands. Environmentalists had explained to me that time was of the essence: a major reclamation project needed to begin immediately. My staff was upset that a settlement proposed by the city's chief lawyer shortchanged the city and would not provide enough money to repair environmental damage. As comptroller I had to approve any settlements by the city, and I let it be known that this one was not acceptable. The city's lawyer resisted renegotiating at first, but the city was able to secure an additional $1.1 million. The wetlands restoration turned out to be so successful that it has become a model for the nation.

But what was Exxon going to do to see that its careless acts stopped? Ultimately, the *Valdez* spill cost Exxon at least $10 billion. It might have been much cheaper for Exxon to build double hulls on its oil tankers and improve its training and screening of employees than to pay these enormous costs and lose public confidence. How was the company going to avoid more accidents, stop polluting, and ensure sound environmental management? And what about other oil companies?

People concerned about Exxon's environmental failures began to meet. In brainstorming about how to influence the companies to undertake sound environmental management, energy for shareowner activism mounted. A nonprofit group emerged called CERES — Coalition for Environmentally Sound Economies — and I agreed to serve as a member of the advisory committee.

CERES soon created a set of environmental principles, a kind of ten commandments of environmental responsibility. Originally known as the Valdez principles, they were basic, simply written guidelines for corporations to adopt and implement. For example, they called upon corporations to minimize pollution, reduce energy usage, reject health and safety risks to employees, communities, and consumers, and conduct a yearly environmental audit.

CERES wanted the city pension funds, as shareowners, to ask our corporate executives to agree to follow the Valdez principles. If the corporations refused, we would use our power as shareowners to take the issue to other stockholders for a vote at the annual meeting. The issue could be aired publicly. If our proxy resolution passed, the corporate leaders would be obliged to agree.

Exxon was first to be presented with the Valdez principles. I joined other representatives of institutional investors in a meeting with Lawrence Rawls, chair of Exxon, in spring 1990. We asked him to make a commitment to the environmental principles, to no avail. CERES approached other major oil companies — Occidental Oil, Champion. None would agree.

Then one New York City pension fund decided to file proxy resolutions. We weren't going to go away.

The clout of pension funds when they decided to push for proenvironmental action cannot be underestimated. If company executives know that their big institutional investors — ones with millions of dollars sunk into the company — will be standing up at annual meetings waving green proxies and raising earth-minded concerns, they ultimately will be forced to respond.

Our determination finally paid off when New York City funds negotiated an environmental agreement with Sun Oil in 1993, the first Fortune 500 company to endorse the Valdez principles.

With the model of the Valdez principles in mind, we used our corporate investments as a way to create a dialogue. Faced with a disturbing practice of anti-Catholic bigotry in hiring in Northern Ireland, I was quickly drawn to the possibilities of using our corporate ownership to champion antidiscrimination efforts, in this case, the McBride principles. The McBride principles called upon companies doing business in Northern Ireland to stop discriminating against Catholics.

I was attracted to the issue largely because of Seamus Naughton, a constituent in my district when I was first elected to Congress. Seamus was a wonderful young man with a brogue so thick that I needed to translate in my mind whenever he spoke. A member of the Northern Irish Civil Rights Association, he took it upon himself to educate me about the problems of Catholics in Northern Ireland. He opposed the violence of both the Catholic Irish Republican Army and the Protestant militants. But he passionately wanted to stop discrimination against Catholics in the north and to find a peaceful way to fight the oppressive majority rule. When he invited me to speak at a dinner in Brooklyn, I was drawn back to the poetry of William Butler Yeats, especially the haunting words of "Nineteen Hundred and Nineteen": "Now days are dragon-ridden, the nightmare/ Rides upon sleep: a drunken soldiery/ Can leave the mother, murdered at her door . . ." With lives still being taken in bombings and shootings, Yeats's words resonated. When I later became comptroller, I silently thanked

Seamus, whose nonviolent commitment I shared, for teaching me about the problems in Northern Ireland.

Local companies in Northern Ireland consistently refused to hire Catholics. Several large American companies, including a major car manufacturer, had set up operations there and blindly followed the local practice of discriminating against Catholics. There was no law against this, but I had no doubt that bigotry was bad for business. A company that discriminated in its hiring would ultimately suffer the consequences in terms of negative publicity, consumer boycotts, and violence. Bigotry translated into lost dollars and cents.

I saw how harsh life could be for those on the "wrong" side in Northern Ireland when I went there in 1990. I was riding in a car with Bernadette Devlin McAllister, known internationally for her courageous political work, when British soldiers forced us to pull over. Pointing rifles at us, they surrounded the vehicle and ordered us out. I tried explaining that I was an American on an official visit, but the officers gruffly demanded our identification and began questioning us. They had opened the trunk to get at our luggage when finally the commander relented and let us proceed. This type of harassment was constant for Catholics, I learned.

In the month or so before I took office, my predecessor had succeeded in getting one company to accept the McBride principles. We felt that we had a strong argument to make through our stock ownership in American companies operating in Northern Ireland. I asked the companies to reject discrimination voluntarily and to agree to the McBride principles. By the time I left the comptroller's office, two dozen companies had consented. Observers in Northern Ireland later informed us that our actions had helped reduce the levels of discrimination and paved the way for peace.

As shareowners, we were able to force action on religious discrimination of a different kind. A city pension fund owned shares in Baxter International, a major hospital supply company, which had sold its plant in Israel and announced a plan to open one in Syria.

On the surface this transaction seemed too similar to what occurred when companies agreed to abide by a boycott established by Arab nations. Under the boycott, companies owning plants in

Israel were not allowed to open a plant in an Arab country. This was extortion, and American firms were prohibited by an antiboycott law from participating. I was familiar with the law, since I had introduced the first bill on the subject in Congress, along with Judiciary Committee chair Peter Rodino. If Baxter were flouting the law, there would be a range of consequences — bad press and monetary penalties. But was it?

We contacted Baxter, asking for information, and got nowhere. We proposed a shareowner resolution. Although the resolution didn't win, it garnered a large vote. And it also drew attention to Baxter's actions.

Investigations were undertaken by the Illinois attorney general and the U.S. Commerce Department. Baxter, they found, was violating the antiboycott laws. Baxter dropped its plans to build the plant in Syria and agreed not to participate in the Arab boycott or to violate the U.S. law. As a result of our action, it is safe to say that other U.S. companies learned that they might face consequences if they participated in the boycott and were discouraged from doing so.

Our major battle with discrimination, however, came on home turf with a U.S. restaurant chain. One day my press secretary described a company that was firing its gay and lesbian employees. The company, Cracker Barrel Old Country Stores, was a southern restaurant chain in which the New York City pension funds owned thousands of shares.

Should I, as trustee, call this matter to the attention of the pension funds and suggest action? Although discrimination on the basis of sexual orientation was not illegal in most states, depriving people of employment because of their sexual orientation was wrong. Gay and lesbian individuals had a right to work and earn a living. The McBride principles provided a clear example of how we could use the powers of persuasion to end corporate discrimination.

Cracker Barrel had been particularly venomous in its actions. Managers at each restaurant were required to question employees about whether they were gay or lesbian or had anything other than a "normal" lifestyle. Any employee who said yes was fired. One woman named Cheryl, whom I later met, was a kitchen worker in a Cracker Barrel restaurant in Atlanta. She put in long hours and had worked for the restaurant for eight years. She had been promoted along the way and was even training workers at other restaurants. Cheryl had never publicly discussed her sexual orientation. But when questioned by her managers, she told them that she was a lesbian. She was promptly fired.

I thought a bigoted employment policy would hurt the company and our investment in it. When polled, the vast majority of Americans didn't think people should lose their jobs for being gay or lesbian. By promoting a discriminatory employment policy, Cracker Barrel would lose customers and goodwill.

The mayor's representative and the board of the largest city pension fund agreed that we should act. We first tried a nonconfrontational approach and wrote to the president of Cracker Barrel, asking for a clarification of policy. His answer was vague and dismissive. We persisted. Would the company make a commitment against nondiscriminatory hiring? The answer was again unacceptable. We decided to propose a shareowner's resolution calling on the company to stop discriminating against gays and lesbians. The company refused to include the resolution in its proxy materials. We decided to ask the Securities and Exchange Commission (SEC) in Washington to order Cracker Barrel to include the resolution. This, I was convinced, was going to be a routine request to the SEC. I was wrong; the SEC refused. Firing gay and lesbian employees was an ordinary business decision, it contended; as such, no shareowner had a right to raise it at an annual meeting.

The issue was broader than gays and lesbians: it involved religious, racial, and gender discrimination. This was an extremely serious matter. Our whole program against anti-Catholic discrimination in Northern Ireland was in jeopardy.

I talked to our general counsel, Paula Chester. She was an experienced and astute securities lawyer. What, I asked, were our options? She recommended that we take on the SEC in court, saying that we had strong legal grounds. The pension fund board agreed. We sued the SEC.

The Cracker Barrel case was brought in the federal district court in New York and was assigned to Judge Kimba Wood. The judge ruled in our favor, writing an excellent opinion. The SEC refused to stop there and appealed. The initial SEC action was taken under the Bush administration; the appeal was made under the Clinton administration.

The Cracker Barrel case involved downright intentional discrimination. I kept thinking about the impact on Cheryl and other ordinary people. Shareowners should have a right to challenge corporate bigotry. Ultimately, this issue may have to be settled by the U.S. Supreme Court.

When the federal government sided with us, as in the case of the Arab boycott, we were successful; when it opposed us, as in Cracker Barrel, we were not. The SEC can help shareowners assert their rights, and by so doing create a healthy dialogue between the major owners of large corporate shares and the companies' management. But when it comes to bigotry in employment, the SEC has abdicated its responsibility.

Perhaps no issue was more critical from a shareowner perspective than those affecting health and welfare. Tobacco was one such issue. As a former smoker, I admit to being more intolerant of smoking than most. But it seemed to me that the long-term prospects of the tobacco manufacturers were shaky indeed. All that stood between these companies and bankruptcy was the slender thread of the law. Once jury verdicts held the companies liable for smokers' deaths, the damages would be staggering.

As shareowners, we had to decide how to vote on proxy resolutions submitted by other investors. One such resolution called on the tobacco companies to stop advertising that was targeted to young people. Should we support it? Our vote would carry substantial sway. We decided to support the resolution, prompting outraged calls from the tobacco companies. We stuck to our position.

Recent revelations suggest that tobacco companies have been even more devious than we thought. There is speculation that the companies knew how addictive nicotine was and manipulated their cigarettes in dangerous ways. Intentionally or not, cigarette manufacturers hooked the American people on death and are still doing so.

At that time I was not in favor of divesting our stocks in the tobacco companies. By maintaining ownership, we could have some influence over their policies. I have since begun to rethink that. In the case of South Africa divestiture worked. If I were comptroller today, I would fight to divest pension funds from ownership of tobacco stocks.

As time goes by, pension funds will own larger and larger percentages of the corporate world. The questions that we touched on will continue to multiply. What will be the role of funds vis-à-vis corporate governance and corporate policies such as employment discrimination and environmentalism? How will institutional investors respond? Are they simply going to sit back and do nothing, or will they take a more active position? Will they recognize that, for better or worse, they are long-term investors in major corporations? Will they understand the implications, and work to keep corporations on their toes?

With all the attacks on government, here is one way in which public pension funds — read, government — can become the innovator for the nation. The question is, Will those with the power continue down the path we charted?

# 12

## The Movement: Women's Issues

*A*N EARLY-MORNING CHILL PUSHED THE MEMORY OF SLEEP away as I stood in front of an abortion clinic in Buffalo, New York, in 1992. Linking arms with a hundred other people, mostly women, we prepared to defend the clinic. I looked across the street at the Operation Rescue forces massing. Their group was about a third of the size of ours. How many more would join them? How much violence would there be?

Just a few months earlier the antiabortion forces had won a big victory in Kansas, attracting thousands of supporters and shutting down an abortion clinic. Effectuating the Bush administration antiabortion policy, the federal government refused to protect the clinics from terrorists, and other government agencies did nothing. Operation Rescue had then targeted Buffalo, a largely blue-collar city with a sizable Catholic population and a very conservative mayor, for a similar effort. If Operation Rescue's efforts won there, abortion clinics everywhere would be at risk. Sharon Fawley, the savvy and gracious head of the Buffalo National Organization for Women (NOW), alerted activists.

The national women's groups understood the need to stand up to Operation Rescue. Weeks earlier I had seen the preparations. Ellie Smeal's Feminist Majority had begun training in a new tactic, clinic defense. I was always impressed with Ellie's deep strategic sense, and I called to praise her for these efforts. Ellie understood that prochoice women would have to put their bodies in front of the abortion clinics to keep the clinics open.

The issue of choice always hit me in a very personal way. Although I never needed an abortion, I knew it was just a matter of luck. When I was a young woman, abortions were illegal. A college friend was injured in a back-alley abortion. I remember what a risky, dangerous procedure it was, and how nervous women felt, putting themselves in the hands of an unknown doctor who might botch up the whole procedure.

Poor women resorted to self-aborting, endangering themselves even more. My brother, a neurosurgeon, did his training at Columbia Presbyterian Hospital, which was affiliated with Harlem Hospital. He described graphic moments in the emergency room when women writhing in pain were rushed in, desperate for help. They shared a look that my brother came to recognize. From trying to do abortions on themselves, many had horrible infections, sometimes even gangrene of the uterus. Often, he said, it was too late to save them.

Prochoice concerns had marked my first involvement with the women's movement. After Carol Bellamy and I became active in Brooklyn politics, we were asked by women's groups to submit an amicus or friend of the court brief challenging the law in New York State that made abortion illegal. I remember arguing that the ban on abortion violated the Thirteenth Amendment's prohibition against slavery. Antiabortion laws physically subjugated women, controlling what we could and could not do with our bodies.

Although abortion had been legalized for many years by 1992, I knew that if Operation Rescue could shut the clinics down by force, the right to choice would be hypothetical. No other elected officials were going to Buffalo, but I felt a special responsibility to stand at the side of the clinic defenders. The struggle was for every woman, including me.

On that morning in Buffalo the mood was oddly quiet. Operation Rescue couldn't attract a large crowd. On our side we chatted among ourselves, getting to know each other. Then a small contingent of Operation Rescue people broke away, crossed the street, and started toward us. We braced, making sure our arms and legs were firmly linked. We stood at the very edge of the curb, not willing to give one inch. The Operation Rescue people rushed up to us, thrusting their faces only inches away from ours. With a loud shout, one of their people slammed his body against our line, trying to break through it. The line held like steel. The training had worked. The police finally stepped in and arrested the assaultive man. The rest of the group slunk back across the street, and ultimately melted away.

We had stopped Operation Rescue. There had been no serious violence. I looked at the people who had stood their ground, and felt exultant. Ordinary people, women and a few men, took time from work and other obligations to protect the right to choice. Facing the antiabortion terrorists, I was just like everyone else, and it felt good to be a part of a larger effort for justice. That was what the women's movement was all about — working together to push back injustice, bit by bit, in whatever ways we could. Buffalo was a triumph for the women's movement.

When I first arrived in Congress in 1972, I hesitated to call myself a feminist. I didn't know exactly what feminism meant. Of course I believed in women's equality, but I didn't know much about actual discrimination and had even told a reporter during my 1972 campaign that I had never suffered from discrimination.

Although the House and Senate viewed my 1972 election with relative indifference, the tiny handful of congresswomen welcomed me warmly. They were interesting and unusual. Rep. Lindy Boggs, the gracious widow of former House majority leader Hale Boggs, used to say in her ladylike southern fashion that a woman had to be twice as good as a man to get elected. Barbara Jordan, a protégé of Lyndon Johnson, impressed me with her enormous dignity, oratorial skills, and keen political sense. Pat Schroeder, who was a year ahead of me at Harvard Law School, was extremely smart, liberal, and issue-oriented. A brilliant parliamentarian, Bella Abzug earned a national reputation for her energetic leadership. Shirley Chisholm, a spellbinding speaker, had been a candidate for the presidency, and Barbara Mikulski, inches shorter than me, always engaged me with her marvelous sense of humor.

Once in Congress, I began to hear more about women's issues. Learning about the experiences of other women, I began to make sense of some episodes in my life. When I saw women's protests, such as the one in New York City against McSorley's Old Ale House, which refused to serve women, I realized women didn't have to accept the exclusions. Looking back, I was chagrined that my college classmates and I had failed to speak out against our exclusion from Lamont, the undergraduate library at Harvard. When I heard stories about male professors who belittled women in colleges and professional institutions, it became clear for the first time that Harvard professor Barton Leach had humiliated women in my class with his "Ladies' Day" ordeals. I heard more about job discrimination, including the tough time many women law school graduates had getting jobs with Wall Street firms, and understood why I had been turned down, too. Most important, I recognized that I was not alone — thousands of women had had similar experiences.

The women's rights movement drew me into its fold quickly. I knew viscerally that gender discrimination had to change, and as a member of Congress I had to work to help bring down the walls of prejudice.

The Equal Rights Amendment (ERA) soon became an issue for me. It had figured in my campaign against Emanuel Celler because he had blocked it for years, and I had challenged him on it. Passage of the ERA was critical because the Constitution did not fully protect women from discrimination. While racial, religious, and ethnic discrimination were "highly suspect," gender discrimination was not. The ERA would rectify that, and by the mid to late 1970s, only three more states were needed for ratification.

Ellie Smeal, then the president of the National Organization for Women, came to my office in Washington and told me the grim reality of the ERA's prospects. She announced that the ERA was in serious trouble. The amendment would not be ratified in the allotted seven-year time period. And if women had to start all over again by getting approval from Congress and going back to the states, the ERA could be lost for a long time. I listened with a kind of disbelief.

Ellie had a plan to extend the deadline for ratification. Although this had never been done before, her lawyers had researched the issue, and Ellie handed me a thick legal memo. I thought she intended to ask my legal opinion, but she had something else in mind. "We want you to get extension legislation through Congress," she said.

I was flattered to be asked to take on this responsibility. I wanted to do everything I could to see the ERA through, but I held back before committing; I would do it only if I could be sure of the legal correctness. I promised to get back to her. After researching the law, I was able to agree with Ellie's lawyers that Congress had the power to extend the ratification deadline. I went to work on Ellie's brilliant rescue plan.

My first goal was to get the support of the House Judiciary Committee, which dealt with constitutional amendments. That turned out to be easy. I visited Barbara Jordan. She quickly gave her support and agreed to see Peter Rodino with me. If the two of us asked, it would be hard to turn us down. The approach worked. Rodino consented, and so did Speaker Tip O'Neill.

All the congresswomen supported the bill. Luckily, by this time, we had formed the Congresswoman's Caucus, an organization made up of all the women members of the House and Senate. Republican Peggy Heckler and I had started it to focus on women's issues. It seemed logical that if we combined our forces, meager though they were, we would be able to get much more accomplished. At first some congresswomen shied away from associating themselves publicly with a group on women's issues, but ultimately all joined. The ERA extension legislation was our first major test.

Sitting in the "ladies' lounge" off the House floor, the congresswomen orchestrated a strategy. Each of us would lobby our male colleagues personally. Together we read through the roster of House members and discussed who would be the best congresswoman to approach each of them. Armed with our list of names, we all fanned out to corner, to cajole, to persuade. Over the next few days, as I talked to those on my list, I could see the other women at work too, in committee rooms, in the hallways, on the House floor. Talking to our male colleagues, we were very persuasive.

Some colleagues said no or maybe. Ellie Smeal and I developed a strategy to deal with them. Particularly hard-core members were to be won over by grass-roots efforts, mobilizing local branches of the national groups. The congresswomen called a meeting of all the other groups that supported the extension legislation, including the American Association of University Women, NOW, and the League of Women Voters. The House members who hadn't committed themselves were divided up among us. We put all the names of House members on computer and began to track the results.

Our effort would have been relatively simple, except that right-wing forces mobilized against us. Phyllis Schlafly led the charge. When she testified at House hearings on the ERA extension, she ran through the litany of erroneous arguments and supposed ERA evils, insisting that the legislation would force unisex toilets on the country. A major goal of the foaming right-wing effort was to stop the women's rights movement. A few years later President Reagan became the first president in modern history to oppose the equal rights amendment.

Try as they might, Schlafly's forces couldn't succeed in Congress. We were inside the chambers, catching members as soon as the right wing talked to them, making sure that they were still on our side. The congresswomen were so committed that many of our male colleagues tried hard to be helpful.

When the day for the vote came, I knew we had a comfortable lead. I was calm and optimistic. But for a moment the thought crossed my mind that perhaps our male colleagues hadn't told us the truth. Was our head count wildly off base? When the final vote came, we saw that our work had paid off. The extension passed in the House and later the Senate. All the congresswomen were elated.

Sadly, our victory in Congress never translated into the ratification of the ERA. At the state level women were not as well organized, and Schlafly's right-wing forces picked up steam. The seven-year extension period went by without getting the three additional states to ratify, and the ERA is still not part of our constitution.

For the congresswomen, however, our effort on the ERA had other benefits. By strengthening our bonds, we laid the foundation for future work on women's rights. In the next years other initiatives were supported by the caucus, which continued with male and female members working together for important legislation for women.

The Congresswoman's Caucus had been so successful that as soon as I became comptroller in 1990, I decided to create a similar organization in New York. By bringing all the elected women in New York City together — council members, state representatives, congresswomen — we could fashion a more effective agenda on women's rights. Serious problems needed to be addressed. Pooling our resources was especially critical. New York State ranked thirty-fifth in the number of women elected to the state legislature and had no women in statewide elective office, and I was the only woman who held citywide elective office.

In the intervening years between my time in Congress and my election to the comptroller's office, I had been radicalized by my experiences as Brooklyn district attorney. In Congress I had quickly grasped the concerns about employment discrimination, constitutional equality, and the ways that women were hurt by the structure of pensions or social security. But as district attorney I saw the epidemic of violence against women that showed me the extreme view of women as unequal, as objects, as people of lower status and humanity. I knew that much needed to be done.

I couldn't get the New York caucus off the ground. Egos got in the way. One highly positioned woman refused to cooperate because it wasn't her idea. A city council member thought it threatened other things she was doing for women. What worked in Washington could not be done in New York City.

Despite my inability to get other elected women organized, women's issues continued to draw my attention as New York City comptroller. One had to do with unfair treatment of women employees of the city. Brenda Berkman, the city's first woman firefighter, contacted me about an incident that disturbed her greatly. I knew Brenda because her partner headed a community outreach program in the comptroller's office, and Brenda and I occasionally played tennis together in Brooklyn. A bright, scrappy woman who had been a lawyer, Brenda described from time to time the difficult situation of women in the New York Fire Department. At the time that Mayor Dinkins and I took office, there were over 10,000 firefighters, but only 16 of them were women and their numbers were declining. Not one single woman had been hired in the fire department for ten years; none had ever been promoted. Worse still, some male firefighters placed the women under intense and, in several instances, life-threatening pressure. They stuck garbage in the women's lockers, called them ugly names, and tampered with their lifesaving equipment.

What brought Brenda to the breaking point was an incident that occurred when she got her regular physical exam, a normal procedure required of every firefighter. The fire department doctor, a man, had not treated her like every firefighter. In the course of the exam, he began fondling Brenda's breasts.

Brenda immediately complained to the fire department about this utterly inappropriate behavior, but to no avail. Women's groups rallied to Brenda's side, demanding that the fire department do something, and so did I. The fire department did not budge.

The time for the fire department to start an investigation into a sexual harassment complaint was running out. Finally, twenty-four hours before the deadline, the fire department decided to look into the complaint. Its investigation found that Brenda's complaint was valid. As a penalty, the department proposed only that the doctor be allowed to resign. Angered by this cavalier response, Brenda sued the city, and years later she won a settlement.

Brenda's case raised deep concerns about the city's sexual harassment policies at approximately the same time that the Anita Hill–Clarence Thomas hearings in Washington were focusing national attention on sexual harassment in the federal government. After Anita Hill charged that Judge Clarence Thomas had sexually harassed her when she was his subordinate at the Equal Employment Opportunity Commission (EEOC), the country watched a rushed week of witnesses on television. I watched, too, impressed by Anita Hill's extraordinary composure and horrified by the senators' abusive treatment of her.

I identified with the problem that Anita Hill faced. When I was young I had attended an out-of-state conference. One of my employers, who also went, asked me to come up to his hotel room — to review documents. When I entered the room, the man grabbed me by the shoulders and pushed me down on the bed. He then threw himself on top of me. Somehow I pushed the man off and forced him away. About to leave the job, I made no issue of it in the office, nor did I mention it to anyone else. If he had been nominated to the U.S. Supreme Court, as Clarence Thomas was, it would have been difficult to carry Anita Hill's burden. I admired her for having the courage to speak out.

But I also focused on something else that affected Anita Hill's situation: the process. The Senate Judiciary Committee acted as though it did not want to find the truth. As head of the Brooklyn district attorney's huge office, I had dealt with several sexual harassment charges made by employees. It was obvious that a serious investigation had to be conducted. Witnesses had to be located, questioned, their stories checked out. Sexual harassment often falls into a pattern; the offender frequently torments other employees. Just as often, those employees hesitate to come forward. It takes time to identify them, to persuade them to talk, to get at the whole story.

The Senate committee had no intention of doing that. When first informed of Anita Hill's charges, it didn't even think they warranted any consideration. It took a public outcry to force the committee to hold hearings, at which point the committee made only perfunctory preparations.

When the hearing commenced, the Judiciary Committee turned it into a duel between Hill and Thomas rather than a search for the truth. About that time, I received a call about a former employee at the EEOC who wanted to tell me about her coworker's interactions with Clarence Thomas. I asked one of my most trusted aides, Liz Schroeder, who had once served as a congressional intern in my office and later became a lawyer working for me, to call the woman back and talk to her. Liz did. The woman had an explosive story to tell. While her friend was working in a commission field office, she met Thomas in his official capacity when he made visits to EEOC offices. Thomas had propositioned her, using explicit and vulgar language. She had felt abused by the experience. Other women in the office had experienced the same offensive treatment by Thomas, the friend said. After watching the Senate Judiciary Committee's treatment of Hill, the harassed woman refused to speak out publicly. She was thoroughly intimidated by what had happened to Anita Hill and didn't want to suffer retaliation. After having been slammed myself for criticizing a judge publicly, in the incident with Judge Irving Levine, I sympathized with the caller.

I discussed the call with Liz Schroeder. We decided, with the caller's permission, to notify the Senate Judiciary Committee. The woman's information about her coworker was critically important. If true, it could buttress Anita Hill's story and refute Clarence Thomas's sworn testimony. Liz called the Senate Judiciary Committee staff; she also called the offices of Senator Paul Simon and Chair Joseph Biden and informed them in detail of the story. The woman was never called to testify. I was struck by the fact that there were no women on the committee who might have a deeper understanding of the seriousness of sexual harassment.

My skepticism about Thomas's candor was borne out years later when two reporters published a book documenting other instances of sexual harassment by him. Congress's silence in the face of these revelations troubled me. Perhaps someday a courageous member of Congress will call for an investigation into these new allegations to determine whether Thomas, under oath, told the truth to the Senate. Perhaps some courageous prosecutor in Washington will ask to review the records. Perhaps Thomas himself will step down.

But those eventualities are unlikely. With the complicity of the Senate Judiciary Committee, President George Bush succeeded in selecting a mediocre judge whose sole qualification was his willingness to act as a hired gun for the right wing and to decimate equal employment opportunity laws for women and minorities while serving as the head of the agency that was supposed to uphold them. Even Richard Nixon had failed to get by with questionable nominees like Clement Haynsworth and Harold Carswell. The Senate protected the U.S. Supreme Court from them, but it didn't and wouldn't protect the court from the shame of Thomas.

After the Clarence Thomas hearings, I wondered how effectively employees in New York City government were being protected against sexual harassment. Did the city administration get it? Brenda's experience suggested that it might not. I decided to investigate and asked for the records of all city agencies on the subject, to see what claims of sexual harassment had been made and how the agencies handled them. The Dinkins administration turned to stone, refusing to cooperate. Even after a meeting with a deputy mayor who promised assistance, nothing happened. I kept the pressure on for more than a year and threatened to subpoena the city's personnel files.

Eventually one city agency, the Transportation Department, provided us with records. When examined, they revealed an awful history. The agency had consistently ignored employee claims of sexual harassment. In other cases it refused to punish the culprits. And worse still, when victims suffered retaliation for making complaints, the agency took no steps to protect them. In one of my last official acts as comptroller, my office issued a report detailing these problems and calling for change.

Standing alone, I couldn't get the city to pay attention to sexual harassment issues; it simply turned its back. Someday I hope the city's elected women will work together, putting personal agendas and party labels aside and joining their voices in unison to protect the women in New York City who have no power to change the circumstances of their lives.

One of the concerns that caught my attention had to do with the high incidence of breast cancer in New York City hospitals. *New York Newsday* published an article that described unsatisfactory treatment of poor women with breast cancer.

I read the article with interest. My great-aunt Pauline had died of breast cancer. She was a very political, very strong woman, and in her late eighties she was stricken with the disease. She rejected chemotherapy and decided to remain at home through the period of her illness. I visited her while she was sick — and felt a great loss at her death. Because of Aunt Pauline, breast cancer was not a remote threat to me — it stalked almost every family, and one in nine women died of it.

The *Newsday* article recounted the personal tales of women who suffered from breast cancer. I asked Tom Sanzillo, deputy director of my policy office, to find out more about what was really happening to poor women with breast cancer. Tom assigned the research to Barry Skura, a Ph.D. with a specialty in health policy.

Barry went through obscure medical reports, hospital analyses, and demographic charts. He analyzed the reports of breast cancer in city-owned hospitals.

Tom was agitated when he entered my office to discuss the findings. Barry's figures showed that poor women in New York City were dying of breast cancer at three times the national average. Although a greater number of affluent women were afflicted with breast cancer, a higher number of poor women died of it. Barry had taken several demographic maps and laid them over each other. One showed where poor people lived, one showed the incidence of breast cancer, and one showed the deaths from breast cancer. The maps made the point all too clearly: poverty and death from breast cancer were linked.

I shared Tom's feelings. But why were so many poor women generally dying of breast cancer? Tom explained that in many cases, survival from breast cancer is connected to early detection. But poor women couldn't get early diagnosis. And that could be traced, in part, to the fact that poor women relied on city-owned hospitals for health care, and most of those hospitals refused to do early detection tests.

Most city-owned hospitals permitted mammograms only if a doctor could feel a lump in the woman's breast. But by the time breast cancer can be felt, it has already gotten so big that it is more difficult to treat. For that reason the American Cancer Society recommended regular screening mammograms for women — in the absence of any palpable lump — to detect breast cancer at the earliest possible moment. That meant biannual mammograms for women over thirty-five and yearly mammograms for women over fifty or with a history of breast cancer in their family.

These guidelines were completely ignored by most of the city-owned hospitals. And because of that, poor women died needlessly at an extraordinary rate — 3,000 a year, well above the number of people killed by handguns in the entire state in the same time period. My office compiled all of the information we had gathered on breast cancer treatment in city-owned hospitals and released a public report.

My concerns did not stop there. As I dug further into the issue of breast cancer, I encountered more governmental indifference. On one occasion I checked out a whistle-blower's tip that came into our office about a city-run clinic in Brooklyn. The caller said that a $100,000 mammography machine at the clinic sat idle. I paid the clinic a personal visit. In the basement X-ray room sat a brand-new mammography machine in pristine splendor. In the year and a half that it had been owned by the city, it had never once been used. In the meantime women in this impoverished area of East New York were suffering from undetected cancer. After my visit to the clinic, the machine was put in service.

Once the word got out that I had taken on the subject of breast cancer, support groups and women's health advocates were eager to work with me and create a forum for advocacy on breast cancer. They provided me with more and more information each day. Barry checked it all out. There were more shock waves on a national level. Medicare, for example, would cover the cost of a mammogram for older women only every other year, even though the medical guidelines clearly called for yearly screenings. Also, almost all women's health advocates agreed that the death rate from breast cancer could be reduced if women, especially poor women, were reached with more information. The federal government had a program that provided money to target states for just this purpose. Amazingly, New York State — even though it ranked first or second highest in need — had consistently been turned down by the Republican-controlled executive branch. Instead of considering health, the grants were awarded to states with much lower need because of what seemed to be political favoritism. In this case favoritism equaled murder. Why was there not enough money to go around to all the states? Why was breast cancer a pork barrel project?

I knew that the only way of getting action on the governmental neglect of breast cancer depended on informing the public. When we issued our report on the mammography policy in city-owned hospitals, women reporters rallied, calling for change.

In this case, reform did occur. The head of the city-owned hospital system, Dr. Emilio Carrillo, conceded that the system handled breast cancer very poorly. His candor surprised me; so many other city officials I encountered responded to criticism of their agencies by hunkering down and denying the problems. Dr. Carrillo agreed that the policy in city-owned hospitals needed to change and said he would make sure it happened. He was as good as his word, assigning a woman on his staff to follow through. Screening mammograms began, saving countless women's lives. The hospitals even started a women's health hotline.

I spent one day working alongside the staff of the Kings County Hospital's breast center. Behind the scenes the doctor in charge of mammography, a truly dedicated physician, showed me how he read the mammograms. We talked about other things that were needed to improve the program. Out front, my volunteer work assignment was to help the staff with patient intake. There was a huge number of women — we were inundated. I felt good knowing that women patients in city-owned hospitals were finally getting screening mammograms.

Our breast cancer initiatives gathered tremendous support, and each effort bolstered the next. Toward the end of my term in office, an innovative bond sales program suggested by my staff saved the city millions of dollars. I had an idea. Health advocates had suggested that women's health clinics, especially in the city's poorest areas, could have great impact on the lives and welfare of women. I approached the mayor and asked him to allocate $3 million of the bond savings to this project. He agreed. Unfortunately, the women's health initiative was scrapped when a new mayor took office.

The years from 1972 to 1994 marked a deep growth in my awareness of women's issues. I have a much better understanding of the obstacles created by gender bias in our society, and I find that my awareness is still growing.

The progress that has been made for women resembles a light that exposes the cracks in the glass. When I was first elected to Congress in 1972, I thought I was at the front of a tidal wave that would sweep many women into office. I was wrong. The numbers, especially at the highest levels, are still pitifully small. Deeply held views about a woman's "proper" role have constrained women. I once thought it would be simple to eradicate gender bias. I believe now that this may be the most difficult bias of all to eliminate.

# 13

## The Environment

$I$'VE ALWAYS HAD A LOVE OF NATURE. Perhaps it started when my parents took my brother and me on trips through green New England summers, or when we spent long, lazy August days on the far reaches of Long Island. I treasured the many fishing trips in Sheepshead Bay with my father, who rented a small rowboat with an outboard motor for these occasions.

As an adult I biked through rural England; swam in the pristine, warm waters of the Caribbean; sailed my own little Sunfish in Peconic Bay; and rode horses through the countryside in France, Ireland, and across the Rockies. I loved cross-country skiing into the quiet of the winter woods. Nature always relaxed and refreshed me.

I grew up expecting a nurturing, clean environment. The half century of my life has wrought vast and, to me, painful and terrifying changes. Even the most remote stretches of Long Island waters are no longer uncontaminated. Some summers, mysterious blooms of mushroom-colored algae kill off the seafood. From a plane, the brown haze of air pollution can be seen hanging over all our larger cities. Flying from San Juan to one of Puerto Rico's outlying, unpopulated islands, I could actually watch the dreary stain of pollution beginning to spread across a green-watered strait. In the mid-1980s, on a riding trip in Wyoming, I looked for birds and other wildlife, but saw very little.

All of us feel the changes. Our waters are being fished out.

Various plant and animal species are disappearing. Rivers and streams are becoming increasingly contaminated, making bottled water a fact of life for more and more Americans. We all know that the chemicals we use are destroying the ozone layer and changing the earth's climate forever.

My parents' country home was located in a rural part of Long Island, nestled among potato farms. In the early 1980s we, along with our neighbors, discovered that the farmers had used a pesticide called Aldicarb (or Temik) to control insects that attacked potatoes. The trouble was Temik also attacks humans; it is in fact among the most dangerous chemicals to human health. It had leached down through the shallow, sandy soil into groundwater, poisoning it for many, many years. Realizing that the tap water we used for drinking and cooking could also kill us brought home how fragile our safety was, how precarious the environment.

As we have known for some time, our civilization is destroying the fabric of the world that sustains us and allows us to survive. When I read about the cutting down of the tropical rain forests in the Amazon, I have a visceral reaction. I find it harrowing. Like our bodies, the world's ecology is complex and interdependent — almost a miracle, which has taken billions of years to develop. Will we destroy it in just a matter of a few centuries? The forces of destruction are strong. Profits and selfishness prevail. The depredations to the environment proposed by right-wingers and others will leave our children a much-diminished world.

If we are to preserve life, it is up to each of us to act to protect the environment, just as I believe we must act to protect another human being in danger. Even a few who stand up can save many lives.

In the environmental movement there are many heroes. Lois Gibbs is one of them. In 1980 I made a trip to Love Canal that left an indelible impression. Hooker Chemical Company had used the canal in upstate New York as a dumping ground for many dangerous chemicals. Later, property was covered with landfill and a developer built a community of small homes. Birth defects appeared in children who lived there. Lois Gibbs, one of the residents, led a crusade for her neighborhood that, when I visited, was finally beginning to attract widespread attention. Largely because of her efforts, the homeowners were finally moved out and compensated, and Hooker Chemical was sued by the state.

Lois showed me around the neighborhood, speaking all the while about her children and others who had been affected by the chemicals. Her voice was quiet but laced with determination and grit. She took me to a set of hedges. It was the middle of summer, and there were only a few green leaves on them. The rest of the leaves were burned off by poisonous fumes in the air. If chemicals could do this to the leaves, what, I wondered, could they do to people?

Lois illustrated how one person could galvanize a community, alert it to environmental hazards, commandeer the attention of the national press, and bring about change. Her example has inspired many and prevents us from shrinking back from environmental efforts with the excuse, "But what can one person do?"

Throughout my years in public office, I saw that at every level of government opportunities exist to improve the environment. A creative public servant will find the pressure points to make a difference. We can never allow public officials to say that they've done all they can. Nor can we give way to the new Republican bullying that is making an effort to repeal the environmental laws and allow pollution to continue unabated.

When I was first elected to Congress in the 1970s, I felt a special responsibility toward the environment, even though we knew less then about environmental issues. The use of defoliants and napalm in Vietnam disturbed me. I worried about nuclear power plants. Dams were being built needlessly throughout the United States. Money for highway projects was plentiful, but little was available for mass transit. I knew that our throwaway society, pollution mentality, and tendency to negate and efface nature were damaging us.

In 1975 my impulse to preserve instead of destroy led me directly to Ocean Parkway, a street in Brooklyn designed by Frederick Law Olmsted. Stretching from Prospect Park, which Olmsted also designed and which many believe to be the most beautiful of his parks, to the Atlantic Ocean, this tree-lined boulevard had promenades along both sides. On one side was a bridle path; on the other, benches and a bicycle path. I grew up on Ocean Parkway, so it had a special resonance for me.

The city wanted to repave Ocean Parkway. Part of its plan was to narrow the promenades, tear down trees, and put up six-foot-high concrete barriers separating the main avenue of traffic from the promenades. I didn't want this plan, which would destroy one of the city's loveliest streets and cut down hundreds of trees. Wasn't anyone else concerned? I checked around. Few people seemed to know what was coming.

I met with the highway department and struck a deal. If the public wanted the barriers, they would go up; if not, they wouldn't. We agreed to notify the public and hold hearings on the planned alteration. The response was overwhelming. Like me, the public did not want the trees cut down. The highway department capitulated. In the process, I got the department to agree to plant new trees to replace those cut down and additional trees to complement them. More than 1,000 trees were planted, and the stately beauty of Ocean Parkway was preserved.

For very different reasons, I was suspicious about nuclear power plants. Although they were heralded as low-cost, low-risk wonders, I didn't believe there could be no risks from these behemoths. They were too much like nuclear weapons to make me feel comfortable about them.

Since Congress had to approve the regulatory scheme for licensing and inspecting nuclear power plants, I started to look closely at concerns about them. Unfortunately, the nuclear power industry dismissed safety and environmental criticisms — nothing to worry about. Their supporters sloughed off daily maintenance problems, which we later saw turn into disasters at Chernobyl in the Soviet Union and Three Mile Island in Pennsylvania. The plant at Indian Point, just a short distance north of Manhattan, was built on a geological fault, but we were told not to fret about that. And there wasn't a word uttered by their proponents about the problems of disposing of nuclear waste.

Again and again, members of Congress were advised that there were no problems. The federal government subsidized the nuclear power plants by providing insurance. Without that federal subsidy, the plants could not have been built or operated. Still, the cost estimates were vastly understated. The price for decontaminating the plants (which had an active life of only about forty years) was never incorporated. The price for safely disposing of the radioactive wastes was never mentioned.

The dangers of nuclear power were obscured. In the wake of the Three Mile Island crisis, I wanted to get more information out to the public, and I held hearings about New York's Indian Point plant that exposed fiscal and environmental problems. I introduced a bill to tighten safety at the plants, which made some headway. Despite the warnings nuclear power plants continued to be built for many more years, until their excessive costs and serious design flaws became impossible to ignore.

When I became DA in Brooklyn, I discovered a different outlet for my environmental concerns, even though on the surface a crime-fighting operation presented an unlikely home for them. Poisoning air and polluting water were not typical crimes like burglary or robbery. The office had no neat category for environmental crimes, nor much expertise with which to approach them.

But there *were* environmental crimes. Hazardous wastes of every type and dangerous description were dumped in lots and warehouses and waterways in Brooklyn. We found infectious medical waste, PCBs, asbestos, chemicals containing cyanide and arsenic, waste oil contaminated with dangerous chemicals. At first I established an environmental specialty to deal with these cases, and then, in late 1986, I set up a new bureau, the Environmental Crimes and Worksite Safety Bureau, unique in New York State and one of a very few nationwide.

The first environmental case came to my attention because a radio reporter whom I had known for years called me to say that hazardous waste might be stored in an abandoned factory in the Ridgewood section of Brooklyn. We sent investigators out to the site. They found a former electroplating plant with its outside doors unlocked. Inside were metal vats, uncovered, filled with dangerous chemicals. Less than a block away was an elementary school, and children walking to and from school took shortcuts through the abandoned property. We prosecuted the property owners — the first hazardous waste criminal prosecution in Brooklyn. The president was convicted and fined $100,000, and we made sure that one-third of the fine went to clean up the hazardous mess.

We uncovered other dangers. Infectious medical waste was discovered in an old open warehouse in the Gowanus section of Brooklyn — 1,400 bags of blood-soaked pads, syringes, and needles had been illegally dumped. Some of the bags held potentially contagious medical waste from hospital wards, including a jar that warned that any leakage should be reported at once to the Centers for Disease Control. We traced the garbage, and the company that dumped the trash and its president were indicted and convicted, the first such felony prosecution in the state. Afterward, however, in an act of judicial hostility to environmental prosecutions, the judge set aside the verdict, stating that the crimes had insufficient impact on Brooklyn to be charged there. Again and again I would see judges who were unwilling to enforce environment laws.

The 1,400 bags in Gowanus pointed to another serious problem. The laws were too weak to deter the illegal disposal of medical waste. Working along with major environmental groups, we urged the passage of new laws heightening the criminal penalties for the dumping of infectious medical waste, and requiring source labeling that would make it easier to trace the waste. After a summer in which the beaches in New York and New Jersey were littered with medical waste that had washed ashore, both the New York State legislature and the federal government passed laws to crack down on illegal dumping.

The most complicated challenge for our office came in the form of mercury. An enterprising journalist for a small newspaper had reported that a Brooklyn thermometer factory called Pymm exposed its workers to excessive levels of mercury. I read this article not long before I wandered with a friend into a photography exhibit in Manhattan. The work of the socially conscious photographers included images of Japanese fishermen who had been victims of mercury poisoning in a notorious incident in the late 1950s, when a large plant spewed mercury wastes into a bay in Japan. The fish became grossly contaminated, and the fishermen became poisoned from handling the fish and eating them. The photographs displayed the full horror of mercury poisoning. The fishermen were so disfigured that they could have been mistaken for bomb victims. As I looked at the photographs, I kept thinking about the workers in the Brooklyn plant.

Mercury is, obviously, an essential component in thermometers. Because of its potential hazards, strict occupational safety standards had been established for the handling of mercury. The federal agency charged with enforcing these standards, the Occupational Safety and Health Administration (OSHA), had inspected the Pymm factory and cited it for violations of federal safety laws on multiple occasions, dating back to 1972. But the agency had fallen flat on the job. The inspectors did little to enforce their own orders. Worse, they did not find the most flagrantly dangerous violations in the Pymm plant until 1985. Then a former worker who lived in the Williamsburg neighborhood of the Pymm plant approached an inspector and mentioned a "cellar operation."

The cellar was a hellhole that had previously been hidden from the inspectors. In a small basement room a recycling operation for broken thermometers was set up. Any thermometers damaged during manufacture were sent to the cellar in cardboard boxes. Boxes holding hundreds of broken thermometers were stored on the floor. The mercury leaked everywhere, leaving puddles on the floor and vapors in the air. The workers — who were given no protective clothing — gathered the broken thermometers by hand to insert them into a recycling machine that crushed the thermometers, letting the liquid mercury pour back into another vat. The room had neither windows nor natural ventilation of any kind, and the level of mercury exposure was very high.

Even short-term mercury exposure without protection can cause headaches, dizziness, fever, tremors, and lung tissue damage. Intensive exposure could result in memory loss, deterioration of the liver and kidneys, and brain damage. The effects of mercury poisoning have long been recognized, in one way or another. For example, mercury was used in making hats. The Mad Hatter in *Alice in Wonderland* was not a purely fictional creation; people in the hat trade were known for the madness that developed from mercury exposure. But the Pymm cellar was no Wonderland. One worker in the cellar operation had become permanently injured by his exposure to mercury. He had irreparable brain damage and could not even walk unassisted.

Pymm was one of the largest thermometer manufacturers in the country. The workers at the Pymm plant were mostly Latino, spoke little English, were not unionized, and had little or no concept of their rights. They were not the only victims: if mercury got on the clothes of the workers, they could carry it home and contaminate their children and spouses.

Criminal laws had rarely been used to prosecute an employer when an employee was injured or killed by toxic or dangerous chemicals on the job. Yet a serious and dangerous assault had occurred at the Pymm factory. Assault was defined in the law as causing intentional injury with a dangerous instrument. Here a man had been seriously injured because of his work around mercury. The employer in this case knew that mercury could cause serious harm unless proper safeguards were used, and had been notified in the past to clean up its act. Mercury, if misused, was every bit as harmful as a gun or a knife. I thought it fit within the definition of assault.

Another technical legal question needed to be addressed before our office could do anything. Since the federal government had passed federal worker safety laws, could a state be stopped from prosecuting? Sometimes federal laws preempted state laws, and if that were the case here, we could be prevented from bringing criminal charges, no matter how awful the actions of the company, and despite the fact that the Reagan administration was doing little to enforce the federal laws. We could find only one case in the country in which an employer had been charged with a state crime for a worker's injury, and it was on appeal. After research, we were convinced that federal law did not prevent a prosecution in Brooklyn in this case. And that is what I decided we must do.

In October 1986, after a year-long investigation, we presented a case against Pymm to the grand jury. We were joined in this effort by the office of the attorney general in New York State. We charged the two company owners, a foreman, and the corporate entity with assault with a toxic chemical and reckless endangerment of workers. It was a landmark indictment.

I felt a personal sense of mission about the Pymm case. Evan Wolfson was the lead lawyer. He was careful, very bright, and deeply committed. This case was not only about the Pymm company; winning would establish a principle that could protect other workers all over the country. It would send a message to callous employers who deliberately exposed workers to chemical dangers and all other hazards.

The Pymm case went to trial in 1987. The judge assigned to the case was antagonistic to the prosecution. He claimed that the existence of federal laws prevented us from prosecuting employers for criminal conduct related to worker safety. Even before the case went to the jury, the judge publicly announced that he would reverse a decision against Pymm, no matter what the jury did. The jury returned with a conviction — a remarkable victory. The judge wasted no time in following through on his threat, and did in fact overturn the conviction. We appealed. Higher courts sided with us. State criminal laws, the higher courts held, could still protect workers from environmental assaults, whether or not there were federal laws on the subject. We won: employers could not be shielded from criminal liability. The conviction against the thermometer company was reinstated, but the judge imposed a very light sentence. Even that was overturned on a new appeal because of an absurd technical error by the judge, who gave the jurors a copy of the indictment with their jury form, a move that the state's highest court found to be improper.

But the importance of the Pymm case could not be diminished. It set a precedent not only in New York but across the nation. In labor and environmental circles, the Pymm case was widely discussed, and employers began to understand that there could be a greater price than a civil fine if employee health were endangered.

Conservatives today are clawing away at environmental regulation and enforcement. If they succeed, and the federal government abandons workers, Pymm offers local jurisdictions an alternative way to fight environmental crimes. And the Pymm case stands as a warning that, left to their own devices, neither the marketplace nor employers will necessarily provide adequate protection for workers' safety.

My environmental activism rose to a new level when I became comptroller in 1990, and I began to take on a fight against incineration. A young boy named Vito symbolized the importance of this struggle. I met Vito at a proenvironment rally about two years into my term as comptroller, and we became friends. At the event, Vito explained to the crowd that his mother had died of lung cancer. Vito begged for the end of an incineration plan in his neighborhood. To emphasize his point he held up a gas mask, and after the rally he gave it to me. Vito seemed to understand something that city leaders could not: air quality and the rest of the environment are resources that can't be casually bargained away.

I became involved with the incineration issue after gathering representatives of virtually every environmental group in New York City shortly after I was first elected as comptroller. When we convened in the Municipal Building, I asked them to identify the most important environmental issue in the city. "Incinerators" was the immediate answer from nearly everyone.

I didn't know much about incinerators at the time, but I quickly learned that New York City had a massive plan to construct garbage-burning incinerators, including the creation of five new incinerators and the expansion of three old ones. This plan carried an expensive price tag, running into billions. The environmental groups informed me that no one had done serious analysis of the financial or environmental cost.

I was leery of incinerators largely because they had the earmarks of nuclear power plants — expensive and dangerous. My experience in government showed that the bigger the construction program, the more skeptical a person should be about it. Cost issues were clearly in the province of a comptroller. I readily agreed to take up the environmentalists' suggestion and to try to find out the truth about the incinerator program. We would study it, as a prominent New Yorker once said, "without fear or favor."

The questions were real. What were the actual costs of incinerators? Had the expenses in building and maintaining them or the expenditures for handling ash left after the trash burning been adequately considered? Did the incinerators emit any harmful pollution? Were there risks to the city's health or environment? Were there alternatives?

Proincineration attitudes, I soon learned, were pervasive inside city government. A steamroller quality existed — a "don't ask, don't tell" mentality, unquestioning of basic concerns. Needing solid facts from top policy analysts, I asked candidates applying to head my office of policy management about their position on incinerators. Incinerators were indispensable, a settled issue, most said. When I interviewed Bob Harris, a candidate with excellent academic and government credentials, I popped the incinerator question to him. He said he had an open mind. I felt I had an independent thinker, and hired him.

Bob was joined on the policy staff by Suzanne Mattei, a lawyer from Connecticut with an extensive background in environmental issues. The first report presented by Bob and the policy office, which came after many months of detailed research, was a scorching indictment of the incinerator program. It showed that incineration was much more expensive than the city had originally claimed. The city had underestimated building costs, had not considered operational expenses, had failed to anticipate future outlays. Bob's report, I thought, provided the concrete information that the city needed to make appropriate decisions. Not so, I soon found out.

At first the Sanitation Department, the city agency entwined in incineration, tried to ignore our financial analysis. The department finally conceded that the much greater costs we projected were correct but then announced that costs were only a small part of the equation. The real problem, Sanitation now said, was that there was no place else to put the garbage. The department was immovable on the subject, and Mayor Dinkins refused to support a moratorium on the construction of new incinerators, although he had promised otherwise when he ran for office.

I went back to the policy office. If costs alone were not convincing, what, if anything, were the health and environmental risks of incinerators? Now Bob and his staff immersed themselves in a thorough review of incinerator emissions. They found serious hazards. Incinerators generate huge amounts of lead, which can cause brain damage. Children are particularly susceptible to lead poisoning. Building more incinerators in five heavily populated areas and adding lead to the city's air seemed callous, at best. But there was more. Incinerators also spewed out a variety of cancer-causing chemicals and metals such as arsenic, cadmium, and mercury. Mercury immediately spun me back to the Pymm case. And the most controversial emission — dioxin — was being reanalyzed by the federal government because of claimed dangers. Later, the federal government announced that dioxin's perils were far greater than previously known; it could cause cancer, birth defects, and a break-down of the immune system.

I was extremely troubled by these conclusions. They showed that the city was deceiving the public about incinerators, covering up serious health threats. Did people in New York City really want to pay more for the privilege of having their health impaired by incinerators, especially when there were other ways to dispose of garbage? We presented this information publicly in a report called "Burn Baby Burn." Now, I thought, others in top positions in city government would have to be concerned.

I was wrong. The city spurned our health analysis. The incinerator plan was so entrenched that the city could not concede that incineration posed serious risks. Doing so would undoubtedly bring to a complete halt the whole incinerator program, something its promoters were unprepared to consider. Instead officials belittled our research, as well as that of others, while never producing any countervailing information. This ploy worked. A reporter for one major newspaper told us that he believed in incinerators, and his opinion shaped his reporting. He once asserted in a news story that most scientific experts believed incinerators were safe. This was not so. The same paper also published an editorial criticizing me, as comptroller, for being concerned about the costs or health risks of incineration. My challenge to incineration, the paper said, amounted to demagoguery.

I realized we wouldn't get anywhere unless we presented alternatives to incineration. I got the policy office going on this issue. One major solution, Bob showed in his next report, was recycling.

Recycling did not interest the city administration. New York City had practically abandoned any pretense at recycling. In that regard, trendy New York City was far behind the rest of the nation, where people sorted and bagged recyclables without great difficulty and even with pride. Former mayor Ed Koch had once said that New Yorkers would never recycle, as if we had no genes for it. The Dinkins administration was not much better on the subject: it had to be forced by a lawsuit and court order to implement even a modest recycling plan.

No alternatives to garbage burning had been tried. Unnecessary packaging added enormously to the tons of trash. Reduction of waste had worked elsewhere; it was a foreign concept in New York.

It became increasingly apparent that a key reason for the city's unwieldy incineration program was inertia. Since the 1930s, the Sanitation Department had been planning to build more garbage-burning facilities and couldn't bring itself to change, despite compelling new revelations. Newton's laws of physics were at work — an object at rest remains at rest unless outside force is applied. Once the city had an idea, it wasn't going to drop it on its own.

Pressure had to be applied. But in this case, even substantial pressure didn't seem to budge those in charge. What were the forces on the other side? I wondered.

Some of those forces were relatively easy to identify. Construction unions supported the incinerator program because it would provide jobs to union members. The business community was for incinerators. They didn't want "longhair" ideas such as recycling to guide city policy. How could Wall Street oppose a multi-billion-dollar construction program that offered more bonds to under-write? Everyone who would profit from big construction was behind the incinerator program. They didn't like opposition, and taking them on meant taking political risks. On the other hand, the business benefits of recycling or alternative approaches were not apparent. No one considered the consequences of more pollution for economic development and how difficult it would be to retain or attract business.

But no matter what problems we pointed out, the city deflected the issues. For example, after the Sanitation Department declared that there was no market for recycled products and no real purpose in recycling, Bob Harris's office explored the subject. We were able to report that markets could be created. As it turns out, newsprint — which the city used to give away — now commands substantial prices. By failing to focus on recycling, the city let many opportunities pass it by. Recycling industries were developed in New Jersey, for example, and New York actually lost job prospects.

Our criticisms of the incineration program, even though staunchly denied, had at least begun to cause some uneasiness. Jack Rudin, a prominent real estate developer in New York, contacted me. Jack, a very nice man who truly cared about the city, wanted to arrange a breakfast between Sanitation Commissioner Emily Lloyd and myself to see if we couldn't find some common ground. I liked his approach and agreed. When Commissioner Lloyd and I met, I found her to be smart and charming. For my part, I said that the important thing was not a matter of who won or lost in the debate about incinerators, but how we could protect the pocketbooks and health of New Yorkers. I was prepared to be proven wrong, if only her people could show us where we had erred in our analyses. We agreed to have our staffs meet and see what our differences really were. Several meetings took place. In the end the effort was futile. The Sanitation Department provided no evidence that we were wrong and would not shift a millimeter on incineration.

Despite the city's official stonewalling, it understood the truth behind our reports and knew very well the problems posed by incineration. We discovered this from our neighbors in New Jersey.

During the early days of our incinerator controversy, I noticed a newspaper item mentioning a lawsuit New York City had brought to stop the construction of an incinerator in Linden, New Jersey, across the Hudson River. Why was our city promoting incinerators in New York and yet trying to bring a halt to another state's incinerator across the river? Maybe the newspaper article had been mistaken. I asked the policy people to get copies of the legal papers. Incredibly, New York City was arguing that pollution from the New Jersey incinerator would harm New York residents. The city was taking my point of view on the other side of its harbor. This was one of the most remarkable examples of municipal doubletalk, a tale of two incinerators with a truly Dickensian twist.

Information about the suit, I believed, would finally expose the duplicity and irrationality of New York City's incinerator strategy. Again, I was too optimistic. After we held a press conference, the city disingenuously claimed that the New Jersey plant burned medical waste, which differed from the ordinary garbage that New York City incinerators would burn. This answer, however, glossed over the much more significant point. Although medical waste and garbage may not look alike or even smell alike, their chemical composition is very similar, and that meant that the products left and pollution emitted after burning would be similar, too. Obfuscation triumphed.

Nonetheless, our reports seemed to have some impact. Concerns about incineration were growing in the public at large and city council. When Mayor Dinkins went ahead and presented to city council a program for the construction of new incinerators, the plan was scaled back considerably. The administration gave up the idea of building incinerators in Queens and the Bronx. Still, the mayor wanted to burn 9,000 more tons of garbage each year. That meant building an incinerator in downtown Brooklyn at the Navy Yard and remodeling two other Brooklyn incinerators to increase their capacity. I recognized this strategy, too — divide and conquer. By concentrating all the incinerators in one borough, the mayor could persuade council members from other boroughs to support him. The council members whose districts were not affected would no longer fight him. Brooklyn members of the city council who opposed the incineration plan were largely isolated, joined only by a few Manhattan council members. The plan passed.

This was by no means the final scene. Finally the winds began to shift. An important success came in Bensonhurst, where I met Vito. Part of the city's plan was to modernize an incinerator in Bensonhurst so it could burn three times as much garbage as before. Bensonhurst, a mostly Italian community, was not known for its environmental activism. But when we alerted them, residents became concerned.

One of the big problems with the Bensonhurst incinerator had to do with the possible release of dioxin. The city kept no records of dioxin emissions, but it did have records of the temperatures at which the garbage was burned. Low burn temperatures strongly suggested the presence of dioxin, but the city refused to release records showing the burn temperatures until we threatened to issue subpoenas. When we did get them, the records suggested the release of dioxin into the air, a frightening conclusion.

We asked the city and state to study whether any incinerators were emitting dioxin. Both refused. As far as I could tell, no government agency wanted the public to know about the real health hazards of incinerators.

We continued to investigate. To our surprise, we found that

the Bensonhurst incinerator had in fact been tested for dioxin in November 1990. The dioxin releases had been dramatically higher than the state safety level permitted. The city knew the results but never told anybody. And the city continued to run the incinerator for another nine months, despite the certainty that it was damaging the health of people in the community. As it happened, the incinerator was closed down only because it broke.

The degree to which the government would support policies that harm the public health was astonishing. Do officials at the highest levels think, "I am not going to let them stop my program come what may"? Is it a power play? Are they afraid of admitting an error? Or are there financial interests at stake — promises of jobs or campaign contributions — that make rational decision making impossible?

The city planned to reactivate the Bensonhurst incinerator without doing an environmental impact statement. The incinerator was located next to a grammar school and a children's amusement park, the Nellie Bly Amusement Park. We argued that an environmental impact statement was necessary. The city balked, but the state called for a public hearing when the city applied for a state permit to begin construction.

The hearing was scheduled at a local junior high school in Bensonhurst. My staff, local politicians, and environmental and neighborhood groups got the word out to the community. When the hearing opened, the auditorium was jammed with more than 500 people, upset about the incinerator plans. A Vietnam vet dressed in camouflage uniform protested the potential release of dioxin: he had lived with it in Vietnam, and he didn't want to live with it in his neighborhood. Vito, then eleven, stood up to the entire city bureaucracy and described the dangers of incineration. And eventually Vito and the environment won. After I filed a lawsuit together with environmental groups, the city capitulated and agreed not to build in Bensonhurst unless it completed an environmental impact statement.

Activists were also becoming more vocal in other communities. In the Bronx people began to fight against environmental racism. Studies showed that incinerators were located more often in minority and economically distressed communities, placing the burden of health hazards on poor people or African-Americans and Latinos. Community groups in the Bronx brought a legal challenge to a private medical waste incinerator, and I joined with them. This incinerator too had been built without ever getting an environmental impact statement, but the community had not realized the danger until after the incinerator appeared on the scene.

Local opponents of the Navy Yard incinerator in Brooklyn kept up their opposition, too. One effort to block the incinerator originated with Revolutionary War maps, which showed that the incinerator would be located on top of the graves of American soldiers starved to death by the British. At the next rally at the Navy Yard, new faces joined in the anti-incinerator crowd, including members of the Daughters of the American Revolution (DAR) and the American Legion. Armed with this newly discovered information on the burial grounds, we asked the city to halt all further preparations for the Navy Yard incinerator until the historical issue could be investigated. The U.S. Interior Department did nothing, and the city refused.

Meanwhile another community grew increasingly vocal in its incinerator resistance. A strong Hasidic community in Williamsburg, a section of Brooklyn, rallied against the Navy Yard incinerator. Once, on a visit to the neighborhood, community leaders took me to a Hasidic girls' school. At the school I looked at rows and rows of young faces; there must have been 1,000 girls crammed into the cafeteria. As I walked outside, I realized that the new incinerator would be located virtually across the street. How coldhearted could the city be? (The Hasidim, I was convinced, would throw their bodies in front of a bulldozer before allowing the incinerator to be built.)

As much as any issue I had dealt with, the battle to stop incinerators showed just how difficult it was to change the course of a vested government policy. With facts and good organization, we made some inroads. The mammoth five-incinerator construction plan was reduced to one incinerator, the Navy Yard incinerator. But as a practical matter that is dead, too. Under mounting public pressure, a new administration agreed not to go forward without a new environmental impact statement, which would doom it anyhow. A new administration has postponed even that one. But the city administration still has done nothing to come up with a long-range waste disposal plan for the future, meaning that the crisis will continue to build, perhaps until rational planning becomes impossible.

The incinerator program has died down — not necessarily because the city administration acknowledged that incinerators were wrong but because communities made them politically unpopular. Is it possible that the interests behind incinerators have lost the day? I wouldn't count on it. Only the continuing activism of alert and vocal opposition will stave off those whose self-interest or financial gain would overlook the hazards posed to the public.

# 14

## Campaigning

*I*N MY CAREER I'VE RUN in some twelve political races, seven of them spirited, contested campaigns. I've won and I've lost. I'm not sure there is any formula for predicting the outcome. Nor am I sure our system serves the voters — or the candidates — well. The cost of campaigns puts liberals, women, racial minorities, young people, and nonestablishment candidates at a disadvantage. And rarely do voters get to hear the real issues discussed in a thoughtful way.

The Greeks had an instructive myth for people holding office. Hercules undertook to wrestle with Antaeus, whose mother was the earth goddess. As long as Antaeus kept his feet on the ground, he could not be beaten. As soon as Hercules lifted him up, he lost.

Keeping your feet on the ground is essential in politics. You can't lose contact with those who elected you. Complying with that dictum, however, is not always easy. Campaigning at its best connected me directly with people's concerns and needs. And in a diverse city like New York that also meant listening and learning how others talked, speaking their language in order to express my positions in ways that made sense.

I enjoyed going out and shaking hands in street campaigning. When I ran for DA in Brooklyn in 1981, I developed tennis elbow from shaking so many hands. Person-to-person, I could address problems, fully explain actions that might have been misinterpreted. I also learned about fresh issues. When I campaigned for district attorney, I heard so many complaints about auto theft that I understood how frustrated people felt about the lack of prosecution. Once elected, I started a new auto theft program.

Yet the pace of campaigns stretched me to the limits, emotionally and physically: the stress, the exhaustion, the stakes. I would be up at six in the morning to greet subway riders and get home well after midnight. Sometimes I felt as though everything depended on the outcome — my job, my reputation, my future. The slip of a tongue, a strategic move that might backfire, the possibility of making mistakes, infused every day with tension. There were days when I felt on display every moment. The press trailed me, asking about reactions to anything and everything, from the day's headlines to an opponent's attacks. Keeping calm involved more than the strength of Hercules. And then, of course, there were other times when I couldn't get the media's attention at all.

My family always supported my campaign efforts. My brother Robbie took special pleasure in helping. Charming and handsome, he especially hit it off in senior centers. Seniors delighted in meeting an available doctor who would answer their medical questions as well as discuss political issues. My father enthusiastically buttonholed everyone he met to line up votes. My mother, while less interested in active campaigning, gave me personal reassurance and often joined me for campaign announcements and other events.

Campaigning at its worst pulled me away from people and issues and forced me to spend too much time buried in fund-raising. For individuals without personal wealth, raising funds is essential to running for office. Conducting a low-budget campaign today is no longer possible, at least not in a major city like New York. When I ran for Congress in 1972, I was able to win the all-important primary with $36,000. Mailers were sent to Radcliffe alumnae and Harvard law classmates. Some of my brother's friends pitched in with donations. Helen Buttenweiser, an attorney who had helped me get my first job, also helped secure substantial contributions.

In 1972 we had no polling operation, no media advisor, no TV or radio advertising — I couldn't afford it. A serious campaign now calls for much more money. Polls cost about $20,000 apiece — and you can't have just one. You need one at the outset and then another as the campaign really heats up. Media advisers get a substantial up-front fee and a percentage of the cost of television commercials. Radio and TV advertising is critical and costly. When Nita Lowey ran for Congress in the Westchester suburbs of New York in 1994, her campaign cost more than $1 million.

I never enjoyed fund-raising. I found it difficult to ask others for financial support. Necessity forced me to learn how; not well enough, but I did it. Being a shy person didn't help. My fund-raising director would sit me down on a regular basis with the phone in front of me, and I would call hundreds of people. In political fund-raising, even the most genial conversation comes to the point at which one has to ask explicitly for a contribution. I wondered if the experience was as awkward for the person on the other end of the line as it was for me. I was relieved when potential contributors eased the path by asking me first if they could help.

Contributors sometimes felt free to offer comments on just about everything. I enjoyed feedback on the issues, but I remember how difficult it was to sit through one contributor's criticism of my clothes, laced with sartorial advice that would have made Seventh Avenue collapse.

Other contributors seemed to expect favors, although I can recall one exception. Bruce Ratner, a former commissioner of consumer affairs in New York City, became a successful developer. He supported me in my initial bid for comptroller and even raised money for my campaign. After I took office, I had to vote on a development project of Bruce's in the Rockaways. I considered Bruce to be a very responsible and thoughtful person, but in this case environmental questions arose about the development, and I ended up voting against it. Bruce was angry at my vote. But he still supported me and told a friend that it was important to have people in office who will vote against their contributors. Most contributors aren't as broad-minded.

Fund-raising did have some gratifying aspects. I always received hundreds, sometimes thousands, of small contributions from people of modest means. On more than one occasion I can remember contributors sending a single dollar bill and a note saying they wished they could send more. These sentiments touched me greatly.

A wealthy person who runs for office is much better off. While there are limits on how much an individual can give to someone else's campaign, under campaign finance rules, people can put as much personal wealth as they want into their own campaign. If people have bank accounts on tap, they can empty them to run for office. Raising money is much harder. The high cost of campaigns works against candidates who are independent thinkers and liberals, in particular. They can count on losing support from monied interests.

When I ran for the Senate in 1980, Larry Tisch, who later became the head of CBS, complained to me about my vote on capital gains. I did not support a cut in capital gains tax, which would have given a break on the taxation of investment income, especially important to wealthy people. From Tisch's perspective, his refusal to support me in the general election made sense.

And there is subtle pressure on candidates to conform to the thinking of actual or potential contributors. The need to spend so much time with wealthy individuals or heads of corporations gives a candidate great exposure to their concerns — and not enough time to hear about the needs of ordinary people. Candidates can wind up with a very distorted view of the world. This is not to say that someone running for office shouldn't understand the outlook of wealthy people or the needs of businesspersons. They should. But those concerns shouldn't dominate candidates' thinking.

Support from special interest groups can be just as troubling. Whenever a vote was scheduled in the House of Representatives, lobbyists lined the route to the chamber, clearing a narrow path up the steps of the Capitol. Running up to vote, I could hear the lobbyists cry out like birds of prey: You owe me this one, you owe me this one. Because no one supported me in my first campaign against Celler except friends, I felt that the special interests had no claim on me. No one could say, "I helped elect you, now you help me."

Campaign financing reform is critical if we are to correct some of the most glaring problems the country faces, such as the widening division between rich and poor and the shrinking of the middle class. If there is no alternative source of money for candidates, no relief from the need to raise huge amounts of money, the ultimate consequence is a government that skews its economic policies to the well-to-do.

By the time I ran for Senate in 1980, things had changed dramatically from my early congressional campaigns. I was now running in the second largest state in America, with approximately 18 million people to reach. We had teams of paid campaign advisers and pollsters.

I decided to run for the Senate even though I loved my work in the House. The biggest impetus for my decision came from serving on the House Budget Committee. There I saw the consequences of our country's obsession with the growth in the military budget, slighting domestic needs. As a senator I wanted to be a spokesperson for a different kind of priority that put people before weapons. So much had to be done: our educational system needed to be strengthened; our bridges, roads, and housing demanded attention; women's rights needed to be bolstered. I knew I could have much more power to work for these objectives in the Senate, and wanted to work in that arena.

I understood that the race would risk a lot, since I had to give up my House seat, which was safe. In the back of my mind a strange optimism took hold. Somehow, even if I did lose, things would work out anyway, I thought.

While the incumbent, Jacob Javits, had a record as a competent person of moderate views, I believed I could do a better job and advance a more liberal agenda. I spoke to an old college classmate, Linda Davidoff, with whom I had reconnected when she and I were both elected as state committeewomen in the early 1970s from our respective districts in New York. We shared a reform agenda and held many of the same political beliefs. I knew Linda to be very adept and totally trustworthy. She agreed to run my Senate campaign.

Besides me, the field in the Democratic primary included Bess Myerson, a former Miss America and consumer affairs commissioner of New York City under Mayor John Lindsay. John Lindsay himself entered the race, trying to make a political comeback after his disastrous 1972 bid for the presidency. He had the support of African-American political leadership. The fourth candidate, John

Santucci, had made his mark as a conservative district attorney from Queens. From the outset, my team felt the race was doable: Myerson's credentials were thin; Lindsay had limited support; and Santucci suffered from the light conservative turnout in a Democratic primary. I had the support of the most liberal elements in the state, the antiwar and human rights activists.

Linda organized a grass-roots effort for me all over the state. On the day of the presidential primary in the spring, she placed campaign workers at all the polling places to hand out flyers saying that I wasn't on the ballot that day but would be on it in September. We hitched our hopes to winning over people who were most likely to vote in the September Senate primary.

Myerson had tremendous support from the establishment, including the backing of many political heavyweights such as Governor Hugh Carey, Senator Patrick Moynihan, and Mayor Ed Koch. My media advisers developed a hard-hitting campaign that questioned Myerson's credentials. We focused on whether she had abandoned consumers to represent big business interests such as Nestlé, which was promoting a product in Third World countries that caused many infants to die.

From the start, the New York press covered my campaign harshly, something of a surprise because I had excellent relations with the Washington press corps. I admired the reporting of Woodward and Bernstein on Watergate and had gotten to know many reporters during the impeachment hearings.

My nonadversarial relationship with the Washington press corps stood me in good stead. When I went on one of my trips to observe conditions in Cambodian refugee camps, I managed to get quite a good snapshot of a wizened elderly Cambodian refugee, although I am not a practiced photographer. The Associated Press (AP) wanted to run it and put the photo out on the wires. Soon I had a phone call from Bob Woodward. "I've bailed you out of big trouble, Liz," he said. The Washington Post had decided to use the AP photo of the refugee woman, except, Woodward explained, the caption underneath read "Liz Holtzman in Cambodia." Bob had seen the proofs and, realizing that the old woman was misidentified as me, managed to stop the press run and make a correction.

Once I announced I was running for the Senate, the way I was treated in the press began to change. In an early article on the race, for the first time I read untruths about myself. When the *New York Times Magazine* did an article on the primary, the writer (a television reviewer) cracked that he couldn't imagine me in a low-cut evening gown. I actually thought I looked fine in all of my evening gowns, including the low-cut ones. But I wasn't walking down a runway, I was running for a seat in the U.S. Senate. And no one asked how Senator Moynihan or candidate D'Amato looked in a tuxedo.

During the last weeks of the primary, one of the major newspapers ran a photo almost every day of Bess Myerson, who was the media favorite. After my campaign complained, the paper began to be a little more evenhanded. But another paper used pictures of me that had my front teeth blacked out. After a while I could tell the slant of the story by the nature of the photo.

All the newspaper polls put Myerson ahead. We knew the polls weren't accurate because they measured all voters instead of just those expected to vote in the primary. Nevertheless, the results showing me behind had a ripple effect, denting my ability to do fund-raising. Few people like to contribute to perceived losers. A day or so before the primary, as I campaigned at night on the Brighton Beach boardwalk overlooking the Atlantic Ocean, campaign workers ran up to me with a *New York Post:* the latest poll put me ahead.

We rejoiced on the night of the primary. I won. Our spirits were doubly raised because we had the sense of a miracle. Few had thought I could succeed, and I had done so without a huge amount of campaign funding and extensive establishment endorsements. All of a sudden people I had never seen before appeared. When you win, everyone shows up telling you how hard they've been working on your campaign.

Alfonse D'Amato, a little-known supervisor of the town of Hempstead on Long Island, became my opponent. He won the Republican primary in a particularly ugly campaign, attacking Senator Javits for his poor health and his age.

At that point I was twenty points ahead in the general election polls. Things looked good. A surprise winner, I benefited from a halo effect. Anticipating that the general election would be tough, I took four days of vacation, flying to Bermuda. That was the first mistake.

Instead of resting, I should have been fund-raising. The day that D'Amato won the Republican primary, the Republican party gave him three-quarters of a million dollars, the maximum allotment under the law. The Democrats gave me about one-fifth that amount. We could never catch up to D'Amato on money. I had three strikes against me: being a woman, young, and liberal.

The campaign became muddier when Republican loser Senator Javits decided to run in the general election as a third party candidate on the Liberal party line. His fund-raising drew even more dollars away from me. We didn't have enough funds to get our commercials on television upstate for more than one or two days.

And there were the attacks against me. While I had served with Ed Koch in Congress, he never forgave me for not endorsing him when he ran for mayor in 1977. I had considered an endorsement until he made support for the death penalty the centerpiece of his campaign. I held back, although I never endorsed his opponent, Mario Cuomo, either.

There were times when I enjoyed Ed Koch enormously. He could be very funny. I remember one dinner during a Democratic mini-convention in Kansas City when he regaled Representative Ben Rosenthal from Queens and me with his hilarious stories and offbeat commentary. But I also saw a mean streak in him. He hated Bella Abzug, also a House member, and the two of them were often at each other's throats in New York caucus meetings, and sometimes on the House floor.

When I ran for Senate in 1980, Koch first campaigned with Myerson, churning out nasty personal barrages against me. He dredged up an inconsequential vote in the House on whether to restore citizenship to the Confederate leader Robert E. Lee. I had no animus against Lee, although the effort to undo history more than a hundred years later seemed silly, just as silly as making George Washington a five-star general posthumously, which Congress also felt moved to do. The Robert E. Lee vote, however, arose against the backdrop of the Vietnam War. I had several constituents whose sons were conscientious objectors and had left the United States rather than serve in the war. After the war, they were still not allowed home. One mother had sat in my office weeping. Congress had little compassion for the young men and their families. I took the floor of the House and pointed out that if we felt it important after a hundred years to reconcile ourselves to Lee, a man who took up arms against the United States, then we should reconcile ourselves to the conscientious objectors. I alone voted against the Lee citizenship bill.

Koch used this vote to ridicule me, claiming that I needlessly antagonized southern Democrats. This was not so. I continued to win support from southerners on a huge variety of legislative initiatives, ranging from changing rape laws to catching Nazi war criminals. I never regretted the Lee vote; I only regretted the distortion of it.

Koch pursued his vendetta even after I won the primary. He invited D'Amato into city hall. Then Koch told people to vote for Javits, a move that would clearly hurt my candidacy. Koch helped elect D'Amato in 1980 and has remained close to him ever since.

D'Amato attacked me for my positions against the military budget, accusing me of never having voted in favor of any money for the military. I had voted for budget resolutions with allocations for the military, but I had voted against all military authorization and appropriation bills. I tried refuting D'Amato — that was a mistake, since it put me on the defensive. I should have challenged him to explain his support for waste and fat in the military budget. My advisers wanted me to get into a tank to show I cared about the military. I refused, because the action didn't represent my beliefs accurately. Years later, presidential candidate Michael Dukakis made the opposite decision, put on a helmet, climbed into a tank, and simply looked foolish.

In 1980 the state Democratic party, led by Dominick Baranello, refused to help me. And other Democratic figures remained on the sidelines. Mario Cuomo, for example, made his endorsement on a weekend when there was little likelihood of press coverage, and then couldn't be found afterward to help. Senator Moynihan, on the other hand, actively campaigned for me, even though we did not see eye-to-eye on many issues.

I didn't have the support of the traditional backers of Democratic candidates, and that also hampered my race. Labor unions sat on the sidelines. The New York State teachers union waited until a day or two before the general election to endorse me. The AFL-CIO supported Javits. Since he couldn't possibly win, this amounted effectively to an endorsement of D'Amato.

The lack of evenhandedness in the press coverage continued. No major paper other than the *Village Voice* seriously investigated D'Amato's tenure as supervisor of the town of Hempstead. The *Voice* did an extraordinary job in detailing D'Amato's role in connection with the forced collection of 1 percent of county employees' salaries, money that was then funneled into Republican party coffers in Nassau County. The siphoning of money was no small matter. D'Amato's associate, Nassau County's Republican political boss Joe Margiotta, eventually went to jail on the charges. According to journalist Sydney H. Schanberg, D'Amato testified to a grand jury in 1975 that he knew nothing about the scheme, and several years later — after the statute of limitations on perjury had run out — admitted that he had known about the kickbacks.

As for critical national issues, the coverage was pitiful. The powerful *Times* endorsement went to no one. The consequences were clear — support by default for D'Amato. In 1986 the paper endorsed D'Amato enthusiastically when Mark Green ran against him, running what I dubbed the "ethics schmethics" editorial — in other words, don't bother us with concerns about D'Amato's ethics.

This occurred even though by that time D'Amato had testified as a character witness in a federal criminal trial for a racketeer with close ties to the Mafia. Through the years D'Amato has continued to pile up interesting conduct for a U.S. Senator. Executives of a defense contractor, Wedtech, testified that they gave D'Amato $30,000 in an illegal campaign contribution (D'Amato said he didn't know anything about it). According to Schanberg and another journalist, Joe Conason, a company called Unisys said it made illegal campaign contributions to D'Amato and that the senator's brother had lobbied for its $100 million defense contract, using D'Amato's stationery and office (again, D'Amato said he didn't know anything about it). The Senate ethics committee later criticized D'Amato for allowing his office to be misused.

My 1980 campaign never managed to go on the offensive against D'Amato. We had no coherent strategy. Yet even without a strategy or money, I would have won by a landslide had Javits not run as a third-party candidate. When the ballots were counted, I lost by 1 percent (45–44). Javits took 11 percent of the vote, and polls showed that most of that vote would have gone to me. I still might have had a victory if the Democratic presidential candidate Jimmy Carter, whose campaign began to collapse in connection with the Iranian hostage situation, hadn't done so badly. All in all, 1980 shaped into the year of Reagan and a bad year for Democrats. A number of incumbent senators across the nation lost by 1 percent of the vote, including Birch Bayh and Frank Church. Losing by 1 percent in a three-way race was not such a bad showing in the context of that election year.

One or two pundits complained that I lost the race because I wouldn't approach Javits and ask him to drop out. Whether he stayed in the race because of vanity or because, as some suggested, he thought he would be rewarded with a plum ambassadorship, we'll never know. He was smart enough to understand the consequences of his remaining in the race.

Around 1981 or so, after I lost the New York senatorial election, I found myself standing next to Jackie Kennedy Onassis at a political fund-raiser in New York City. I admired Eleanor Roosevelt as first lady, but I never exactly knew what to make of Jackie. As first lady, she seemed gracious but oddly distant from public issues. At the fund-raiser, she turned to me immediately. "I can never forgive Jacob Javits for what he did. I can't even hear his name without getting angry," she said, referring to the convention center in New York named after Javits. As we talked more, I realized how deeply she cared about political issues, and wished the public had more opportunities to see that side of her.

During the campaign everything is a jumble. Afterward, I always replay the decisions, good and bad. I recount the people and moments and try to analyze what went wrong and where. The 1980 race was a bad loss, and it hit me hard.

When I ran for district attorney in 1981, political sexism was a centerpiece of the campaign against me. The sexism was blatant, talking about how tough DAs had to be and implying that a "girl" couldn't handle the job.

When I first ran for Congress in 1972, there were those telling me that as a woman I had no business going to Congress, that I should stay at home and take care of my family.

After I was elected DA, I had an inkling that sexism continued to play a role in how the press covered me. The press was pugnacious on an almost daily basis. I couldn't help but notice, however, that there were no pounding attacks on my successor, even though many controversies arose.

When in 1989 I decided to run for comptroller, I hoped to work on broader issues again and had actually polled to see if I should run for mayor. Ed O'Malley, who came out of the Queens Democratic organization, was politically savvy and had terrific rapport with people of all backgrounds. Linda Davidoff dug deeply into issues, philosophy, and positions. The raw numbers on the poll for mayor were encouraging, but our pollster warned otherwise. He had been the pollster for Harold Washington, the first African-American mayor of Chicago. He told us there would be tremendous pressure for an African-American candidate to run — in this case, David Dinkins. The pressure would be irresistible, the pollster thought. At that time Dinkins, Manhattan borough president, had not announced his candidacy. If Dinkins got into the race, the pollster said, it would be impossible for me.

Comptroller Harrison Golden declared that he was running for mayor, and his position opened up. I knew I could do a good job as comptroller, particularly with my experience on the House Budget Committee. I could win if I preempted the field, Linda and Ed thought. We talked with Dick Morris, a campaign consultant who had worked on prior campaigns for me and subsequently became an advisor to Bill Clinton. Dick agreed. In mid-December 1989, *New York* magazine announced I was going to run.

As with many of my campaigns, it turned out much harder than it seemed at the outset. Campaigning and communicating to people, I discovered, was more difficult if they had no conception of the job I was running for. People knew what a DA did; they understood generally what a member of Congress or the Senate did; but most people had no idea what a comptroller did.

The early polls showed me way ahead in the Democratic primaries. The perception was that whoever won the primary would most likely win the election, since the Republicans had little foothold in New York City that year. The Democratic political organizations split among the candidates. The Manhattan and Brooklyn organizations supported me; the Queens organization went solidly for Alan Hevesi; Frank Macchiarola got the support of the Bronx and Staten Island. All the newspapers endorsed the other candidates. Ideologically, it made sense for the *Post* and the *Daily News*, with their conservative bents, to endorse one of my opponents. The *Times,* where Hevesi's brother worked as a reporter, dismissed my experience on the Budget Committee and endorsed Hevesi. The lack of newspaper support made my race tighter than I had expected, but I was glad to pull out a strong victory anyhow in the primary, and I skated through the general election.

Disappointingly, my own polling showed lack of enthusiasm for my candidacy in Manhattan's liberal community. Being a prosecutor for eight years had, no doubt, eroded my liberal image. My greatest support came from African-Americans, and I was immensely proud to have such favorable response from the African-American community. It was based, I felt, on my record of standing up against racial bias in jury selection, police brutality, and the demeaning treatment of an African-American rape victim. It was, however, possible, I reflected with Ed O'Malley, that the backing might be ephemeral. Had there been an African-American candidate, I might not have had the same depth of support. This prediction proved all too true when two years later I decided to run for the Senate again.

In 1992 Alfonse D'Amato was up for reelection to the U.S. Senate, and he looked vulnerable. The newspapers had finally begun to report on the scandals in which he had been involved.

Twelve years had passed since my prior Senate race. I felt even more qualified and seasoned. Working in government in New York City gave me a wealth of experience. As DA I had dealt in depth with crime and could bring a real sensitivity to that issue in the Senate. Serving as comptroller informed me with concrete knowledge about the problems of urban areas. I saw up close the consequences of the Reagan budget priorities, which D'Amato had supported with gusto. My city teetered on the edge of fiscal chaos.

The social problems had multiplied. The Clarence Thomas hearings pointed out with brutal clarity the consequences of an all-male judiciary committee. I was prepared to speak out for an urban agenda, a women's agenda, a human rights agenda. In challenging D'Amato, this time I planned to correct the mistakes I made the first time. But you really can't replay history.

There were three other Democratic candidates in the race: Bob Mrazek, a relatively unknown member of Congress from Long Island; Robert Abrams, the New York state attorney general; and Gerry Ferraro, a former member of Congress and vice presidential candidate on the ticket with Walter Mondale in 1984. Initially my standing looked good. Polls early in the year showed me as the strongest candidate to run against D'Amato. I stood substantially ahead of Ferraro and Abrams when matched against D'Amato. I felt optimistic, since I had never lost a Democratic primary. There is always a first, as it turned out.

Piece by piece, the race began to turn into one enormous political disaster. When Mrazek dropped out because of the House banking fiasco, Al Sharpton announced his candidacy. I had been counting on strong support in the African-American community. My campaign knew Sharpton spelled trouble, but polling showed him at only 3 percent of the total. Still, in retrospect, when Sharpton got in, I should have gotten out. In public life it's important to know when to say yes and when to say no. You can back out when you make a mistake, and it's preferable to cut your losses than persist. I unfortunately learned that lesson too late.

I knew I would be facing a tough opponent when Ferraro announced she was running for the 1992 Senate seat. As the first woman ever nominated for vice president on a major party ticket, Gerry had made an historic breakthrough. Millions of women admired that accomplishment. I did, as well, and had worked for the Mondale-Ferraro ticket. I knew that every barrier that fell for women served to open the way for other women. There had been discomfort in 1984 when disclosures about some of Ferraro's business connections and finances were made public. It hurt the ticket, putting Mondale on the defensive. By 1992 those memories had largely faded. People remembered the triumphant images of the nomination and her acceptance speech. Many believed she could win the Senate seat because she was so well known.

I had known Gerry in Congress. She was a friendly person. We sometimes rode the shuttle together back to New York, and we often joked about the bad advice I had given her when she thought about running for Congress. I had suggested that she should get some political experience first, going for a lesser office. Ferraro, who had many political connections in Queens, wisely ignored me, ran, and won. In Congress her politics were more conservative than mine. She supported the military budgets and the MX missile. Our records and experience differed significantly.

Since I had run in a previous primary in 1980 against a different high-profile woman, Bess Myerson, I failed to appreciate that there would be concern over two women running in a primary in 1992. Somehow the public, the press, or both found this very disconcerting, even though 1992 had been dubbed the "year of the woman."

Articles portrayed all the Democratic candidates as having the same views on issues, which was not true. By depicting all of us as different versions of the same candidate, the press made the campaign seem irrelevant. The media paid no attention to any issues. Erasing our political beliefs left the race in the territory of personality.

Gerry walked comfortably on that terrain. I had hoped to engage voters on the issues and the differing perspectives of the candidates. The summer before the September primary proved frustrating. Gerry canceled appearances in forum after forum — at least a dozen times, including several nontelevised debates in which her chair was left empty. The last time I remember seeing her discuss her positions in public was in May at a crowded Soho forum sponsored by WAC, the Women's Action Coalition. WAC, newly formed by women artists and others after the Anita Hill–Clarence Thomas hearings, had a brash and outspoken political agenda. The differences between Ferraro and me emerged clearly at the forum. Ferraro was questioned sharply on her belief in the death penalty, which I opposed, as well as on her lack of support for a key congressional measure on gay and lesbian rights, which I had sponsored. She was challenged for backing a watered-down health plan, while I described my proposals for universal health care, something that this audience strongly favored. After that Gerry would not attend any issues forums.

My campaign tried everything to get to the issues — circulating daily press releases on myriad subjects, from cutting the military budget to my legislative proposal for strengthening women's right to choice. We even put out an issues-oriented video on public access television. Nothing worked.

I knew from personal experience in 1980 how down and dirty D'Amato could be and how ruthless he would be against Ferraro. Little-publicized polls showed that Gerry would have an extremely tough time in a race against D'Amato. By midsummer D'Amato was already pushing ethical questions about Ferraro into the press.

Toward the end of the summer, the media campaigns of the candidates heated up. It was then that I ran an ad asking questions about the child pornographer who had rented space from Ferraro's family's business. The ad was a terrible miscalculation on a political level. I had failed to see how it would be perceived by the many people who felt warmly about Gerry. All of the campaigns in which I had participated, including the one with Bess Myerson, involved a back and forth on difficult issues. I was therefore surprised to be attacked in personal terms with claims that I had been unfair or that it was wrong for me as a woman to challenge another woman candidate.

The ad ran very briefly, and the points raised in it — taken from a *Village Voice* article — were never disputed or answered. Yet throughout the rest of the race, and for a seemingly endless time after it was over, people continued to jab at me for raising these points. And despite the obvious feelings of goodwill toward Gerry, Bob Abrams, when he publicized a report on Gerry's ethical violations from the House of Representatives, had not met with any level of animosity.

Perhaps in a different system, where the voters are exposed to a great deal of information about the candidates, it would be possible to run a totally positive campaign. Every campaign with which I am familiar involves candidates critiquing their opponents. I have always tried to present my own positive program for the office.

Clearly, women won't be able to compete equally in politics if they are expected to abide by some hidden rules of decorum that apply only to them.

Competition between women in politics seemed to make people uncomfortable in that "year of the woman." Women commonly compete in other fields, whether applying for promotion on a job or auditioning for an acting role, and I think that's a healthy sign. No one expected that Martina Navratilova should do anything but play her best when competing in tennis matches against her women opponents. Perhaps someday, when the stereotypes about women's behavior change, women in the political arena will be free to play with the same vigor, no matter who the opponent is.

Gerry and I both lost the primary. She was hurt by it, as was I. Bob Abrams took on D'Amato in the general election. With his $12 million war chest and no primary to worry about, D'Amato succeeded in making Abrams — whose record of integrity was impeccable and solid in sharp contrast to D'Amato's — look dishonest (D'Amato claimed that Abrams had been late on some property tax payment).

I regretted afterward not having dropped out after Al Sharpton entered. I ended up in terrible debt, having personally guaranteed a loan taken out by my campaign. I should have withdrawn when the odds made it seem unlikely for me to win.

If 1992 was the year of the woman, 1993, when I was up for reelection as comptroller, was the year to dump on women and minorities. Despite some lingering resentment about the Senate race, the comptroller's race seemed at first like an easy win. In the late spring, a few months before the September primary, a *New York Newsday* poll showed me with the highest favorability ratings of anyone running for office in the entire city of New York. No one could have predicted that four months later, I would lose the primary to a man so unknown that he used his invisibility during his years as a state assembly member as his campaign mantra: "Alan Who?" he would advertise.

My two opponents were Alan Hevesi, whom I defeated in 1989, and Herman Badillo, a perennial candidate. Neither had any great vision for the office; their only real idea was to attack me. Although

I had been excoriated just a year earlier for raising negative if truthful information against Ferraro, no one questioned their right to assail me with innuendo and falsehoods, which they did with great fervor.

The turnabout that squelched my campaign occurred in the spring of 1993, when the *New York Times* ran a prominent story that seemed to suggest I had shown favoritism to a bond seller. That was untrue. But the charge was a sensational one, and it was doubly harmful to me because it went to the soul of my reputation in public office — my integrity.

The article was about Fleet Securities, a firm that had sold bonds for the city for years and had recently been moved up on the list of sellers from category three to category two. Bond sellers commissioned by the city were grouped into three categories. The most important sellers were known as senior managers. Senior managers designed and managed the bond sales, sold the bonds to other sellers, and accepted liability if the sales fell short. They earned substantial fees for their work. The sellers in the second category, known as comanagers, made a commitment to the senior managers and the city to sell blocks of bonds. The city's bond sales were so large that many firms needed to be involved, and there were about two dozen comanagers. Sellers in the third category included a large number of bond firms from all over the country that sold city bonds on occasion, whenever the opportunity arose. Although the analogy is by no means exact, the top bond managers could be compared to the architects and financiers of a housing development who build the houses, then design sales campaigns and sell the homes to large brokers. The comanagers are like real estate firms that buy a block of homes or take on responsibility for managing the sale of a group of properties. The third category of bond sellers are comparable to independent brokers who are authorized to sell houses if they can, but are not under any obligation to do so.

I considered the selection of the top managers to be very important and worked with Darcy Bradbury, my deputy comptroller, and her staff to make sure that the city selected the best senior managers. For the second and third categories, Darcy and her staff evaluated the sellers' capabilities and, using publicly distributed standards, chose the best on their own. In 1993, Darcy felt that Fleet Securities, which had the best record of sales among the third category of bond sellers, should be allowed to sell a greater volume of bonds, in essence promoting it to the second level. On the recommendation of the mayor's office, Fleet had already been selected as a second-level seller for the city's Health and Hospital Corporation. The mayor's office also had to approve the city's bond comanagers and agreed with Darcy's proposal to promote Fleet.

The *Times* article suggested that Fleet was upgraded at my urging. This was untrue. I had delegated to Darcy the choice of the lower-level bond sellers. But by juxtaposing the Fleet Securities selection with another, unrelated event, which also had nothing improper about it, the article made it seem that I was doling out favors.

The unrelated event was a $450,000 loan that my Senate campaign had taken out nine months earlier from Fleet Bank. Campaigns frequently take out loans. The loan complied with the strict guidelines of federal election laws. This was a loan at a standard rate of 1 percent over prime, which had to be paid back in full. But the *Times* went on to suggest that I had gotten a special rate. Moreover, I had personally guaranteed the loan, placing all my assets, including my Brooklyn home, at risk. The implication was that Fleet Bank had done me a favor, and that in return, I made sure that Fleet Securities, its affiliate, got more business from the city.

In the Abscam sting, when FBI agents pretending to be rich foreigners had bribed members of Congress and taped their conversations, one corrupt lawmaker was pushed to say who else might be bribable. "What about Holtzman?" the agent asked. "Don't bother," the crook was recorded as saying; "She's too honest to trust." In Congress, as DA, I had put politicians in jail for crooked acts. Now, this record was in jeopardy.

As a result of the press, the city's Conflicts of Interest Board (COIB) asked the Department of Investigations (DOI) to look into the matter. This request was made public, although all aspects of the proceedings are supposed to be confidential. I was not concerned about the investigation itself. I knew that nothing wrong had occurred and that no favoritism had been shown. My campaign advisers were very worried. Although they knew nothing untoward had happened, they were convinced that politics could influence the investigation.

The media would discuss nothing else during the comptroller's race. I wanted to talk about my four years as comptroller and what I had done for the budget, building affordable housing, protecting the environment, and upgrading women's health care. But I had little success in steering press coverage onto the real issues.

In the meantime I was paying the price of challenging corruption during my years as comptroller. People whose contracts I questioned — for example, the holders of the overpriced school bus contracts to which I had objected — dumped hefty donations into my opponent's coffers.

The DOI continued to conduct an investigation that seemed designed to cause me maximum harm. Under normal procedures, the DOI investigates claims and makes a confidential report on its findings to the Conflicts of Interest Board, which then makes a public ruling on each case. But the DOI director, Susan Shepherd, who was under fire for her slowness, announced a few days before the primary that the report was complete. Normally, even the completion of a report is considered confidential information.

I could not obtain a copy of the report; I wasn't even allowed to see it. But now the Conflicts of Interest Board also had an unusual announcement: I could make the report public. The clock had ticked to practically hours before the primary.

I felt trapped in an impossible situation. Investigators are supposed to refrain from affecting an election. In 1980 federal prosecutors delayed the indictment of Nassau County's Joe Margiotta until after the U.S. Senate election to avoid influencing the Senate bid of his political associate, Alfonse D'Amato. I had taken a similar position of noninterference as district attorney when Mario Cuomo was running for governor in 1982. Shortly before the election a newspaper reporter, Jerry Capeci, called to find out whether my office was conducting an investigation into a possible crime. The crime had nothing to do with Cuomo, but realizing the investigation might have hurt Cuomo in the election, we refused to comment to Jerry.

The DOI, however, was proceeding very differently, making a public announcement and forcing me to make an untenable public decision just before election. If I declined to make the report public, I knew that the voters would react angrily to what could seem like a cover-up of information. I could lose the primary. On the other hand, I had no idea what was in the report. If the report were filled with inaccuracies and misstatements of fact, I could also lose. I decided to wait. The primary results came in showing Hevesi as the top vote-getter and me as second, but neither of us had a sufficient number of votes under primary rules to be declared the victor. The comptroller's race geared up for a primary runoff.

In the two weeks between the primary and the runoff, I had the report released. Nothing in it supported the allegations of favoritism on my part. The report confirmed that I was not personally involved in the selection of Fleet Securities.

Despite those conclusions, the report came up with a new claim. It created a standard that had never been applied to a public official and applied it to me. The report said that I had committed "gross negligence" (later overturned by an administrative judge) in failing to check whether Fleet Bank was doing business with the city before my campaign applied for the loan and in failing to remove myself formally (I had removed myself informally) from the decision to upgrade Fleet Securities. So it came down to an issue of semantics — had I removed myself formally from deciding Fleet's fate or simply removed myself?

I lost the race in the primary runoff. Soon after, the mayor lost the general election, which meant that the DOI director lost her job. One of the people who wrote the DOI report against me did find other city employment and was named to a top spot in the office of Alan Hevesi, my campaign opponent.

Darcy Bradbury, who had made the decision to upgrade Fleet Securities' business for the city, went on to become the assistant secretary of the U.S. Treasury Department overseeing the nation's bond sales. She passed through every security check, background check, and personal integrity grilling that the FBI and Secret Service could muster up.

After two and a half years, both an administrative judge and the COIB finally ruled. They agreed that the campaign loan was not at favorable rates, that I did not personally recommend the promotion of Fleet, that there was no preferential treatment in Fleet's selection. But they both found I should have removed myself formally from the selection process to avoid any impression of favoritism to Fleet. Crediting my good faith, the judge imposed no penalty; later, the COIB assessed a fine.

I did learn a thing or two about friends and enemies in that campaign. At one point during the race, the *Daily News* used its entire tabloid front page to call for my ouster. The next day I received a call from Cardinal John O'Connor. I had first met the cardinal during a parade, which in New York tradition stopped at St. Patrick's Cathedral. Before his aide could introduce me, the cardinal said "Hello, Ms. Bellamy." I knew he had confused me with Carol Bellamy, a former city council president. Carol and I often laughed about how people mixed us up, even though we really didn't look much alike. After the cardinal realized his mistake, he was very apologetic.

When the cardinal called me after the *Daily News* attack, it was Rosh Hashanah. I returned the call after going to the synagogue. The cardinal was very gentle. He said, "I always thought of you as a person of integrity, and I wanted to share in your pain." I could barely hold back the feelings surging through me of gratitude at his kindness.

There was, I realized, a much more complex person behind the robes, a man who could reach out to people who differed ideologically and try to comfort them in a time of crisis. He was very conservative on issues such as abortion and gay and lesbian rights, and I had consistently, and unapologetically, opposed him on those points. But after that I took pains to mention to people how generous the cardinal had been to me.

I have reflected a great deal about our methods of campaigning and have come to the conclusion that they have to be changed.

Candidates cannot get elected without getting out their messages. The media does not inform voters about candidates in ways that are useful, that tell what they have done and fairly portray what they plan to do. To communicate with their potential constituents, candidates have no choice but to buy space in the very same media, and at premium prices. And that brings the need for huge amounts of money to the fore.

Raising campaign money puts candidates in difficult positions and can create appearances of corruption, and in some cases the actuality of corruption.

Cutting the cost of campaigning would begin the process of reform. With a lower expenditure ceiling, more people could compete. Public financing would help, as well. It would reduce candidates' dependence on special interests and the wealthy for contributions. Television time, for example, could be paid for through vouchers bought with public financing. And public financing would allow candidates and incumbents more time to listen to the voices of those who currently feel disenchanted with their elected representatives.

In the end, I can't really think about modern-day campaigns without experiencing the pain of my last one. Losing was unfortunate, but it was not the worst. What I couldn't understand was the way I was vilified. In the comptroller's race I was often called a "witch" — by politicians and journalists. How had I deserved this ire? I had stood up for my principles, trying to make the world a better place. I always worked to try to help people. How had my intentions, my record, all I had done, been turned upside down? I had certainly made mistakes, but not the ones attributed to me. Many of them lay in trying to squeeze another minute out of the day, another issue onto a jam-packed agenda.

Was it that I had not kept my feet on the ground like Antaeus in the myth? Or was it perhaps that being a strong woman inevitably provoked such sharp responses? Antaeus, after all, was a man. The very term "witch" rings with the history of strong women who were demonized. In criticizing the media coverage of me, *Village Voice* writer Alisa Solomon wrote, "A woman with power, who helps women without serving as a man's assistant . . . that's the 400-year-old definition of a witch." Would I have been treated the same had I been Elliott Holtzman instead of Elizabeth?

Although my mother had warned me early on that politics was a dirty business, she has been kind enough not to repeat these sentiments. My father tells me that twenty years of giving myself to public service is more than enough.

In my last days at the comptroller's office, staff members gave me a copy of a poem by Marge Piercy, "For Strong Women." I often read poetry. Poetry reflects the deepest honesty with words. In politics, words are often debased and used to deceive. Poetry provides an antidote. Parts of Piercy's poem say, "A strong woman is a woman determined to do something others are determined not to be done. . . . She is trying to raise a manhole cover with her head. . . . Her head hurts. . . . A strong woman is strong in words, in action, in connection, in feeling. . . . Strength is not in her, but she enacts it as the wind fills a sail."

Since I left office, I often wonder whether our society, culture, and politics are sufficiently advanced to make room for strong women, especially liberal ones.

# 15

## Conclusion

*D*URING ELECTIONS, I SOMETIMES THOUGHT of Aleksandr Solzhenit-syn. Although far too conservative and nationalistic for my taste, he dealt brilliantly with the issue of human courage in his writings. In *The First Circle*, Solzhenitsyn describes how the protagonist, a scientist sentenced to a laboratory facility in the Gulag, is con-fronted with a moral dilemma. If the prisoner is willing to collabo-rate with the authorities, he will get better rations, extra clothing, more comforts. If he refuses and cannot be bought, if there is no material thing that is dearer to him than his conscience, then he is free.

Reading *The First Circle* helped me understand that if you are willing to give up your elected position for your principles — as unpleasant as that outcome may be — then on a moral plane, you are free.

When I took a controversial position, I consoled myself by say-ing that as an elected official in a democracy, you have to do what you think is right. If the voters disagree, they can throw you out of office.

Understanding that democracy was at work didn't make los-ing elections any easier. I discovered nothing redeeming about political defeat.

Being out of office after twenty years of public service, of frenetic activity and extraordinary stress, has its undeniable rewards. My life has become almost normal.

Being out of office, however, has not dulled my reaction to what is happening today in our country. The right is on a rampage. Their program: rip out environmental safeguards, blow up guarantees of income for poor mothers with children on welfare, grenade Medicare for the elderly, bomb worker safety programs, nuke the reforms of Roosevelt and Johnson. In the name of new ideas, they want to rocket back to the 1920s — or the beginning of the century, if they can just destroy the income tax. The right wages war on the poor, women, and minorities. The right exploits race as a decoy for anxious middle-class voters.

Newt Gingrich is, to me, an almost Dickensian caricature, except that he can exercise real power. Sounding like Mr. McChokeumchild, he wants to take children from poor mothers and put them in orphanages. Our secretary of health and human services meekly agrees to take children away in cases where mothers refuse to take government-specified training courses. As DA I learned that if the family can't protect the child, there is no guaranteed safe alternative. Taking children away from nonabusive parents leaves the children hugely vulnerable. And what right does the government have to take children away from a mother solely because of her poverty?

The lack of real resistance to the right, the fatalistic acceptance, the political hush, is dismaying to me. The alternatives, whether at a city, state, or federal level, seem virtually nonexistent.

Many proponents of welfare reform, for example, blame the nation's problems on poor women. I understand the bitterness about welfare, particularly among working people who have to struggle harder than ever in order to enjoy a middle-class standard of living.

But to "end welfare as we know it" requires more than hollow slogans. Draconian proposals to extract penalties and cut off children won't solve the problem. Effectively reforming welfare will require a recognition of the sexism that underlies the current system.

Welfare began in the 1930s, when many mothers stayed at home and raised their children. They were financially dependent on their husbands or partners. Since women's dependency was commonplace, when the provider died or fled, an alternative source of support for the mother had to be found. If the husband wasn't there, welfare created a substitute dependency — the government. Welfare never tried to make women independent. It accepted a woman's dependency as the norm.

How do you change sixty years of entrenched thinking? The key lies in improving women's self-esteem, which is essential for women to take control of their lives. If we want independence for women, we will need to begin a serious, sustained, broadly based effort. This will include improving education for girls (and recognizing how low expectations for girls' performance in American schools have become a self-fulfilling prophesy); changing media images that make women feel that their only value is as sex objects; providing inexpensive contraception and ready availability of abortion, including RU-486 and the like, so women can plan for wanted children; offering better job training; enforcing antidiscrimination laws, including those against sexual harassment; and providing quality day care for children of poor and middle-class mothers, a problem in a society that pays zookeepers more than child care workers.

Instituting these programs will not be easy. Our country is still ambivalent about strong and independent women. While women have made many gains, so few have real power or control. There is still no equal rights amendment to the Constitution. Iowa voters turned down a state equal rights amendment in 1992. Some of the criticism of Hillary Clinton is related to the feeling that she has abandoned her "gender role," and that tells us much about the barriers that block true equality for women. I, too, have often felt the hostile response to a strong woman in my own political career.

Neither poverty nor the problems associated with welfare can be solved unless society produces enough jobs for all adults to be self-sufficient.

A similar superficial reasoning also characterizes the discussion of health care reform. Every European country has a health care system that works fairly well. Managed care, the alternative proffered here, places cost above cure. In some instances medical decisions about permitting certain treatments are made by insurance company clerks. Hospitals' policies of ousting mothers who have just given birth after twenty-four hours have finally prompted legislative remedies. But the parameters of the debate are wrong. No one seems to be seriously considering the systems that have worked elsewhere or addressing the very real fears of the millions of Americans who are uninsured and underinsured.

Turning programs over to state and local governments, the most recent craze, is the same states' rights debate that began before the Civil War. As comptroller of New York City, I saw the city's capacity to run programs. It was not impressive. The city couldn't do any better than the federal government, and in some instances it does far worse. Government on a local level has a hard time attracting the most competent people and is far more open to blatant corruption than the federal government.

What can we do to oppose this turn to the right?

The vote is the ultimate power. The people can say no. Unfortunately, too many people adversely affected by the right's rampage don't vote. Only a comparatively small percentage of Americans voted in the 1992 elections that brought the right to power in Congress. If more people vote, right-wing extremism is less likely to succeed.

When government officials are doing wrong, it is important that people speak out. Silence will be misinterpreted as acquiescence. A single letter expressing opposition can have an impact.

But that is clearly not enough. More liberals and progressives need to seek office. Admittedly, here is where my own personal reservations take hold. I'm not sure I would encourage any liberal friend to seek elective office. Much as I was motivated by the excitement of making government work for people, much as I was thrilled by the ability to do things to help those in need, the frustrations were infinite, and the sacrifices enormous.

Some sacrifices, like personal wealth, have been unimportant to me. I never cared about becoming rich. Other sacrifices have truly been a loss, like spending more time with family and developing friendships, which too often wither in the frenzy, anxiety, and lack of privacy in a public life. Relationships need nurturing —

time and care. And that is next to impossible in the midst of relentless campaign cycles or with the demands of endless community meetings, emergencies, and late-night strategy sessions. Time for expansion of the soul is all too rare, as well. In Congress, after we finished working on impeachment, life returned to a more orderly schedule. There were at least regular vacations, including a break for almost the entire month of August. In my other positions the days and nights ploughed into one another with little chance to pause. I missed many personal opportunities.

There were other sacrifices. Even though Eleanor Roosevelt warned every public woman that she would need a skin as thick as that of a rhinoceros, none of us can develop that. Few people are immune to criticism. It drains psychic energy and takes time from other important activities. After returning to New York City as DA and comptroller, I was weighed down by incessant newspaper attacks, many of which were unjustified, and some downright silly. The stress of being in public life in New York was so constant that I never had a proper chance to open up the more jovial side of my personality.

Speaking out undoubtedly drew reprisals. But the choice of silence was worse. Speaking out against a corrupt judge who permitted the humiliation of a rape victim in court made the New York judicial system so upset that it not only chided me but changed its rules to prevent other lawyers from criticizing a judge in public. And as for corruption, speaking out against it in New York City brought such anger from those who had fed contentedly at the public trough that they poured vast energy and money into throwing me out of office.

As Emily Dickinson wrote, "Assent — and you are sane — demur — you're straightway dangerous — . . ." If you challenge the powers that be, no matter how polite or courteous you are, you are a threat. The powerful will strike back.

So why should decent, idealistic people run for office? Why should they pay the price of press scorn, false attacks, and loss of privacy? And how can they win, given the present system of campaign financing and the high cost of elections?

A system can't be thoroughly reformed, I know. But what,

then, is the alternative? Those of us who care simply have to keep struggling. We will lose some skirmishes, perhaps many, in the effort to create a more just society. But we will win some fights, too.

For the moment, though, I am tending my garden, both literally and in the Voltairian sense. After twenty years of public service, it is time for me to put down my own roots and tend the blossoms of friendship and love. And who knows what that renewal will bring?

# Acknowledgments

$M$ANY PEOPLE HELPED MAKE THIS BOOK possible. First and fore-most were Dan and Joanna Rose, longtime patrons of the arts, who urged me to write about my experiences in government — and provided the friendship and support that make it impossible to say no. Mark Mirsky also strongly encouraged me to take on this project; his enthusiasm was infectious, and his advice, whether about a literary agent or the Talmud, was readily available and invaluable.

Friends and former colleagues — Judith Ames, Barbara Baer, Rebecca Folkman, Maerwydd McFarland — as well as my mother undertook the time-consuming task of reading the entire manu-script with a red pencil. Their thoughtful comments improved the book enormously. Others read parts of the manuscript and made important suggestions: Darcy Bradbury, Zachary Carter, Linda Davidoff, Rhea Dignam, David Eichenthal, John Jonas, Irena Klep-fisz, Ibby Lang, Richard Laskey, Sylvia Lerner, Nancy Ludmerer, Bob Mazur, Norman Redlich, Dennis Roberts, Tom Sanzillo, Liz Schroeder, Jim Schweitzer, Marilyn Shapiro, Bob Sheehan, Anne Stone, Barbara Underwood, and Evan Wolfson. I am also grateful to Andrea Bernstein, Skip Enders, Tony Freedman, Aviva Futurian, Jim Ledbetter, Suzanne Mattei, Ed O'Malley, Eli Rosenbaum, Men-achem Rosensaft, Lionel Rosenblatt, and former representatives Billy Lee Evans and Ed Mezvinsky for sharing their reminiscences and observations. Emily Rosenberg and Lynda Downey helped with photographs, Larry Barton graciously permitted use of his wonderful cartoon, Marlene Rehkamp located archival materials, and Norma Lusardi tracked down former employees. Dick Morris added perceptive comments.

I appreciate the useful suggestions of my agent, Jennifer Lyons, and the helpfulness and unflagging enthusiasm of my editor, Jeannette Seaver. David Martyn and Dick Seaver, as well as everyone else at Arcade Publishing, worked hard and cooperatively. The staff of the Arthur and Elizabeth Schlesinger Library at Radcliffe College, the depository of my papers, provided valuable assistance, as did the staff at the Jimmy Carter Presidential Library. My thanks go as well to the New York Foundation for the Arts and its employees.

My special gratitude is reserved for Cindy Cooper, who agreed to write this book with me — a commitment that involved long hours, lots of research, and many, many drafts. She met the challenges with great patience and good humor. I particularly valued her excellent writing skills, as well as her good judgment. Her efforts were aided by Jennifer Clarke and her agent, Carol Mann.

Sir Isaac Newton once said that if he saw farther it was because he stood on the shoulders of giants. Unlike Sir Isaac, I don't claim to have seen farther than others, but my successes in government and politics could not have been achieved without many extraordinary people with very broad shoulders. My family and closest friends provided love and comfort during the good times as well as the crises. I was also fortunate to have had wonderful staff, in both my government positions and my campaigns, who taught and inspired me. We shared a sense of commitment and adventure — and often had a great deal of fun — as we took on impossible challenges and tried to make government just a little fairer and better. I cannot thank those who worked with me enough.

I am humbled by the willingness of so many to take time from important commitments in their lives to assist me once again in writing this book. Their affection and concern has meant more than they will ever know.

I would also like to express my appreciation to those who played an important role in the events that shaped the book. In my campaigns, Mark Alcott, Judith Ames, Paul Asofsky, Barbara Baer,

Barbara Berger, Brenda Berkman, Dale Best, Leonore Blitz, Karen Borack, Mary and Patrice Cheasty, Michael Churchill, Linda Davidoff, Harris Diamond, Pam Elam, Al Fagin, Dan Feldman, Judy Flecker, Barbara Fife, Alan Fleishman, Sylvia Frank, Helen Henkin, Caroline Herron, Tracie Holder, Irena Klepfisz, Wynn Kramarsky, Sheila Levin, Marcia Levine, Esther Lopato, Patsy McCook, Patsy McNevin, Joe McDonald, Margo May, Angela Montevago, Ed Miller, Libby Moroff, Michael Nairne, Ed O'Malley, Marilyn Shapiro, John Speziali, Susan Thomases, and Carol Ann Weisenfeld all worked tirelessly through thick and through thin. My uncle Norman Ravitz designed the campaign fliers and buttons for my first two elections, Dick Levy created brilliant print ads, and I benefited greatly from my other media advisers and pollsters: Carter Eskew, Tubby Harrison, Bill Knapp, Paul Maslin, Dick Morris, Hank Scheinkopf, Doug Schoen, and Bob Squier. I am grateful to my congressional staff, including Judith Dollenmayer, Linda Donnelly, Aviva Futurian, Michael Greenberger, Anne Harvey, John Jonas, Joanne MacBeth, Liz Schroeder, Jim Schweitzer, Marilyn Shapiro, Bob Sheehan, Rod Smith, Teresa Spigone, Anne Stone, Leah Wortham, and Andrea Zedalis, and to the staff of my Congressional District Office, Judith Avner, Mary and Patrice Cheasty, Stanley Collander, Dan Feldman, Linda Feldman, Tony Freedman, Ibby Lang, Sylvia Lerner, Miriam Trokan, Donna Samuels, Joan Soloway, and volunteers Thelma Newman and Sydell Berman. In the District Attorney's Office, I was fortunate to work with Zachary Carter, Mary Cheasty, Debra Cohn, Rhea Dignam, Harry Dodds, Bill Donnino, Richard Laskey, Jim Ledbetter, Sylvia Lerner, Bill Miller, Patty Nolan, Ed O'Malley, Len Sabatino, Liz Schroeder, Zachary Tumin, Barbara Underwood, and all the bureau chiefs and deputies, including Barry Aaron, Dale Campbell, Laura Drager, Vincent Fay, Mark Feldman, Mike Gary, Edna Handy, Bob Kaye, Judy Kluger, Barbara Newman, Marc Schindelheim, Arlene Semaya, Alan Teichman, Alan Trachtman, Bob Vinal, and Bob Winter, as well as Lois Raff, Peter Weinstein, and Evan Wolfson. My thanks also go to those who served on transition teams or advisory groups for the DA's and Comptroller's offices, including Karen Burstein, Tony Bruan, John Burton, Billy Cobbs, Debra Cohn, Pat Corbin, Drew Days, Steven Fenster, Marc Fasteau, Dale Horowitz, Laura

Banfield Hoguet, Phil Hyman, Mark Moore, Bernard Nussbaum, Candace Straight, David Trager, Carol Ann Weisenfeld, and Peter Zimroth. As Comptroller, I benefited greatly from the help of Roger Anderson, Brian Baxter, Manny Behar, Joe Benitez, Darcy Bradbury, Paula Chester, Pam Elam, Rhea Dignam, John Gilliam, Dick Halverson, Beverly Hamilton, Bob Harris, Dixie Hathaway, Steve Kagan, Alexandra Lowe, Donna Marris, Suzanne Mattei, Barbara Mehlsack, Ed O'Malley, Michael Poretsky, Marlene Rehkamp, Tom Sanzillo, Liz Schroeder, Marc Schindelheim, Anne Strahle, and Jim Tatum; those who worked with the media, including George Artz, Andrea Bernstein, Carter Eskew, Glenn Goldberg, Louis Haber, Shirley Katzander, Maerwydd McFarland, Jeff Soref, Ned Steele, Jim Vlasto, Nancy Young, and Amy Wilentz; and those police officers who provided security, including Eddie Cordina, Joe Delfino, George Guida, Tom Hawkins, and Carol Weinberger. I also wish to thank Mary Greenebaum and Diana Ladas for their help when I worked in the Mayor's Office. I am deeply grateful to George Katz, Robert Mazur, Bernard Nussbaum, Norman Redlich, and Wachtell, Lipton, Rosen and Katz, and to Dan Kolb, Nancy Ludmerer, Tim Mayopolous, Lisa Hone, and Davis, Polk, & Wardwell for their extraordinary representation in legal matters.

I also want to express my appreciation to the countless government officials, community activists, and just plain ordinary people who helped me at various times in my career, including in particular Edward M. Kennedy, one of the finest U.S. Senators, former representative John Burton, Mort Olshan, and Max Palevsky, and those with whom I worked on the issue of Nazi war criminals — Beatte and Serge Klarsfeld, Martin Mendelsohn, Eli Rosenbaum, Alan Ryan, Neal Sher, Rabbi Paul Silton, Simon Wiesenthal, and many Holocaust survivors, such as John Ranz. Given the frailty of memory and the incompleteness of documents, individuals must have been omitted from this list. My apologies to them. Sadly, my dear friend and former employee Sylvia Lerner and my mentor George Katz did not live to see the publication of this work.

Although this book and my years in government benefited immeasurably from the counsel and aid of many people, in the end the shortcomings, both literary and political, are mine and mine alone.

# Index